PEN & INK
ILLUSTRATION SHOWCASE

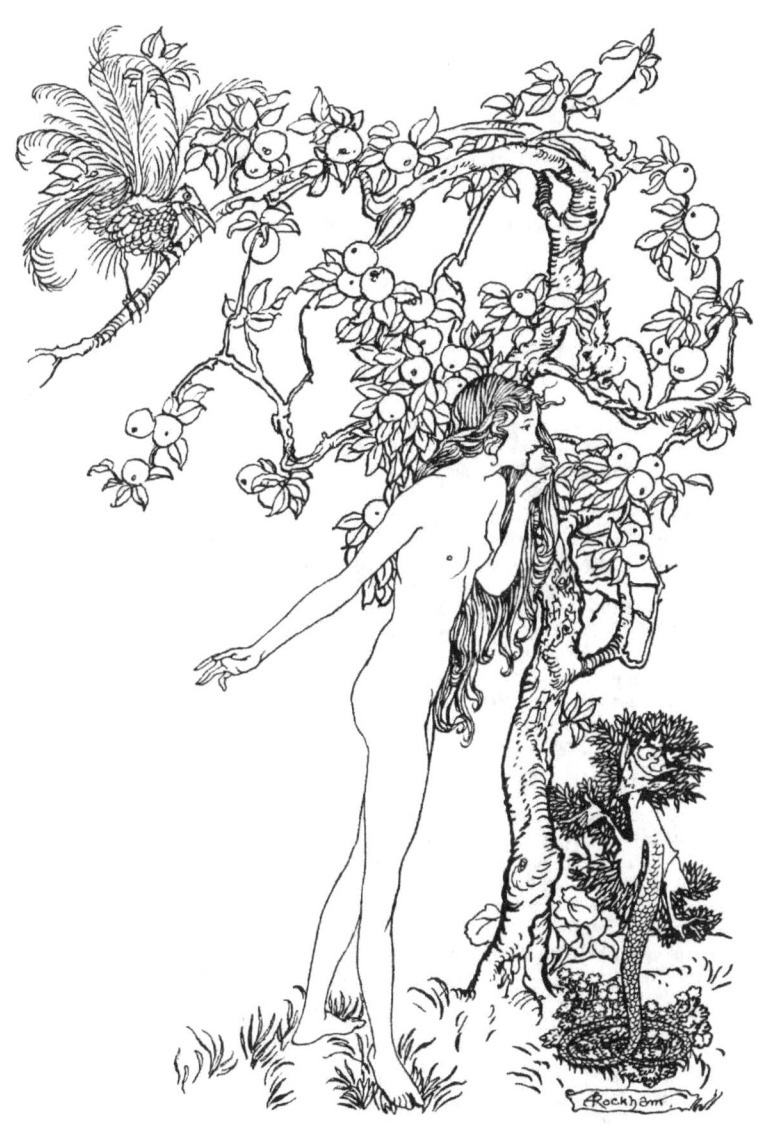

REDCREST PUBLISHING

Compiled and edited by Steve Archibald

Copyright © 2019 Redcrest Publishing

All rights reserved

ISBN: 978-1-9996677-4-0

Bibliographical Note

This Redcrest Publication is an original compilation of illustrations from the following works: Eene halve Eeuw, 1848-1898 (1898 ed); The Poetical Works of John Keats (1884 ed); Hamlet (1922 ed); Modern Pen Drawing: European and American (1901 ed); Andrew Lang's Crimson Fairy Book (1903 ed); Andrew Lang's Brown Fairy Book (1914 ed); Andrew Lang's Animal Story Book (1904 ed); Andrew Lang's All Sort of Stories Book (1911 ed); Pen Drawing and Pen Draughtsmen (1920 ed); Aesop's Fables (1916 ed); Alice,s Adventures in Wonderland (1907 ed); Peter Pan in Kensington Gardens (1906 ed); Rip Van Winkle (1905 ed); The Land of Enchantment (1907 ed); The Fairy Tales of the Brothers Grimm (1909 ed); The Rainbow Book (1909 ed); Princess Mary's Gift Book (1914 ed); Altes u. Neues von Herm Vogel (1902 ed); Heldensage Deutsche (1892 ed); Plume Crayon Fusain (1911 ed); Early English Prose Romances (1904 ed); The Magazine of Art Volume 24 (1901 ed); The Lost World (c.1912 ed); King, of the Khyber Rifles (1916 ed); Collier's Magazine (August 1920, March 1917, April 1913 ed); A Midsummer Nights Dream (1914 ed); A Hundred Fables of La Fontaine (1900 ed); Fairy tales from Hans Christian Andersen (1899 ed); Old-time stories (1921 ed); The works of Mr. Francis Rabelais, Vol 1 & 2 (c.1904 ed); Gibson New Cartoons (1916 ed); The Studio International (1898, 1899 ed); Allegories (1898 ed); Fairy Tales and Stories (1900 ed); The Story of the Weathercock (c.1895 ed); Alice's Adventures in Wonderland (1910 ed); The Cloud Kingdom (1908 ed); Make Believe (1896 ed); The Big Book of Nursery Rhymes (1903 ed); Dream Boats and Other Stories (1920 ed); Rubaiyat of Omar Khayyam (c.1900 & 1920 ed); A Dream of Fair Women & Other Poems (1900 ed); Sintram and his Companions (1908 ed); Sartor Resartus (1898 ed); Fairy Tales from Hans Andersen (1910ed); The Inns of Court & Chancery (1908 ed); The Poems of Coleridge (1906 ed); The Rape of Lock (1896 ed); Under the Hill (1904 ed); More English Fairy Tales (1922 ed); Celtic Folk & Fairy Tales (c.1890 ed); More Celtic Folk & Fairy Tales (1895 ed); Shakespeare's Sonnets (1899 ed); Boys' and Girls' Bookshelf (Vol 4,19,20 ed); Greek Fairy Tales (1912 ed); Chicago Daily News (sept 1898); The Tachypomp and Other Stories (1874 ed); The Kaiser's Garland (1915 ed); The Works of William Shakespeare Vol.5 (1889); St. Nicholas: For Young Folks. Vol.25 Parts 1 & 2 (1905 eds); Battles of the Nineteenth Century Vol.II (1901 ed); Salomé (1892 ed).

Other picture credits
ARTHUR RACKHAM (Title page). HENRY OSPOVAT (Introduction page).
PERCY J BILLINGHURST (Atrists page).

Redcrest Publishing
9 Chalfont Close, Hemel Hempstead, Herts. HP2 7JR

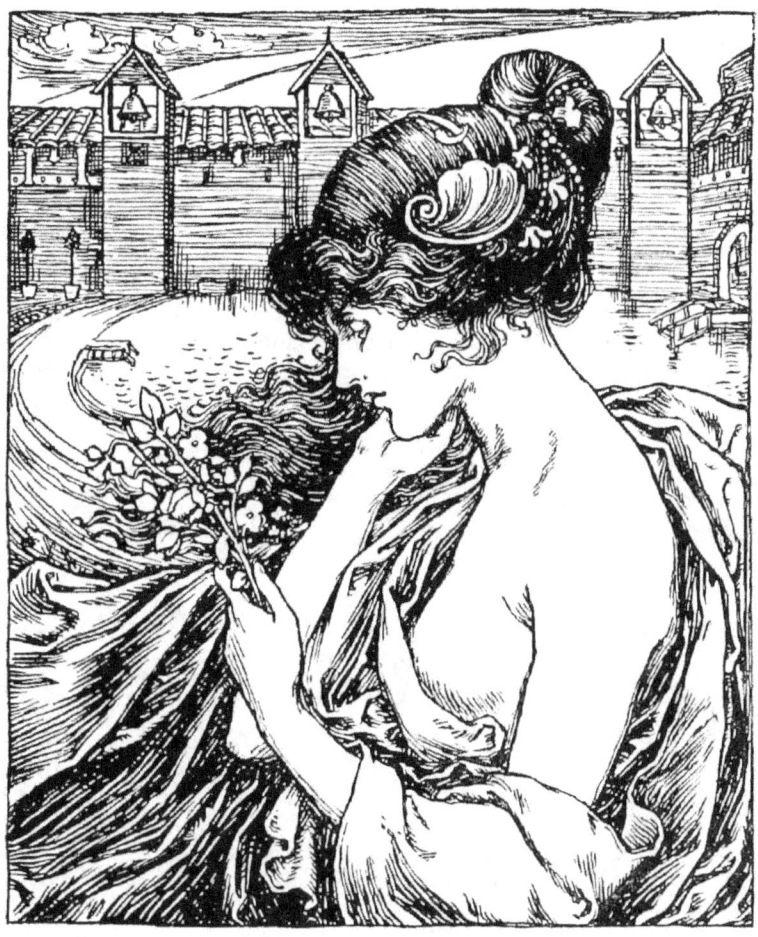

INTRODUCTION

Pen and ink artwork has been a popular form of art and illustration for well over a century. The art form reached it's height in publishing at the end of the 19th century through to the first part of the 20th. During this period many artists came to the fore in a 'Gold rush' of illustrated books, magazines and newspapers.

This book includes a selection of over 120 superb examples from some of the early masters of the craft. In total this showcase includes works from 48 excellent artists and illustrators. The examples come from not just the well known artists, but also artists you might not be familiar with. Probably the best known of these are Arthur Rackham, Charles & Heath Robinson, Aubrey Beardsley, Charles Dana Gibson, Percy J Billinghurst, Joseph Clement Coll, Franklin Booth, Edmund J Sullivan and Harold Nelson.

In most cases the images are from scanned examples of the published work which the author has digitally cleaned and adjusted to show the images as near to the original as possible. All the images are beautifully reproduced in a large size so the reader can study the different styles and techniques of the different artists.

THE ARTISTS

RONALD BALFOUR
(1896-1941) English.............Pages 5, 65

W HEATH ROBINSON
(1872-1944). English............6, 7, 8, 9, 10, 11, 12

CHARLES DANA GIBSON
(1867-1944) American..............13, 14, 15

ARTHUR RACKHAM
(1867-1939), English...............16, 17, 18, 19, 20, 21, 22

CHRISTINE DRUMMOND ANGUS
(1877-1920) English.........................23

AMELIA BAUERLE
(1873-1919) English.....................24, 25

HERMANN VOGEL
(1854-1918) German...............26, 27, 28

ALEXANDRE DE RIQUER
(1856-1920) Spanish........................29

C E BROCK
(1870-1938) English....................30, 31

WILLARD BONTE
(1877-1943) American..................32, 33

FRANKLIN BOOTH
(1874-1948) American......34, 35, 36, 37

FREDERICK O'NEILL GALLAGHER
(d.1937) Irish........................38

LOUIS F MUCKLEY
(1862-1926) English...........................39

FIDUS (HUGO HOPPENER)
(1868-1948) German................40, 41

HAROLD NELSON
(1871-1946) English..........42, 43, 44, 45

W. R. WENCKEBACH
(1860-1937) Dutch...................46, 47

PERCY J BILLINGHURST
(1871-1933) British...................48, 49

ROBERT ANNING BELL
(1862-1933) English....................50, 51

JOHN AUSTIN
(1886-1948) English....................52, 53

VAINO BLOMSTEDT
(1871-1947) Finnish.........................55

HENRY J FORD
(1860-1941) English..........56, 57, 58, 59

JOSEPH CLEMENT COLL
(1881-1921) American........60, 61, 62, 63, 64

HANS TEGNER
(1853-1932) Danish................66, 67, 68

HENRY F FARNY
(1847-1916) American........................69

W G BAXTER
(c.1856-1888) Irish............................70

JACQUES ONFROY BREVILLE (JOB)
(1858-1931) French.............................71

CHARLES ROBINSON
(1870-1937) English..............72, 73, 74, 75, 76

FREDERIC REMINGTON
(1861-1909) American.....................77

EDWARD T REED
(1860-1933) English.........................78

CYRIL GOLDIE
(1872-1942) New Zealander................79

DUGALD S WALKER
(1883-1937) American.....80, 81, 82, 83

EDMUND J SULLIVAN
(1869-1933) English........84, 85, 86, 87, 88, 89

GORDON BROWNE
(1858-1932) English................90, 91, 92

THOMAS MAYBANK
(c.1869-c.1929) English....................93

HERBERT RAILTON
(1857-1910) English................94, 95, 96

GERALD METCALFE
(1871-1929) English........97, 98,99, 100

AUBREY BEARDSLEY
(1872-1898) English......101, 102, 103, 104

JOHN D BATTEN
(1860-1932) English........105, 106, 107, 108

HENRY OSPOVAT
(1877-1909) Russian.............108, 109, 110

PETER BAUER
(1871-c.1941) German.......................111

LOUIS RHEAD
(1857-1926) American......................112

LUCY F PERKINS
(1865-1937) American...............113, 114

GEORGE SOPER
(1870-1942) English........................115

FREDERICK RICHARDSON
(1862-1937) American......................116

RICHARD KNÖTEL
(1857-1914) German........................117

REGINALD BIRCH
(1856-1943) English-American.......118, 119, 120, 121

L A SHAFER
(1866-1940) American......................122

JOHN R NEILL
(1877-1943) American..............123, 124

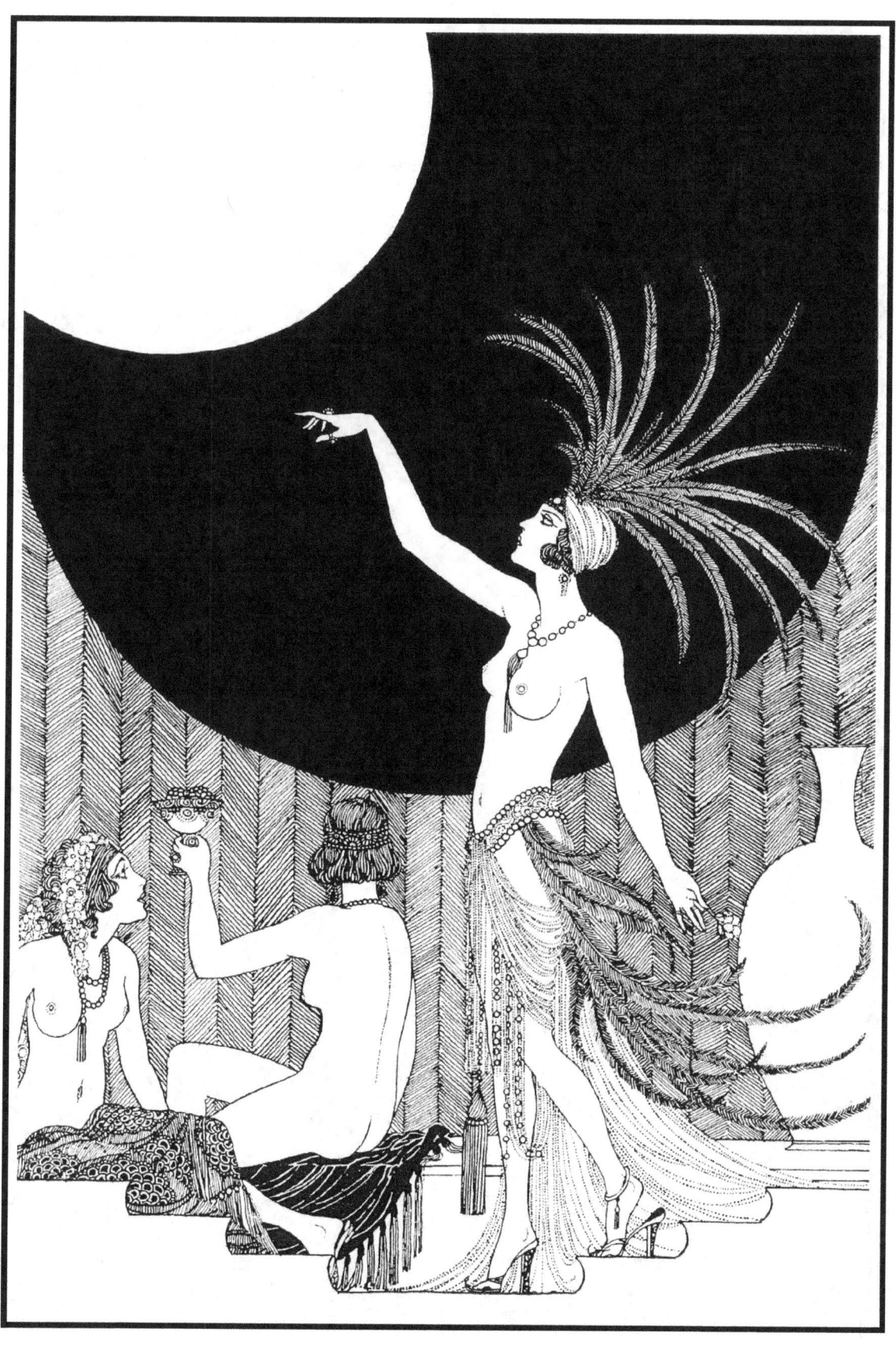

RONALD BALFOUR: Illustration for 'Rubáiyát of Omar Khayyám'

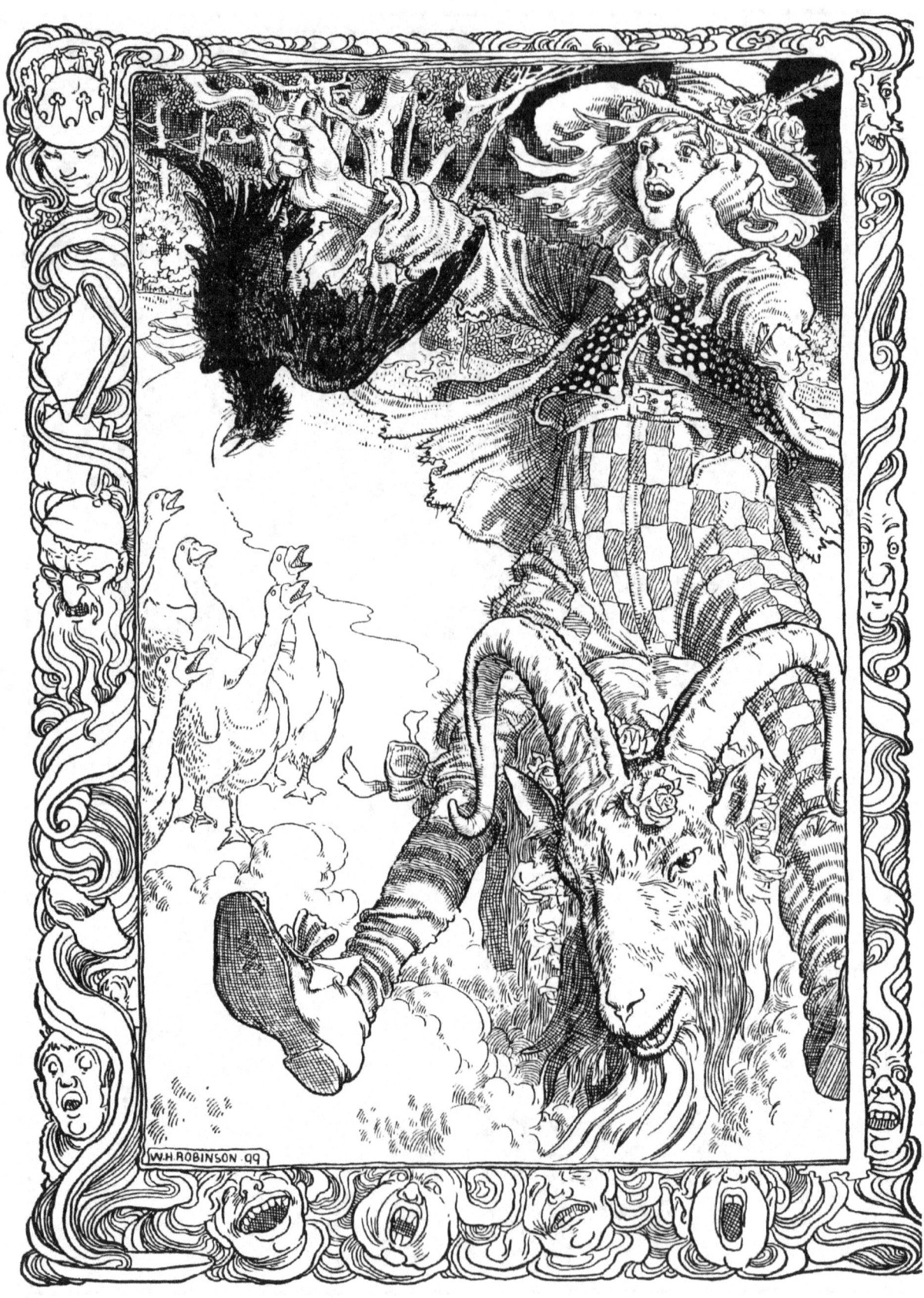

W HEATH ROBINSON: Illustration for the 'Hans Clodhopper' story from 'Fairy Tales from Hans Christian Andersen'

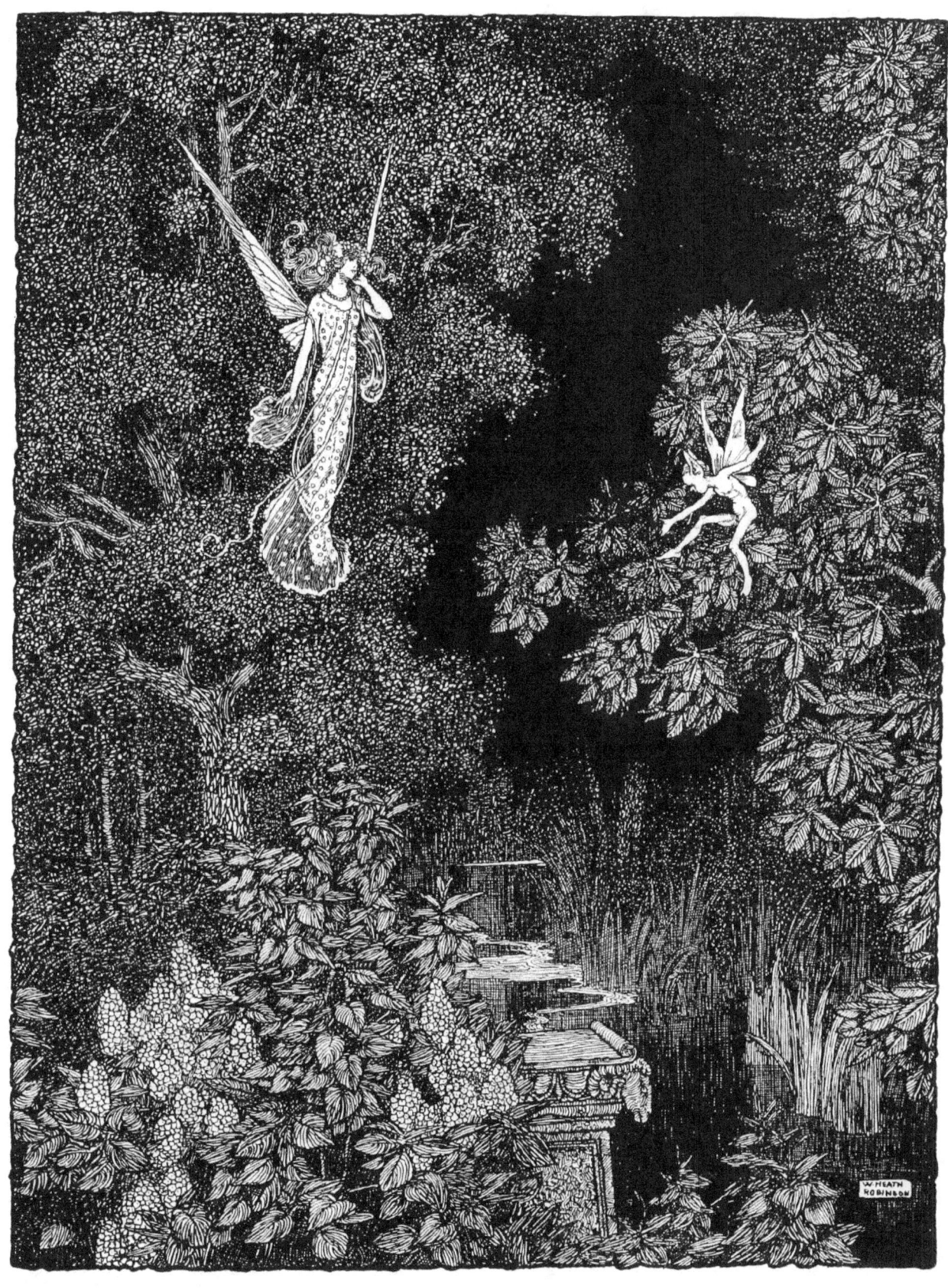

W HEATH ROBINSON: Puck. "How now, spirit! whither wander you?"
From 'A Midsummer Nights Dream'.

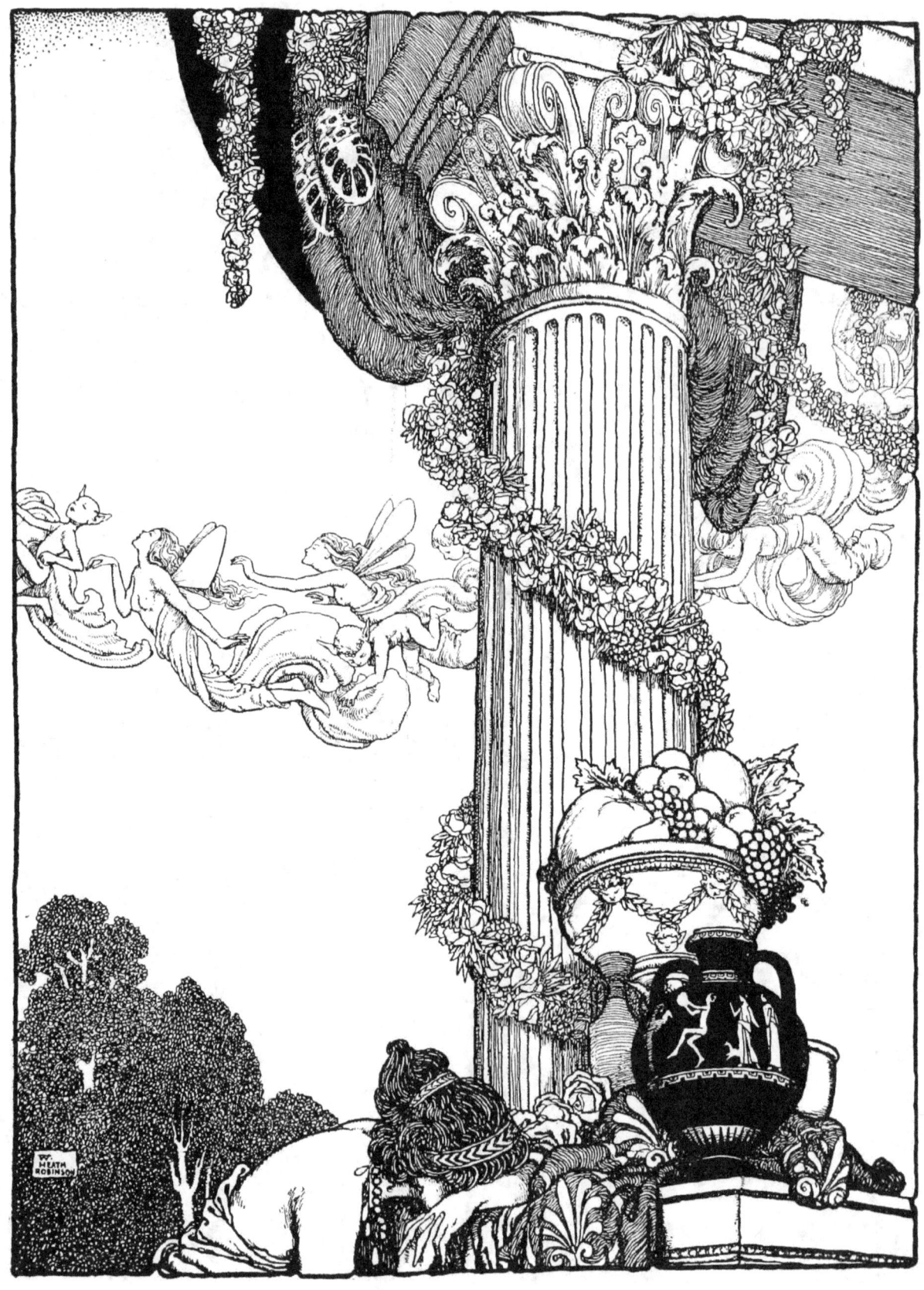

W HEATH ROBINSON: Lysander. "...and she, sweet lady, dotes, Devoutly dotes, dotes inidolatry, upon this spotted and inconstant man". From 'A Midsummer Nights Dream'.

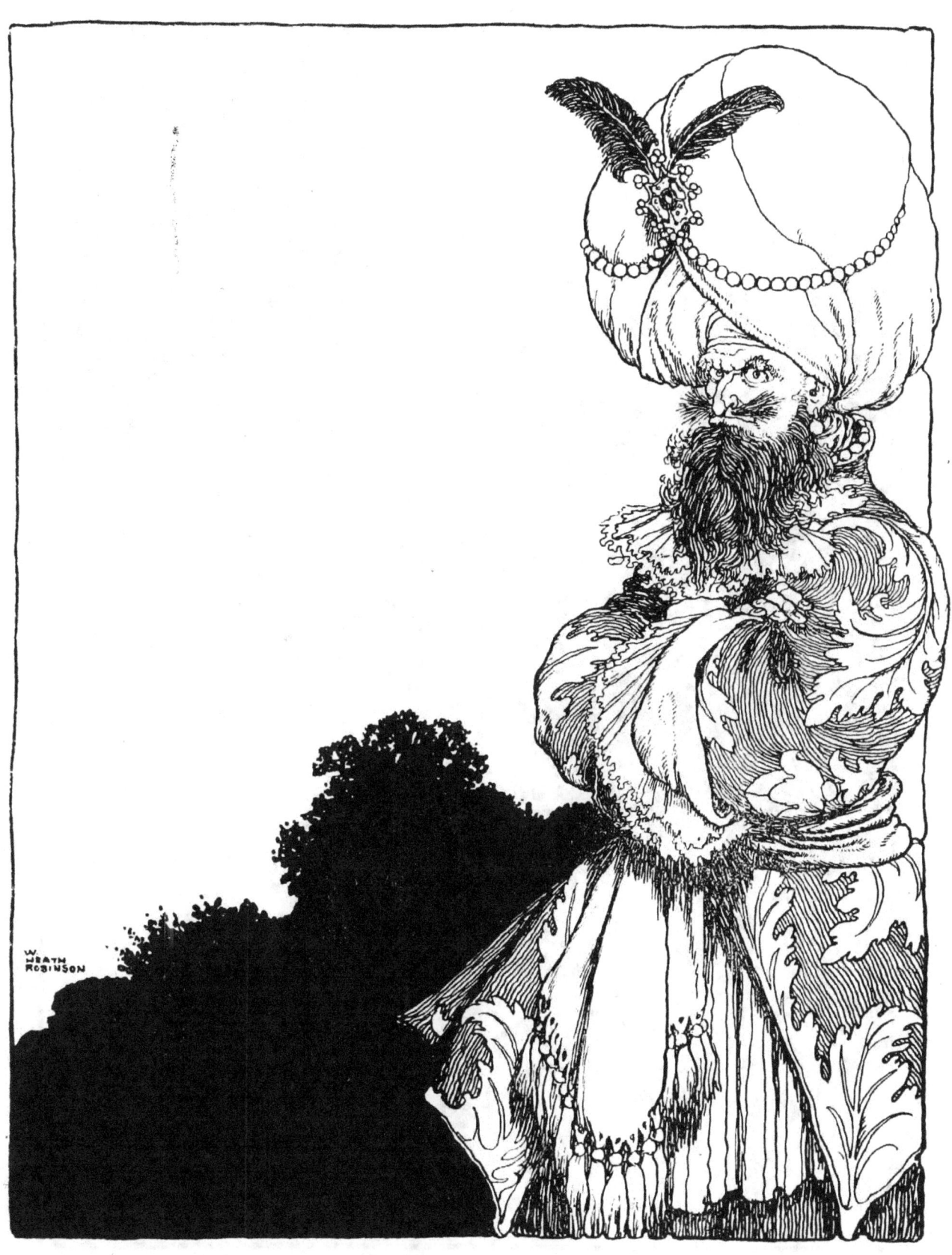

W HEATH ROBINSON: Blue Beard
From 'Old Time Stories'.

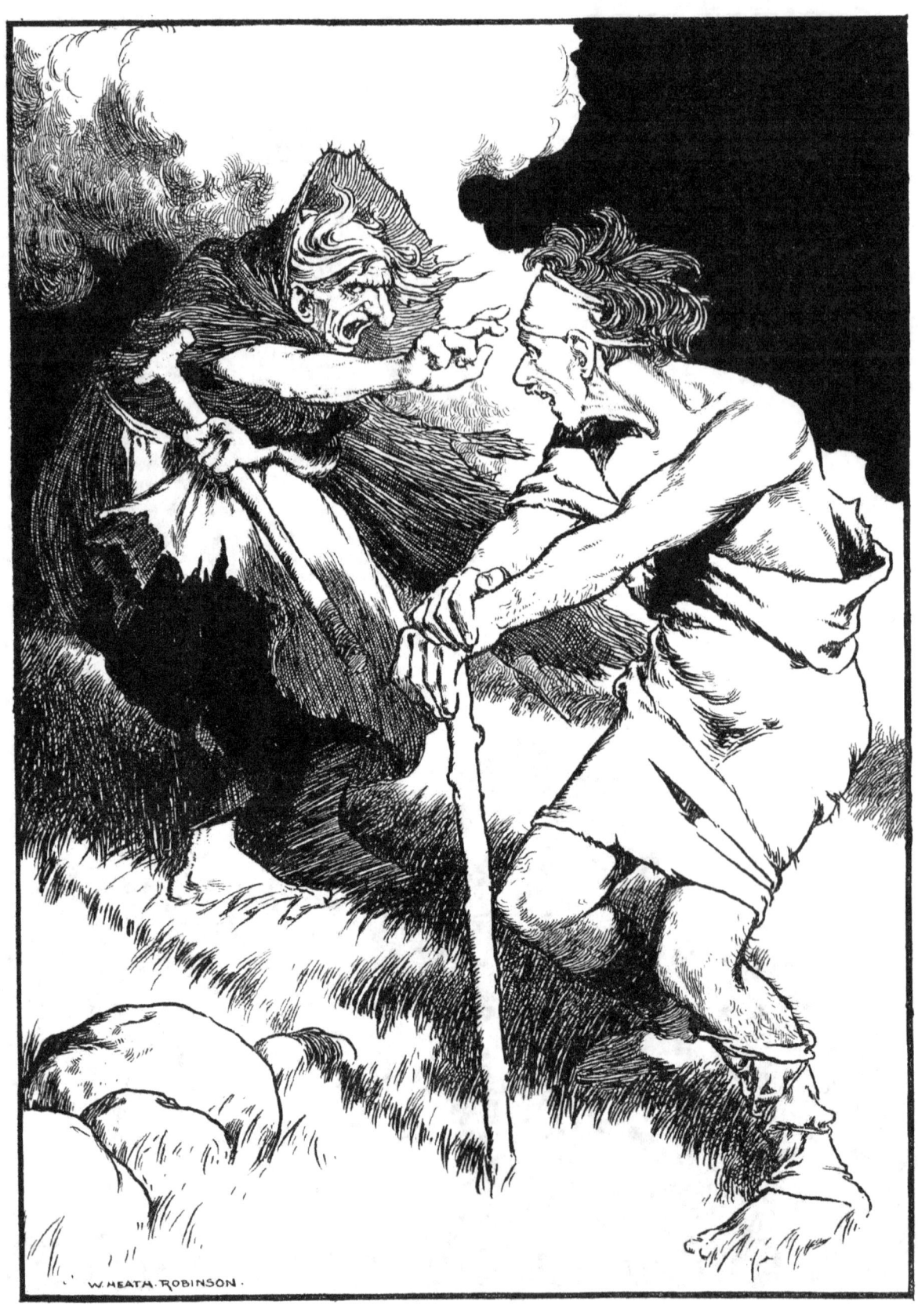

W HEATH ROBINSON: Was foretold by an old Lourpidon hag, that his kingdome should be restored to him at the coming of the Cocklicranes. From 'The Works of Mr Francis Rabelais' Volume 1

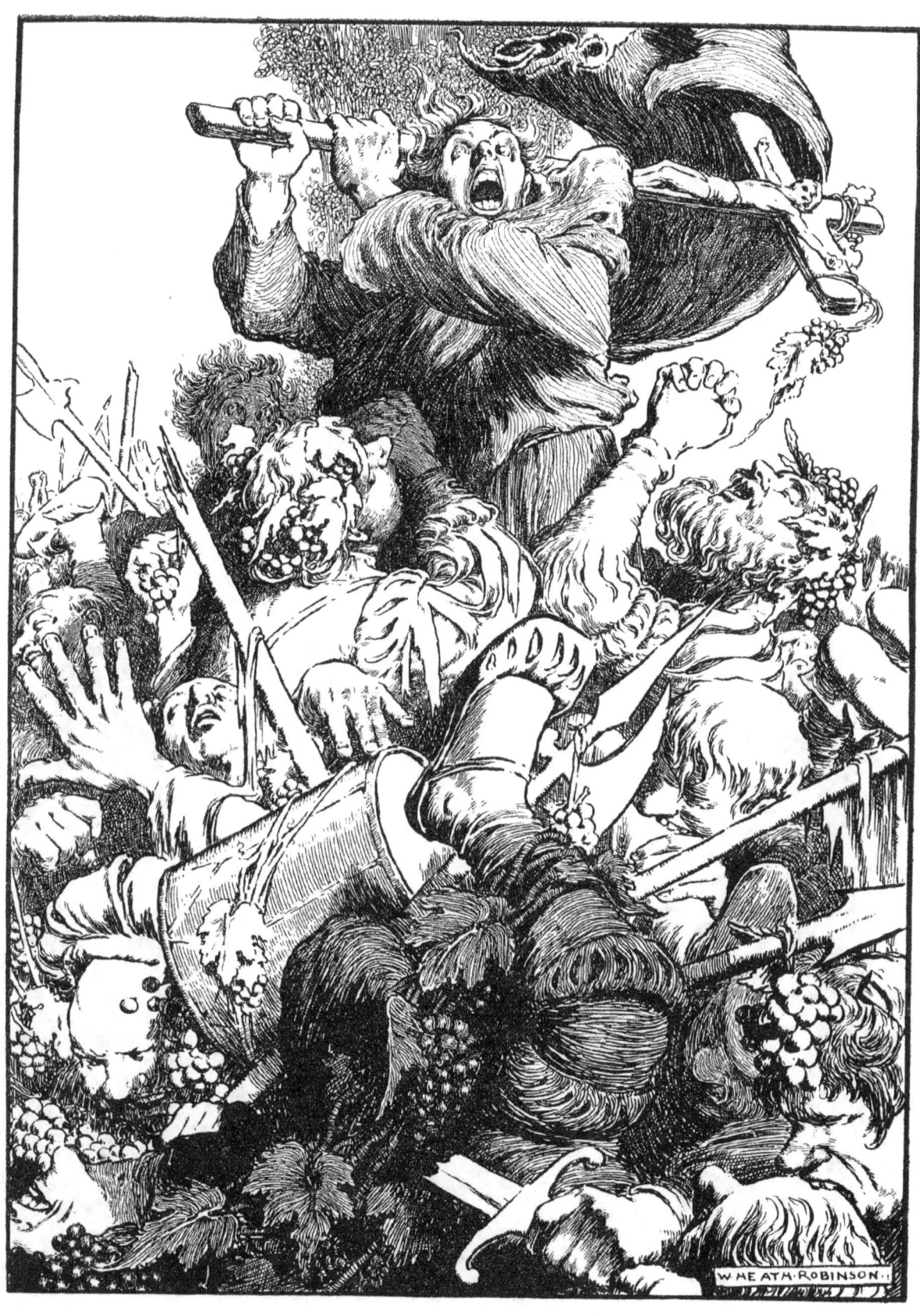

W HEATH ROBINSON: They fell down before him like hay before a mower.
From 'The Works of Mr Francis Rabelais' Volume 1

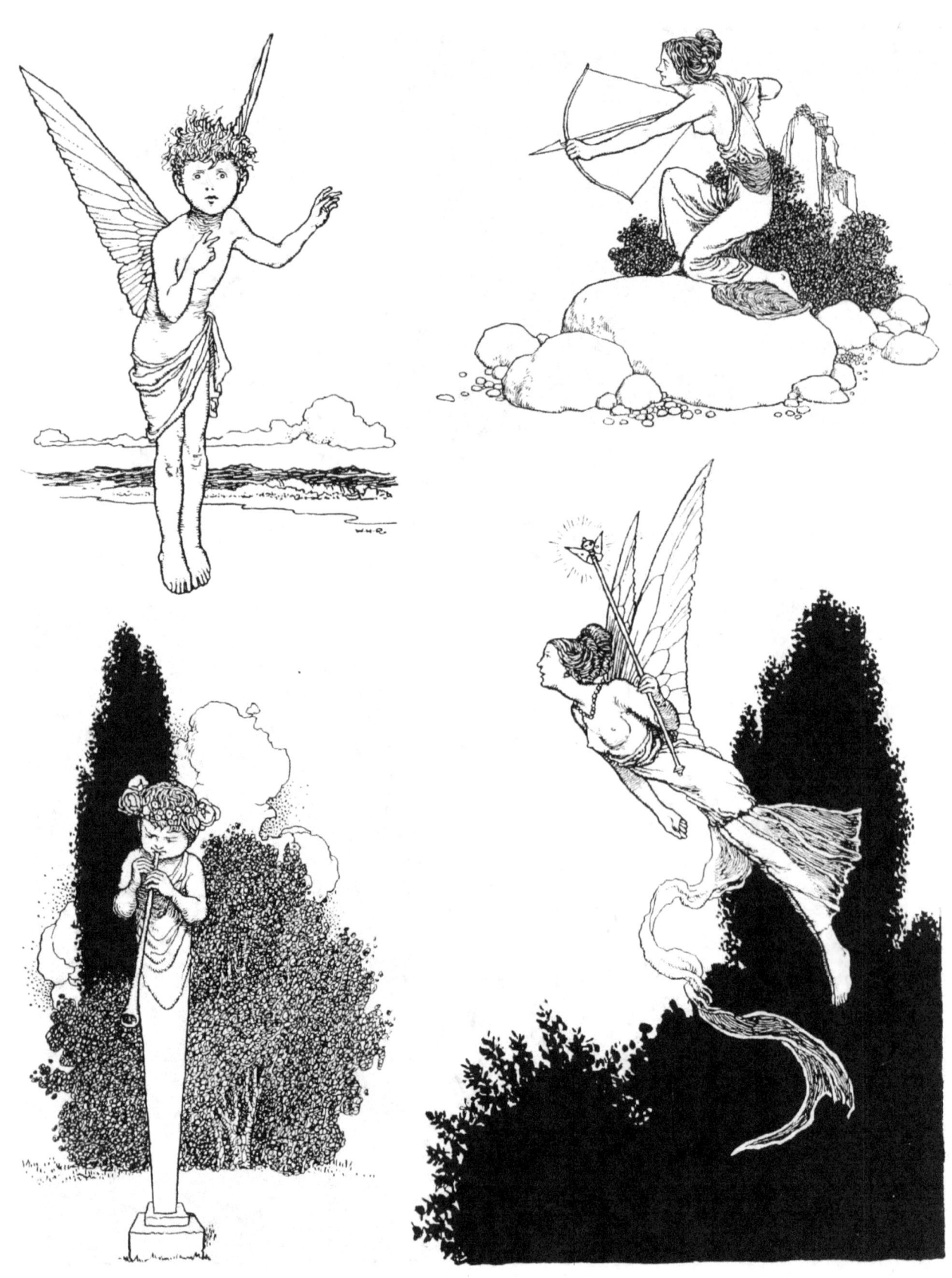

W HEATH ROBINSON: In-text drawings from 'A Midsummer Nights Dream'.

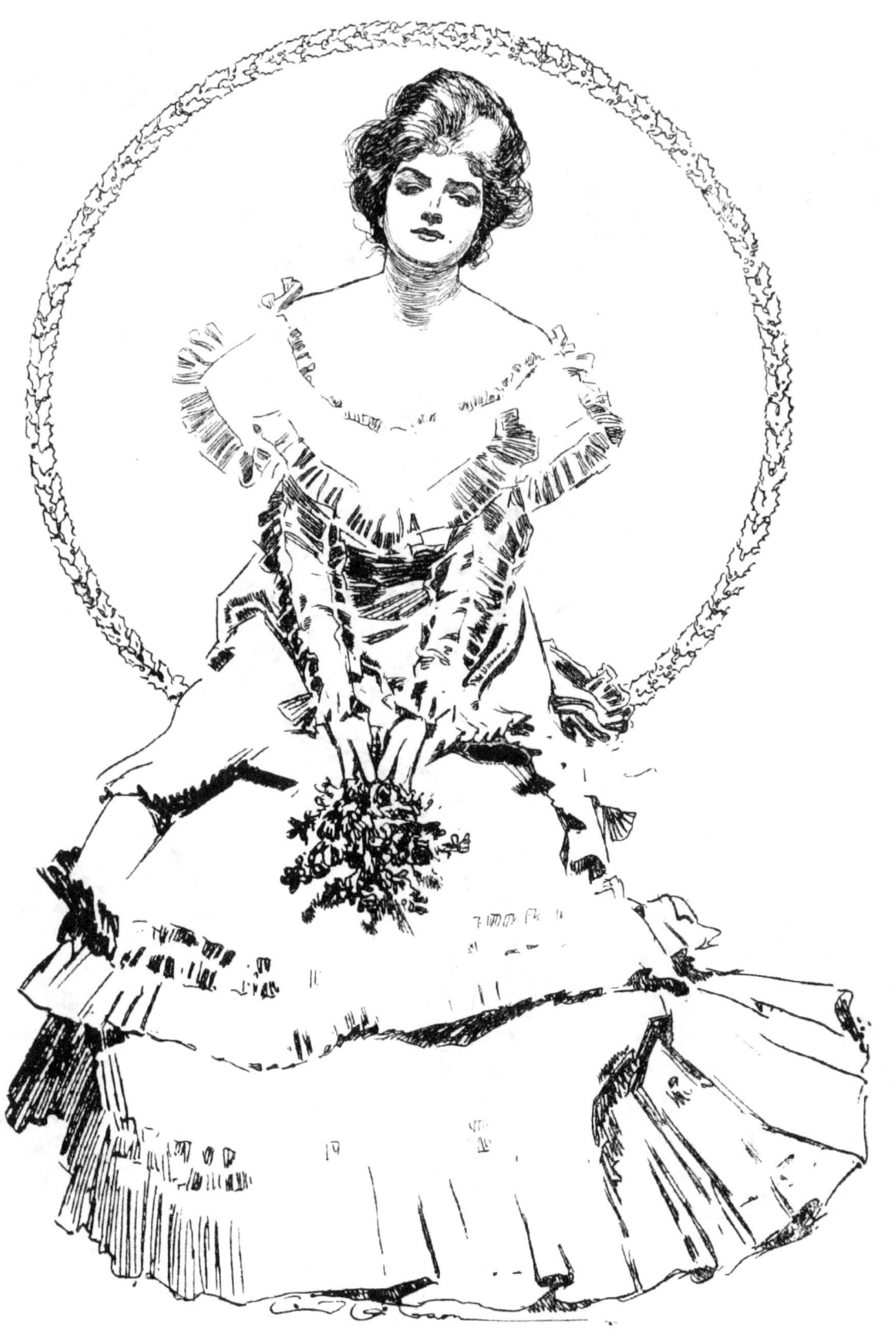

CHARLES DANA GIBSON: Illustration from 'Modern Pen Drawing: European and American'.

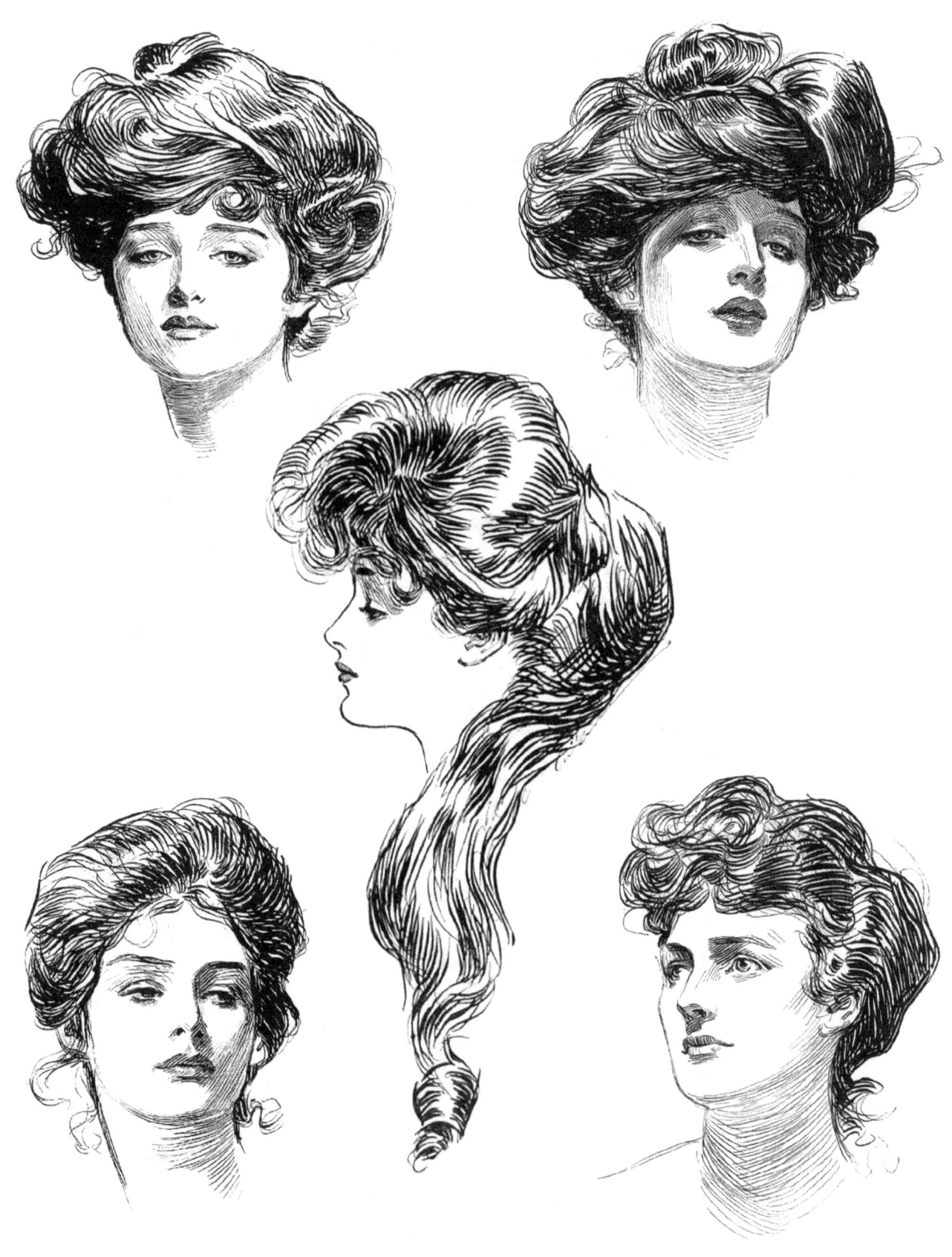

CHARLES DANA GIBSON: Examples of Gibson's stylish women

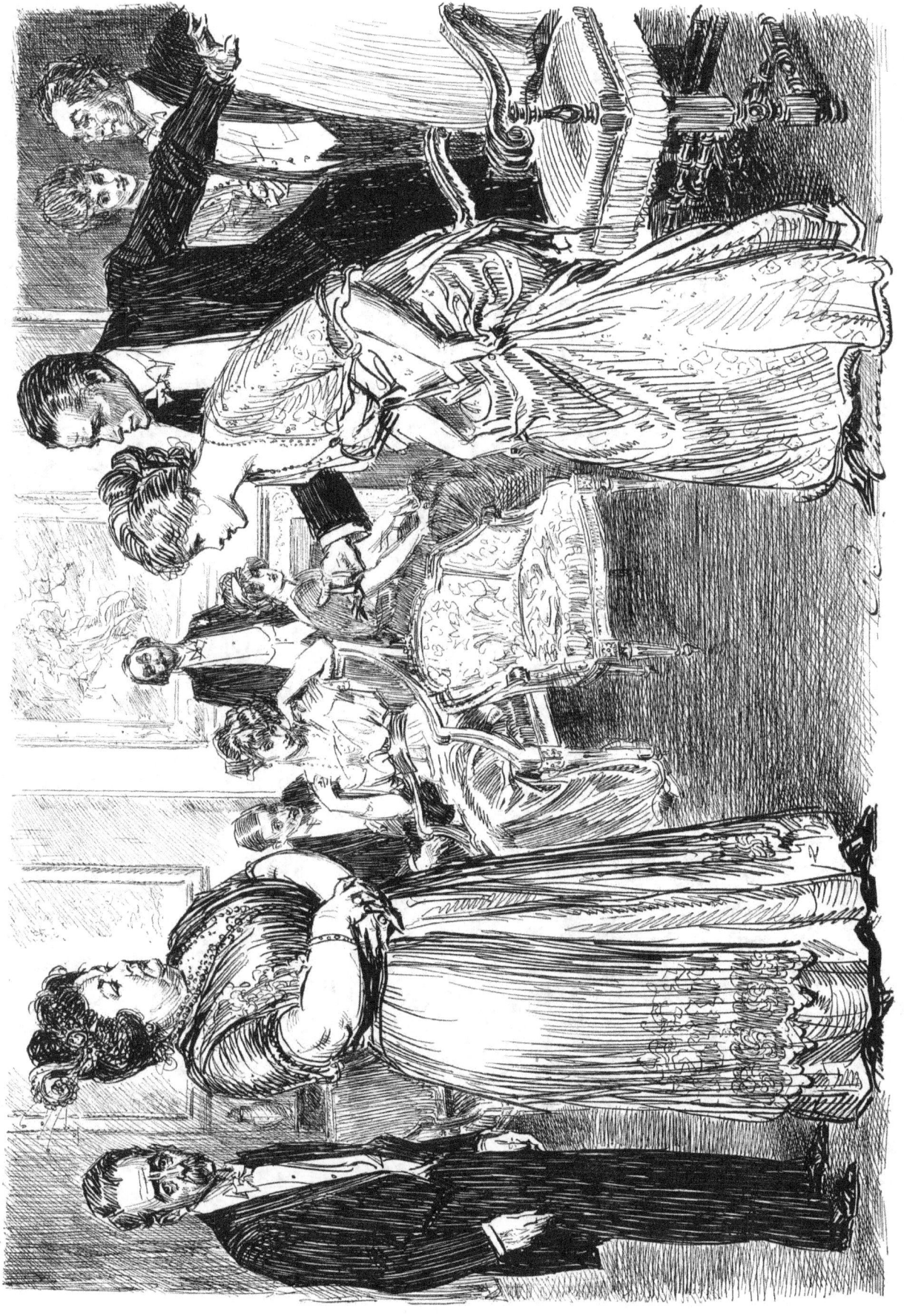

CHARLES DANA GIBSON: Illustration from 'Gibson New Cartoons'

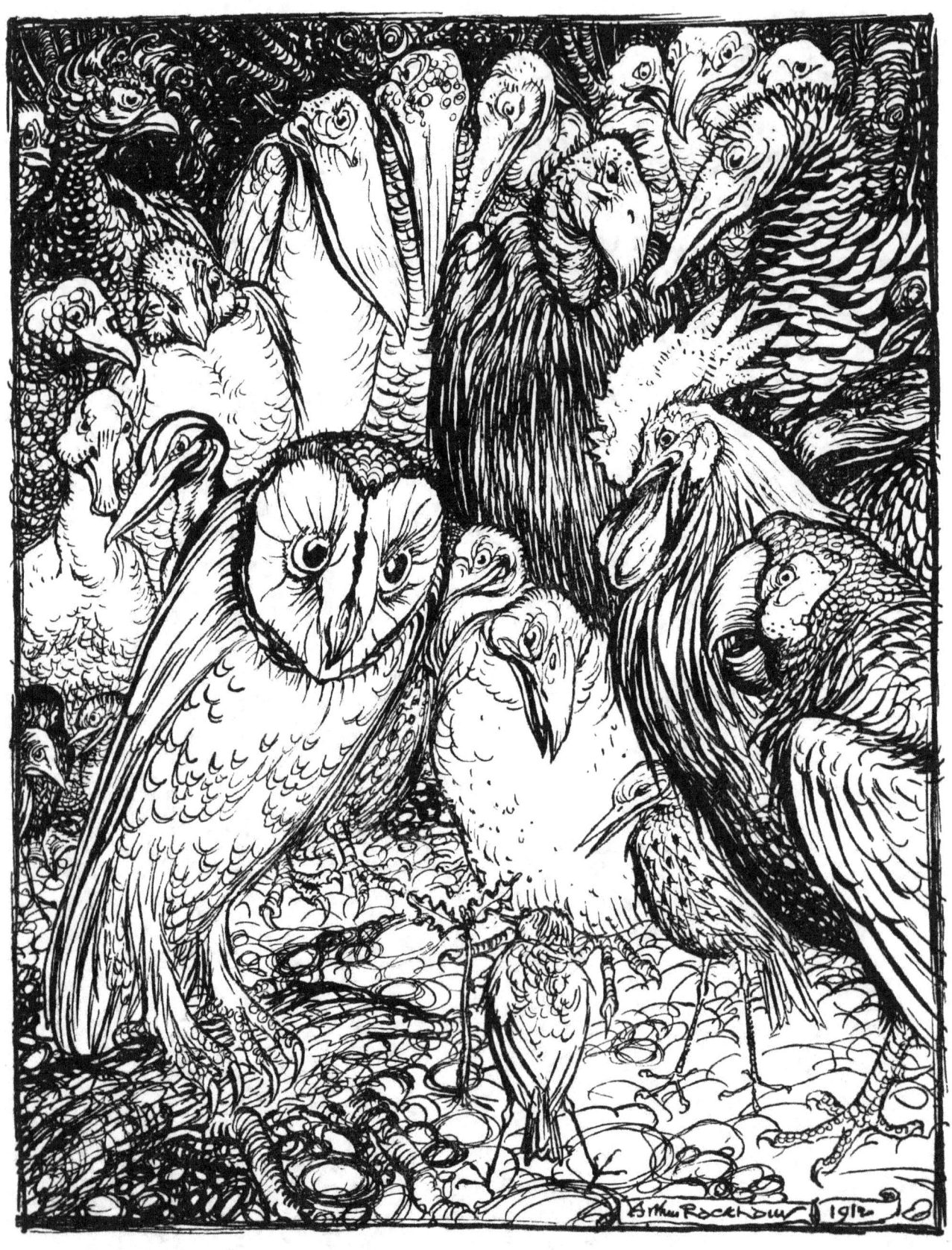

ARTHUR RACKHAM: The Owl and the Birds from 'Aesop's Fables'

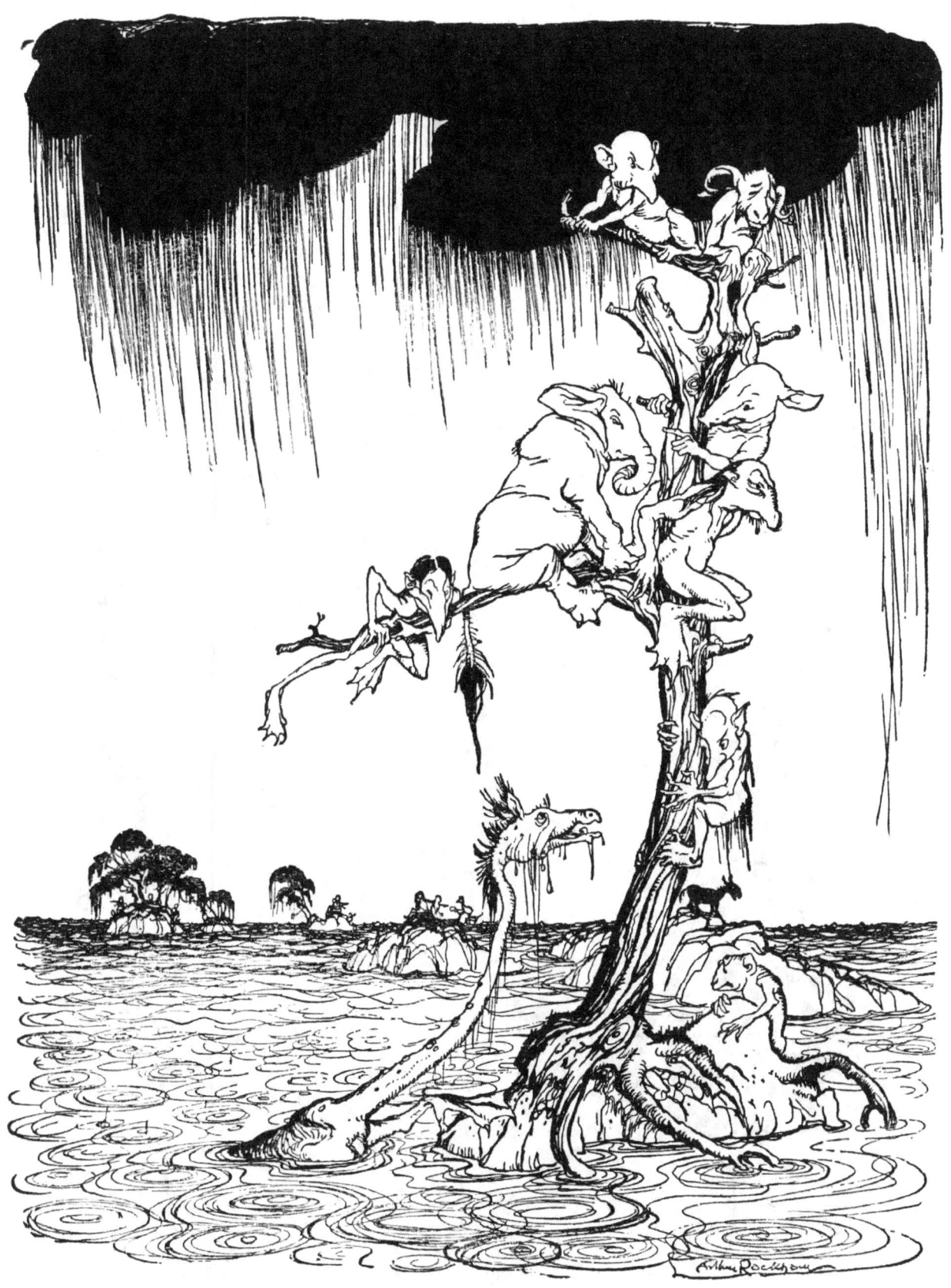

ARTHUR RACKHAM: "The animals, you know, were not as they are now"
From 'Princess Mary's Gift Book'

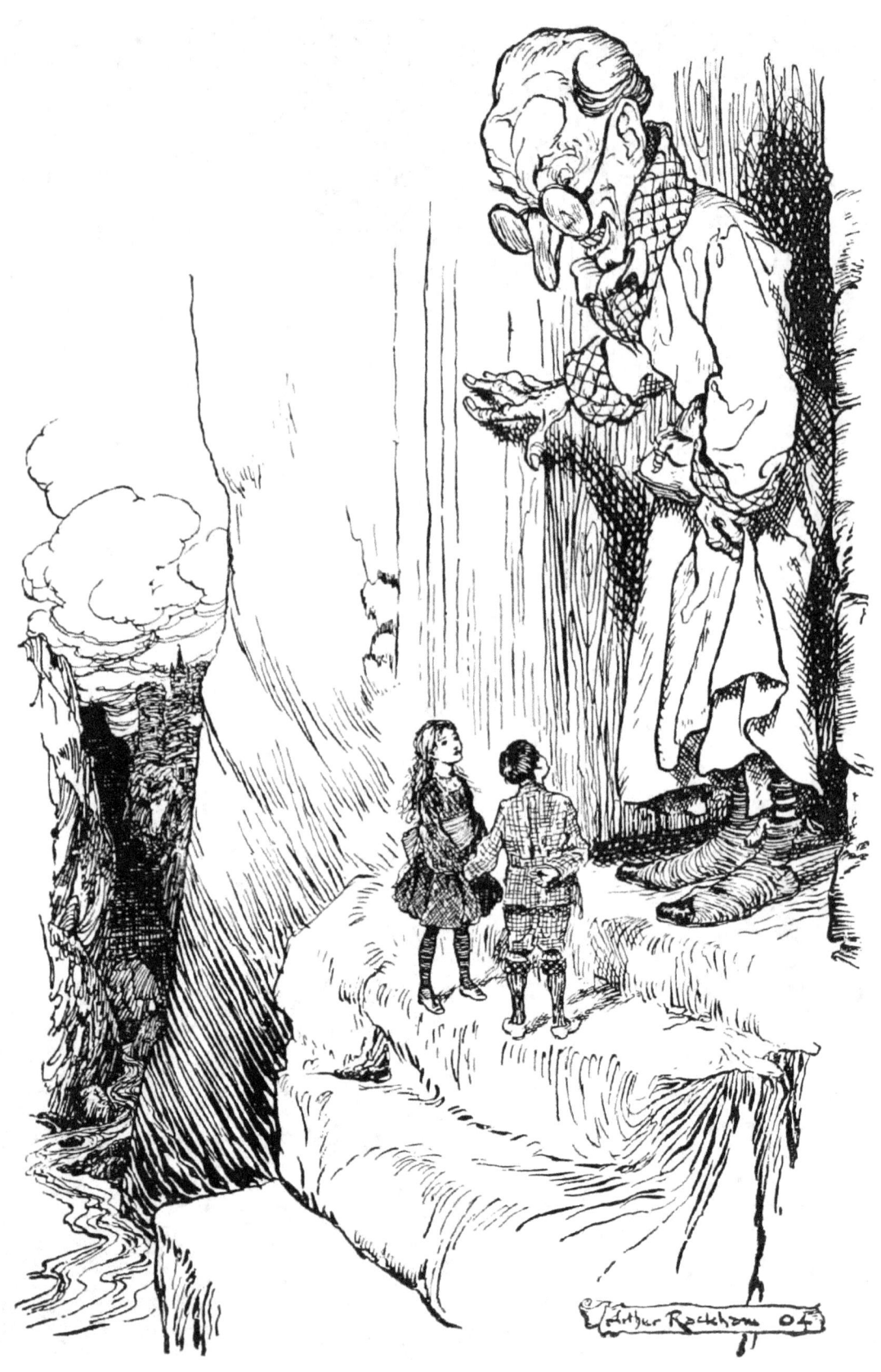

ARTHUR RACKHAM: "So you've come to see the Wizard," he said.
From 'The Rainbow Book'

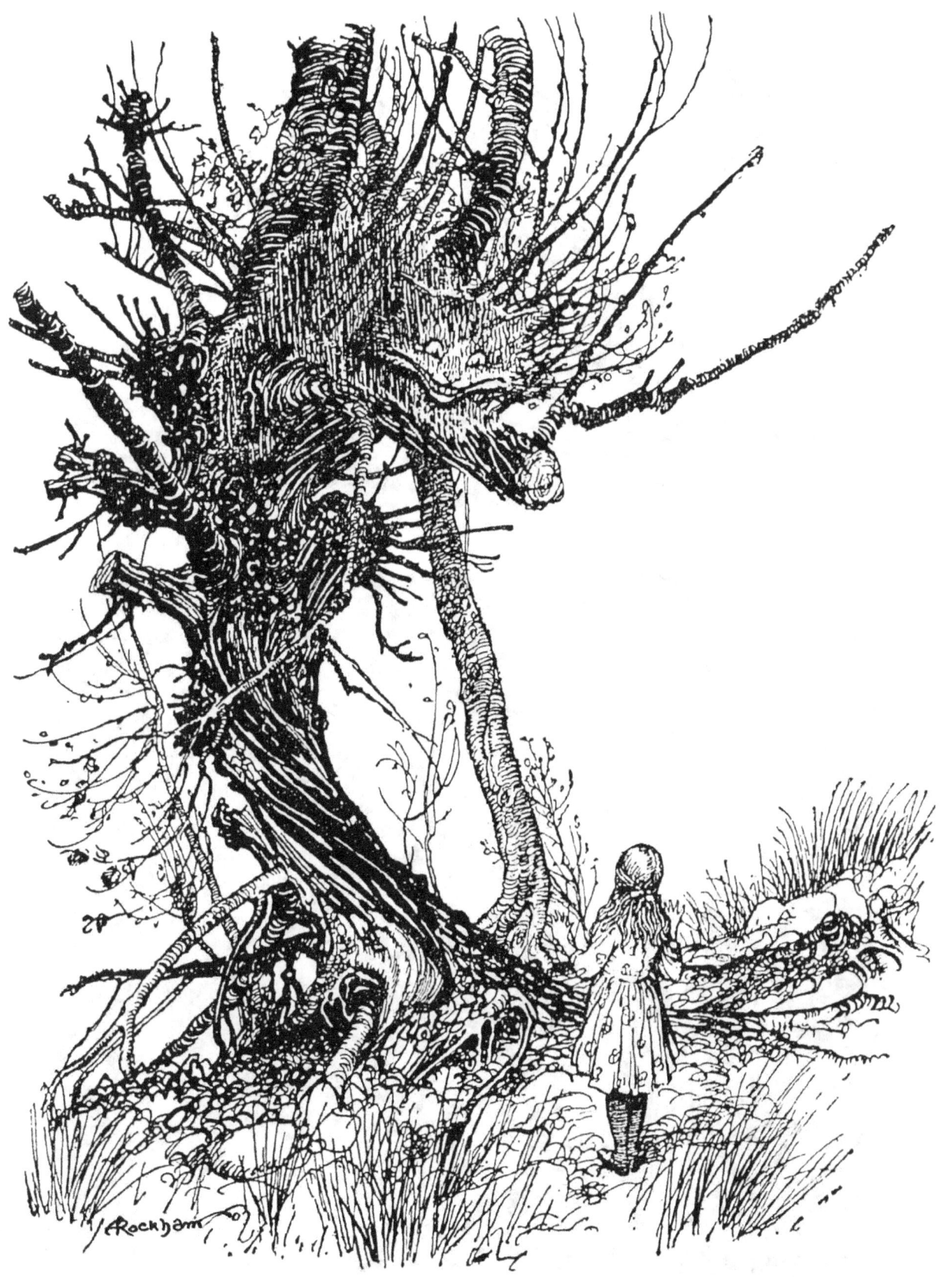

ARTHUR RACKHAM: Alice and the Cheshire Cat from 'Alice's Adventures in Wonderland'

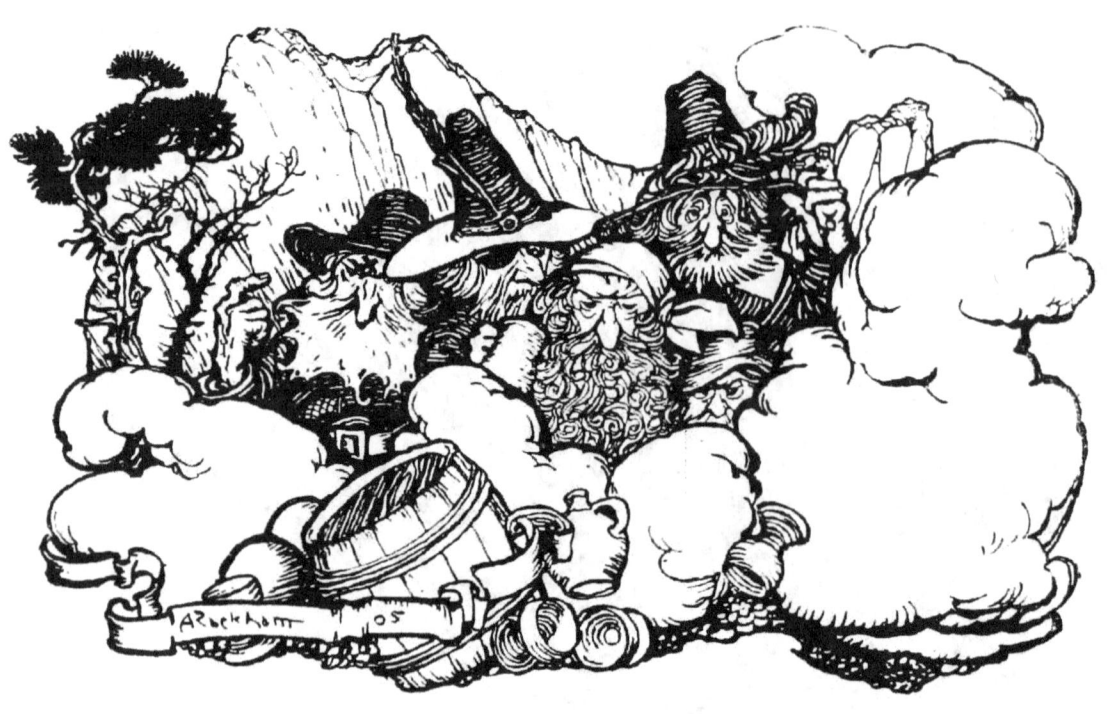

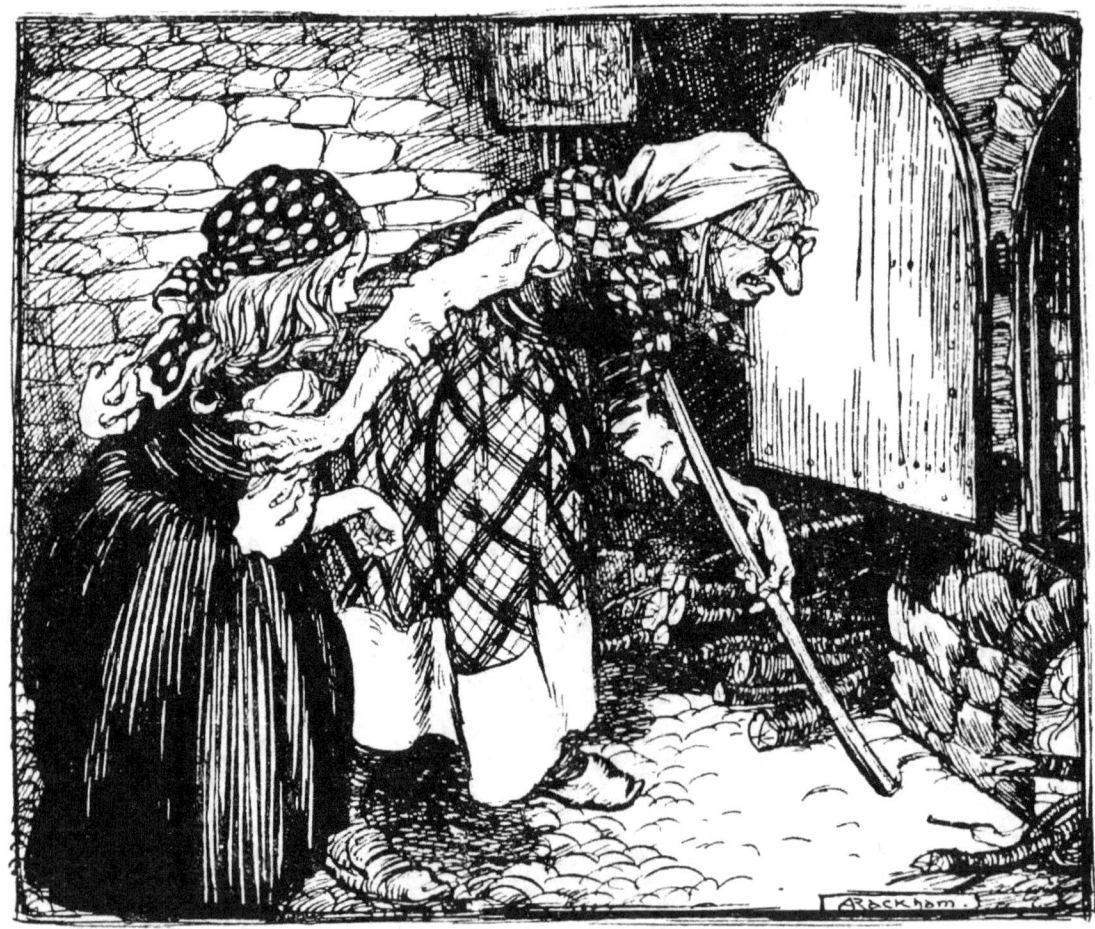

ARTHUR RACKHAM: In-text drawings. Above Top, from 'Rip Van Winkle'.
Above, from 'The Fairy Tales of the Brothers Grimm'

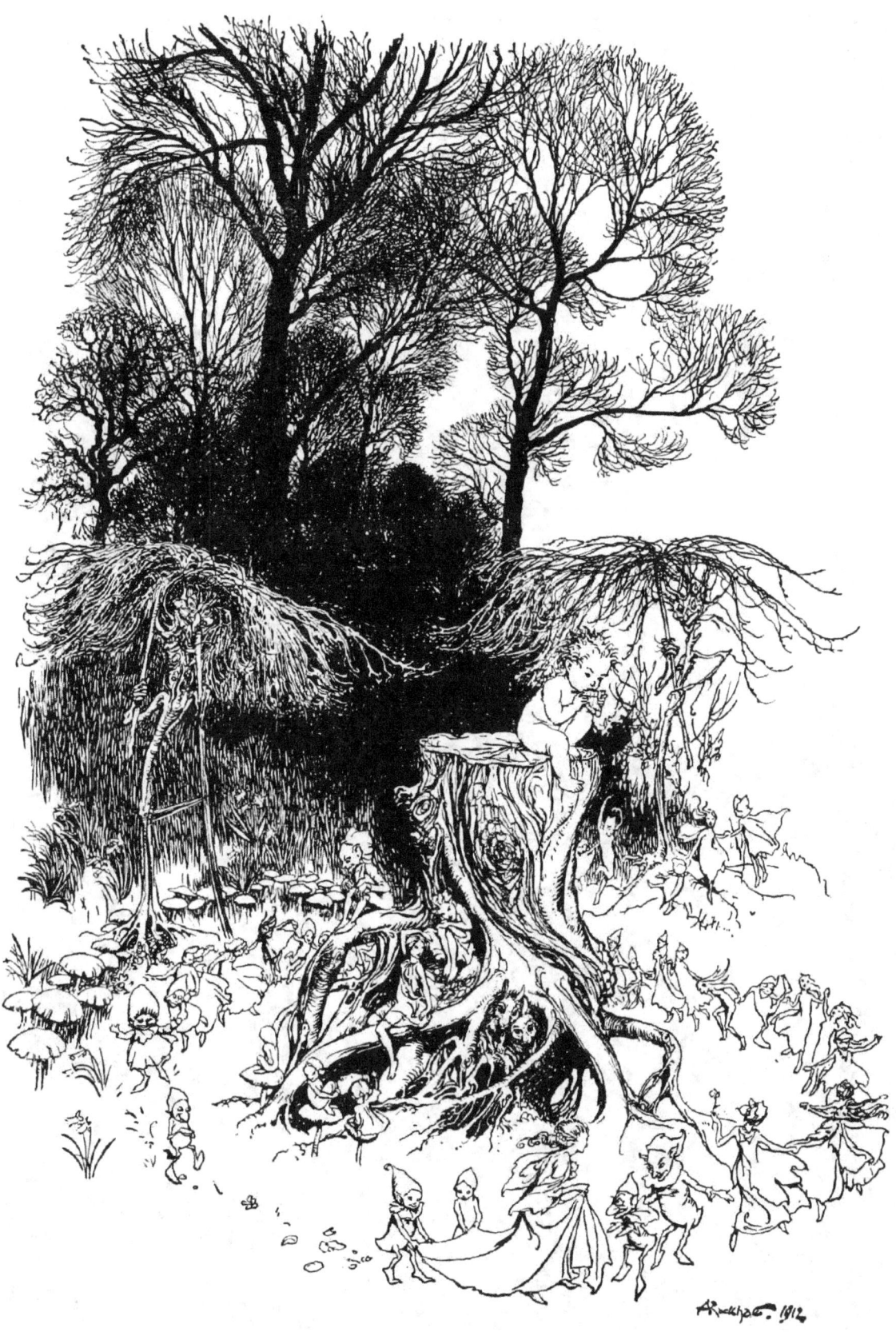

ARTHUR RACKHAM: A Fairy Ring. From 'Peter Pan in Kensington Gardens'

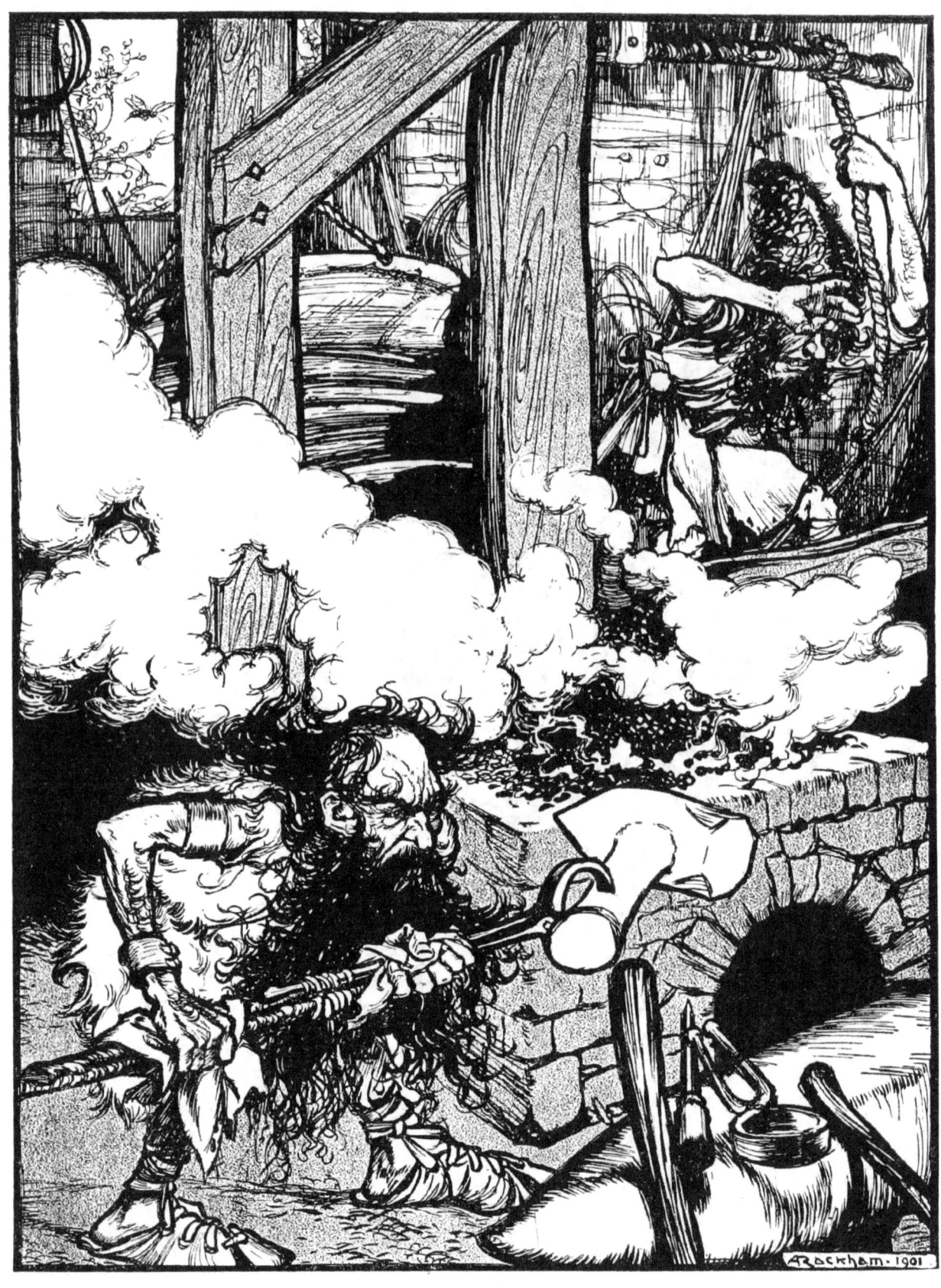

ARTHUR RACKHAM: Once again the buzzing fly came in at the window.
From 'The Land of Enchantment'

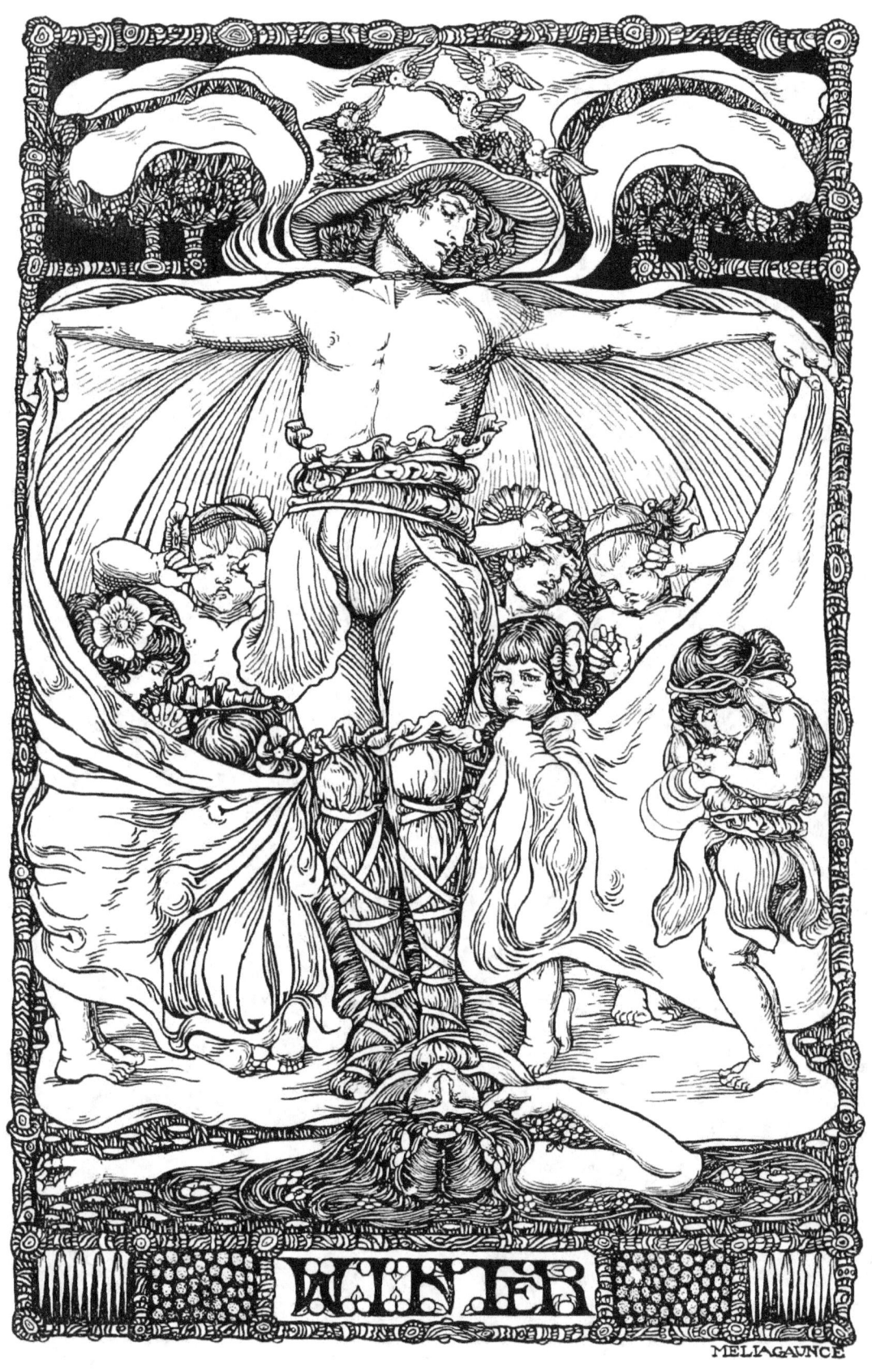

CHRISTINE DRUMMOND ANGUS (alias Meliagaunce): Competition winner from 'The Studio International' 1899

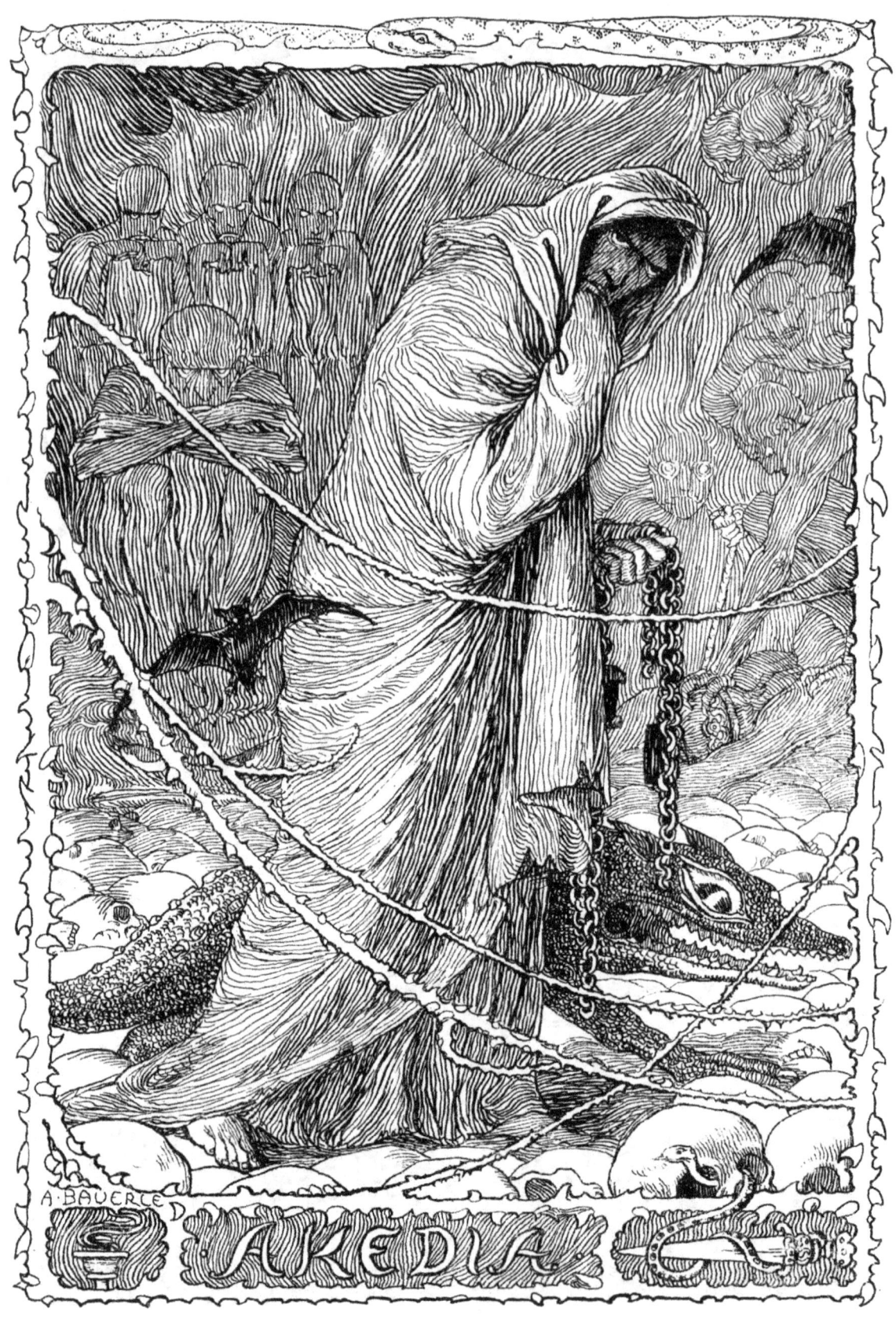

AMELIA BAUERLE: Akedia glided forth. From 'Allegories'

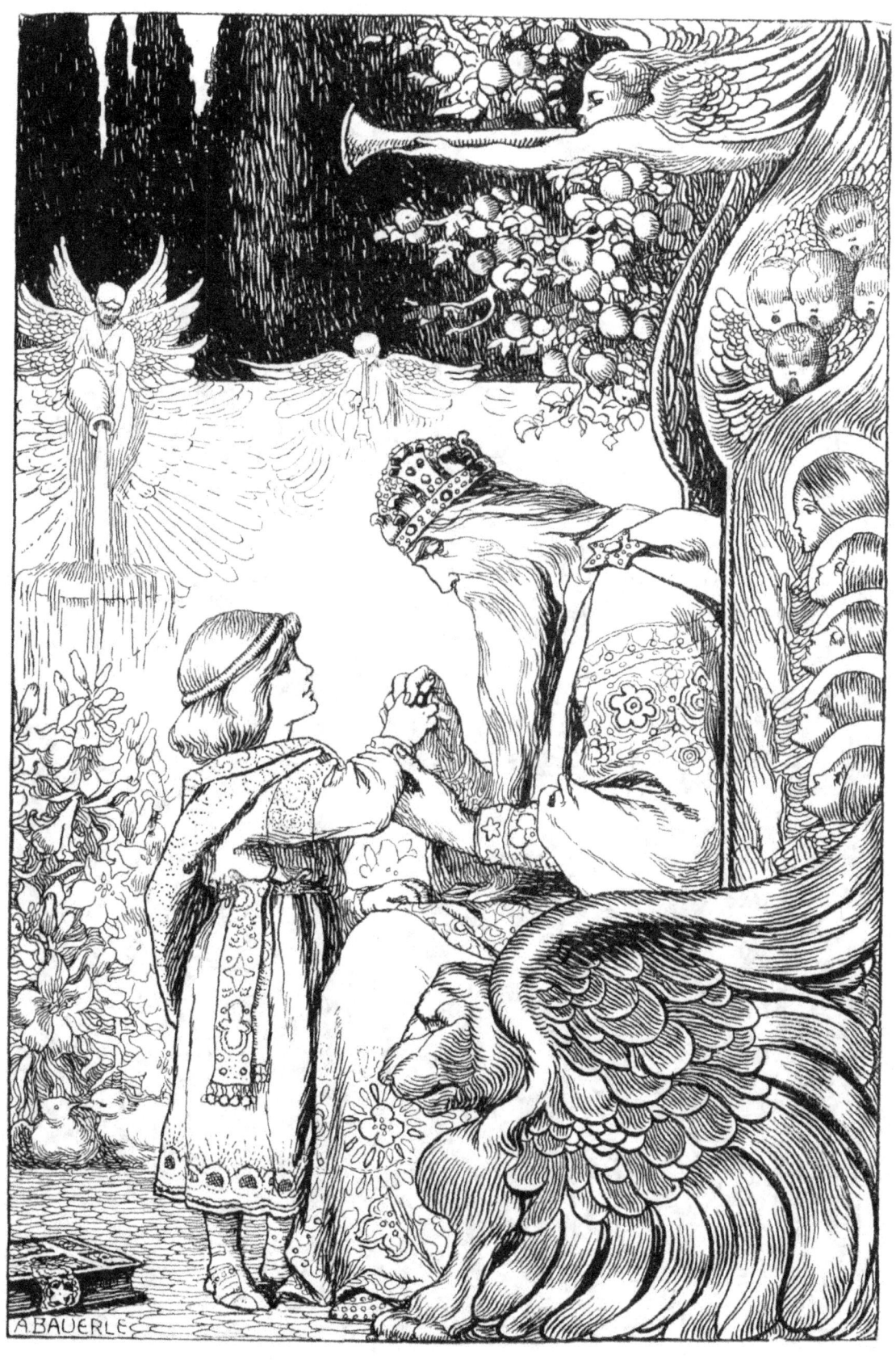

AMELIA BAUERLE: King Elyon and Paedarion. From 'Allegories'

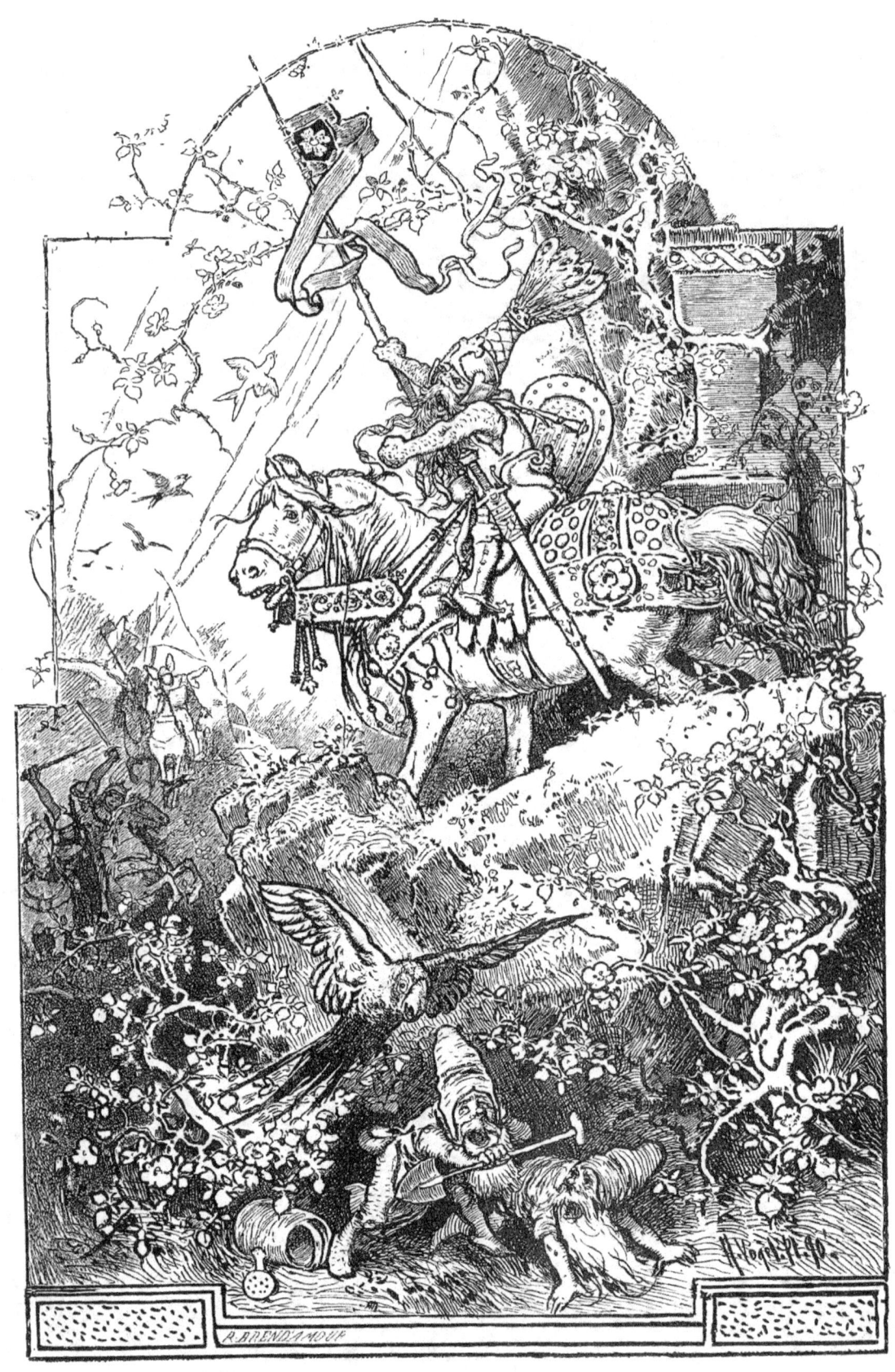

HERMANN VOGEL: King Laurin.
Illustration from 'Heldensage Deutsche' (German Historic Sagas)

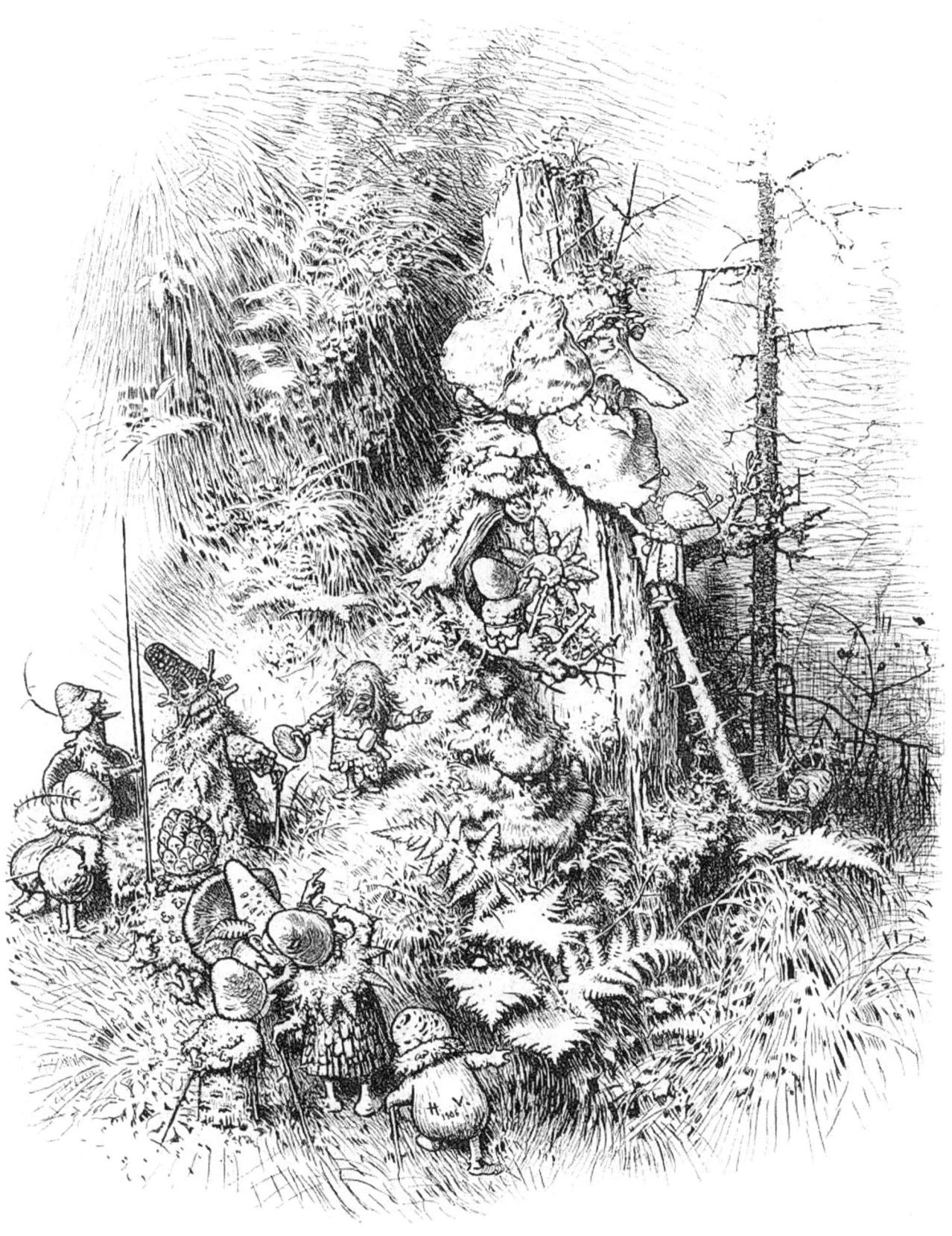

HERMANN VOGEL: His Majesty King Wichtelmann's court sculptor.
From 'Altes u. Neues von Herm Vogel' (Old and New from Herm Vogel)

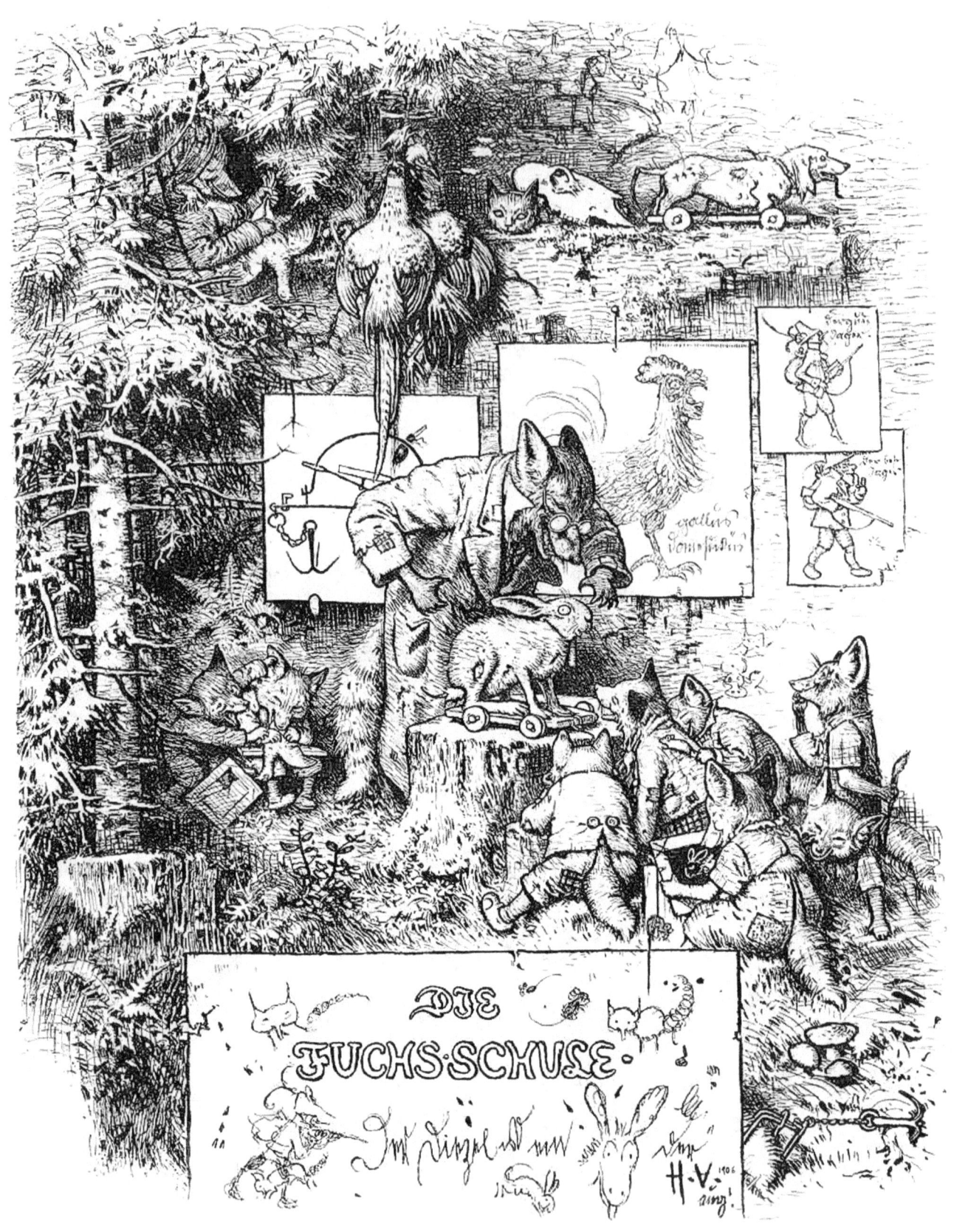

HERMANN VOGEL: The fox school.
From 'Altes u. Neues von Herm Vogel' (Old and New from Herm Vogel).

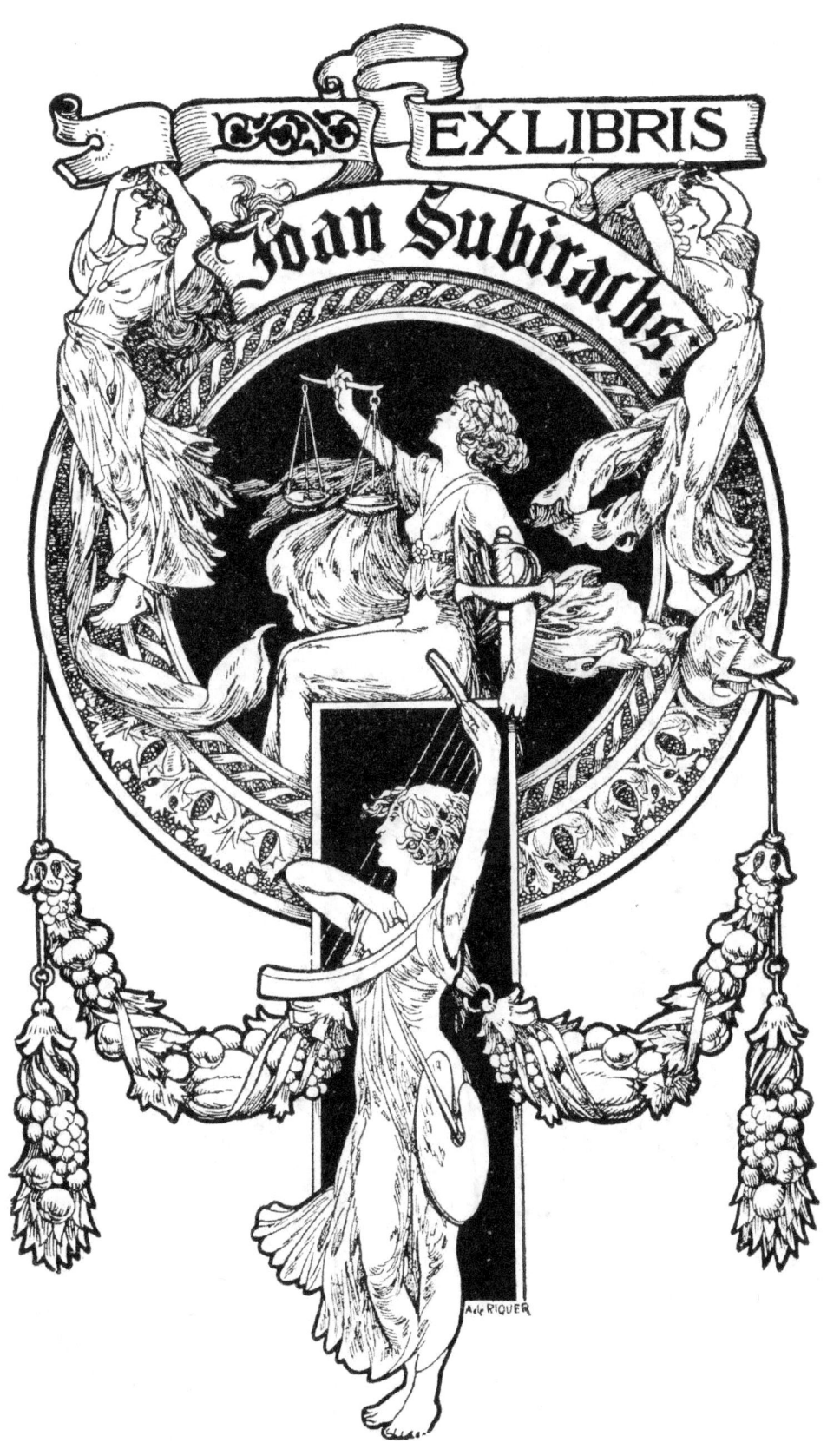

ALEXANDRE DE RIQUER: Design for a Book-plate

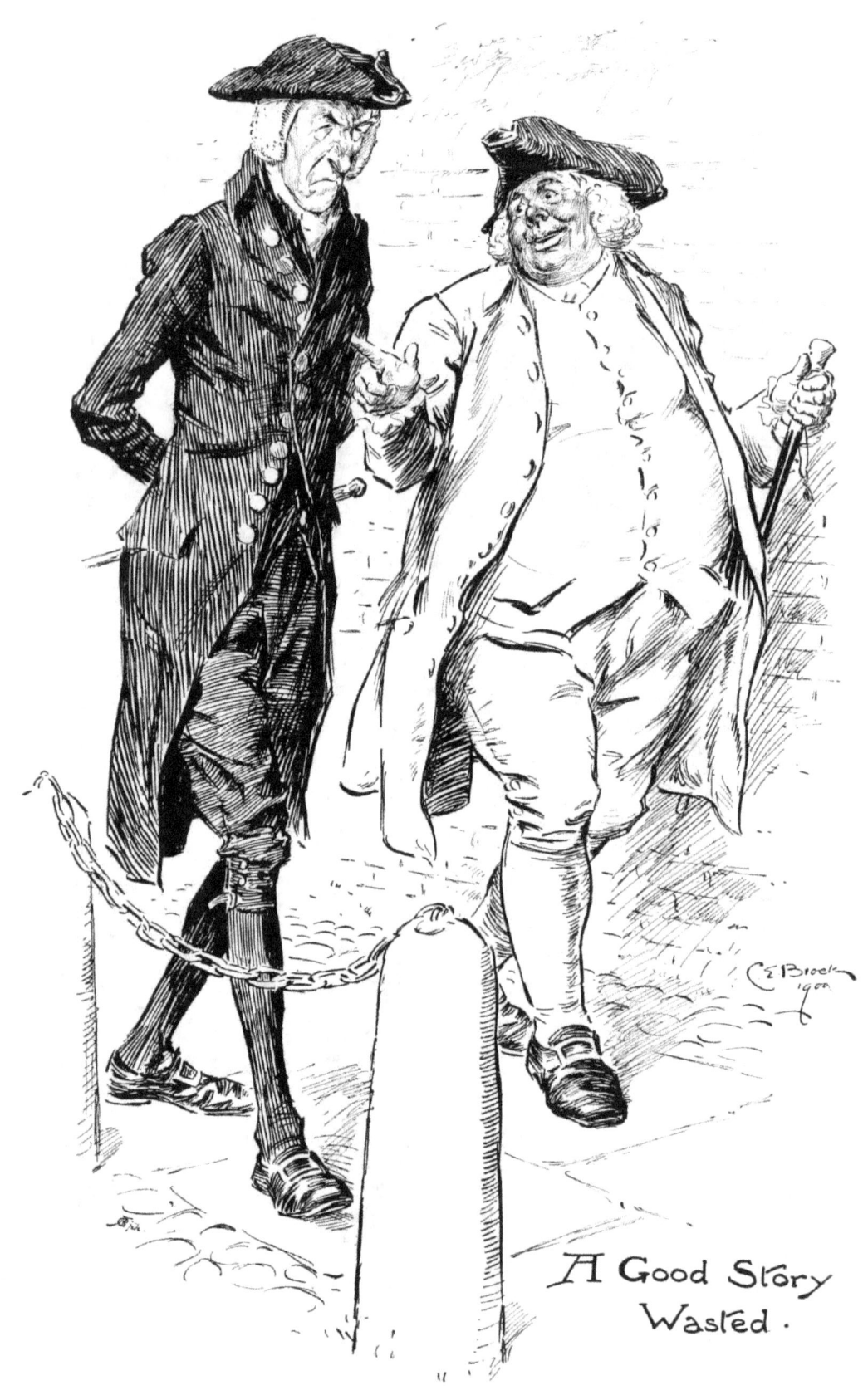

C E BROCK: A Good Story Wasted. From 'Modern Pen Drawing: European and American'

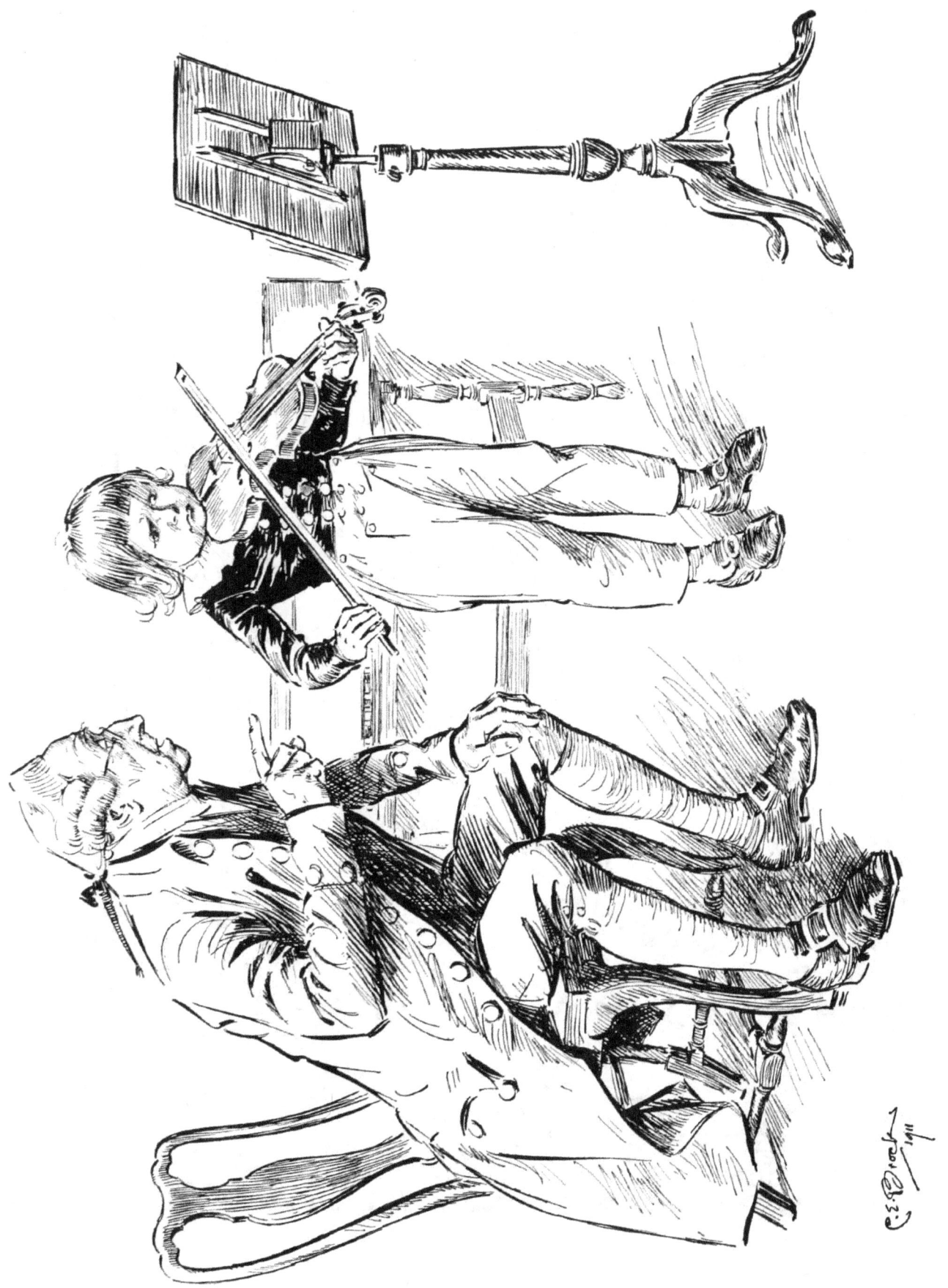

C E BROCK: A Music Hater. From 'Plume Crayon Fusain'

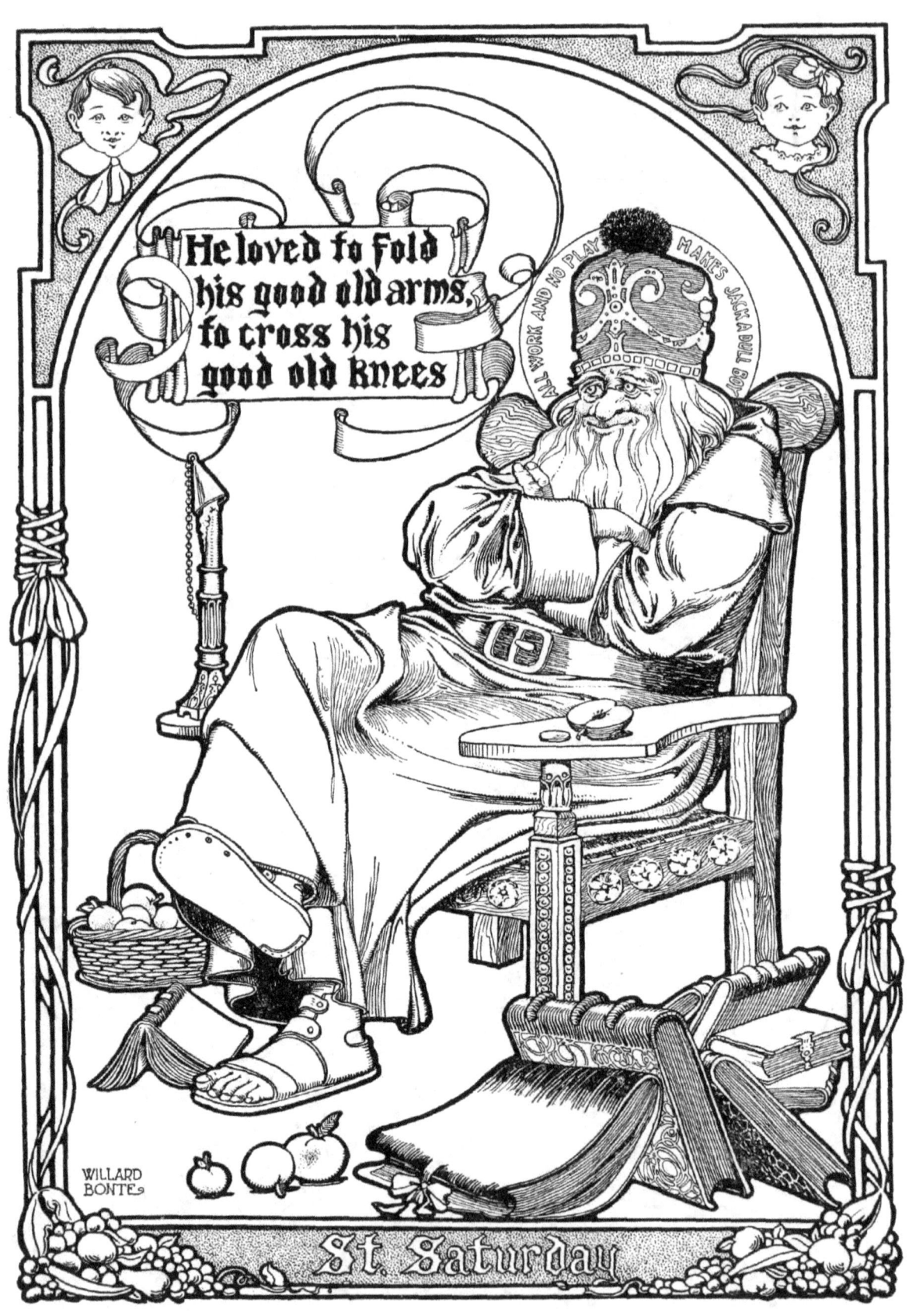

WILLARD BONTE: Saint Saturday. From 'Boys' and Girls' Bookshelf' Vol 20.

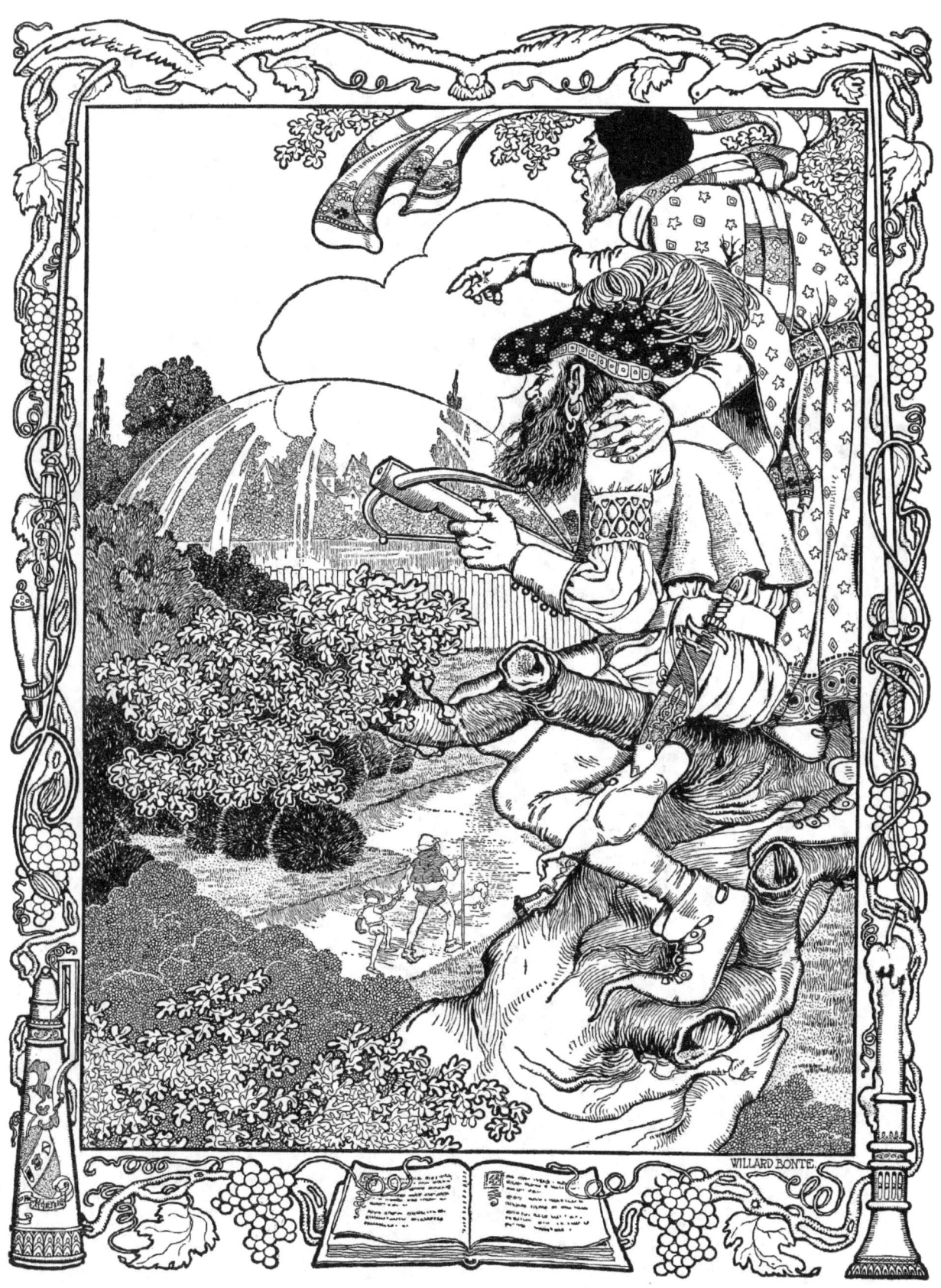

WILLARD BONTE: The Baron took a crossbow and prepared to shoot.
From 'Boys' and Girls' Bookshelf' Vol 19.

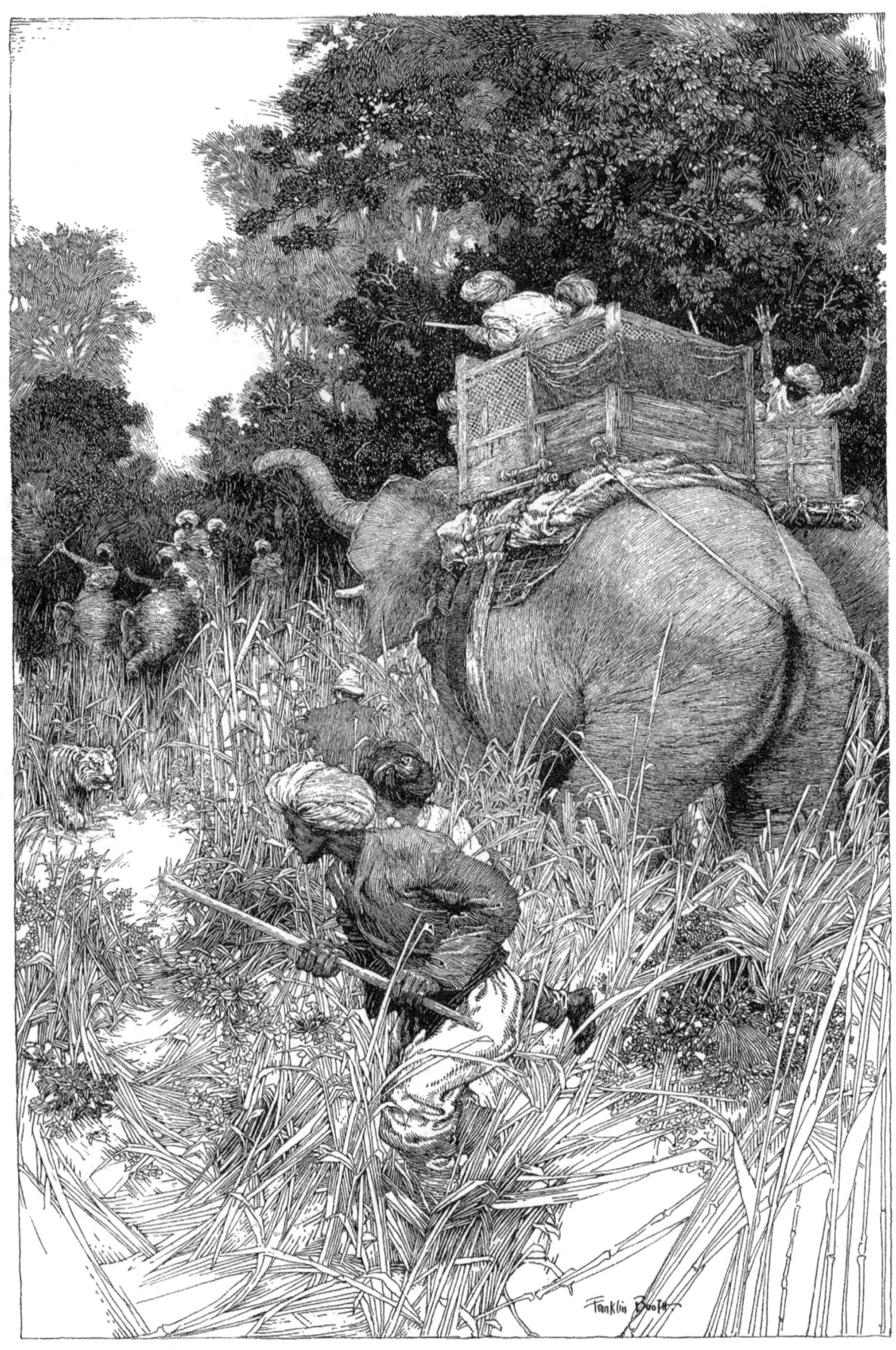

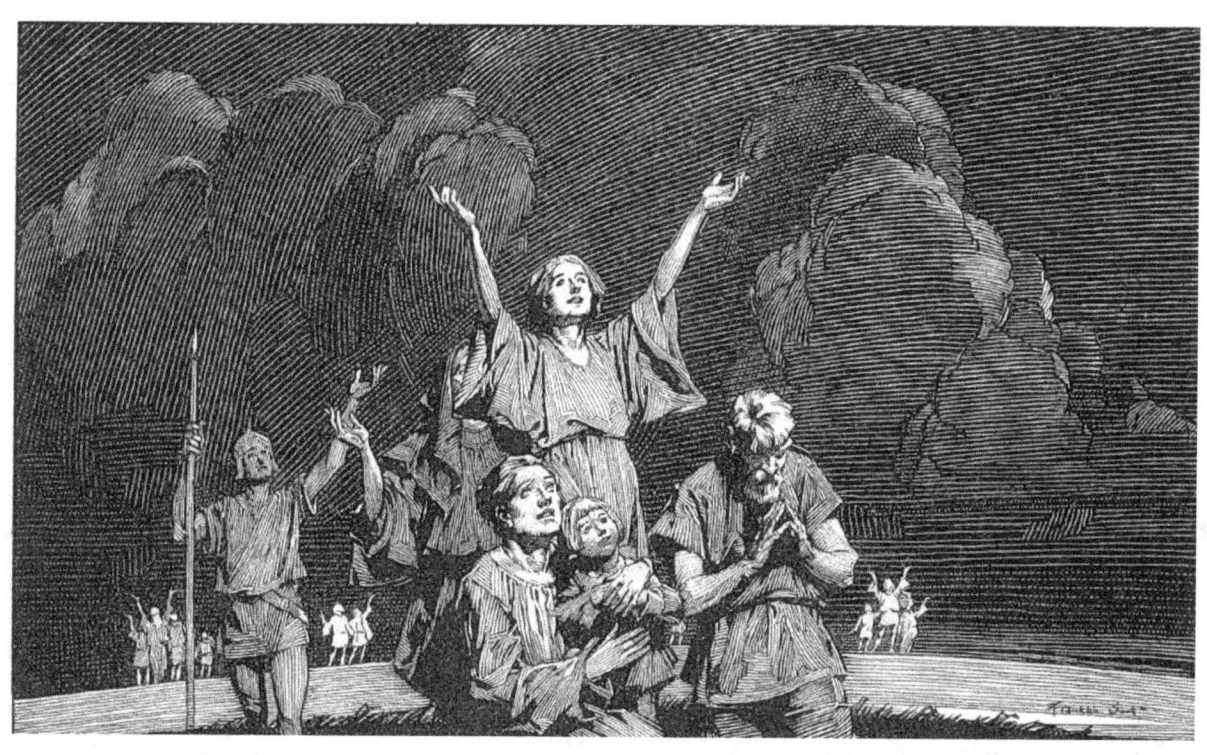

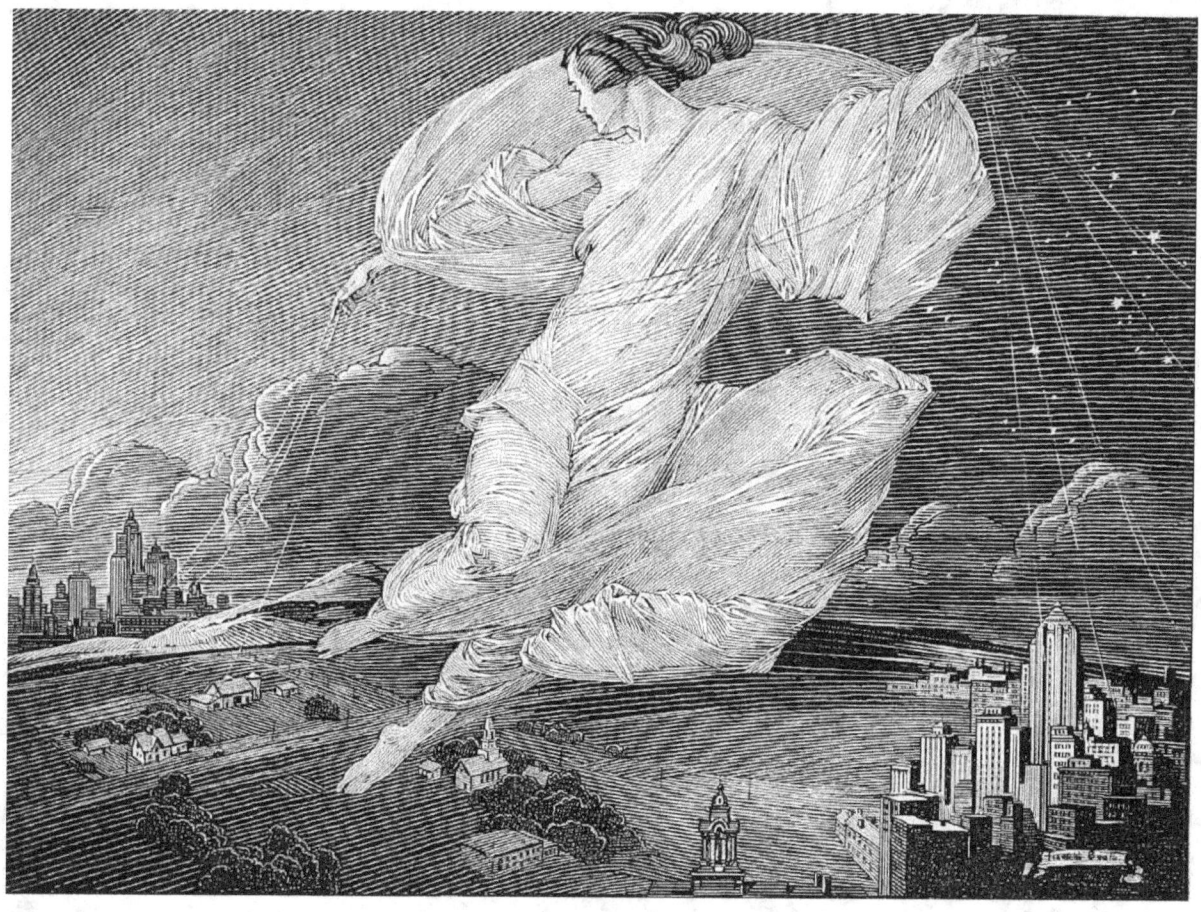

FRANKLIN BOOTH: Left, 'Tiger Hunt'. Above top, 'An Easter Prayer'. Above, 'A Continent is Bridged'.

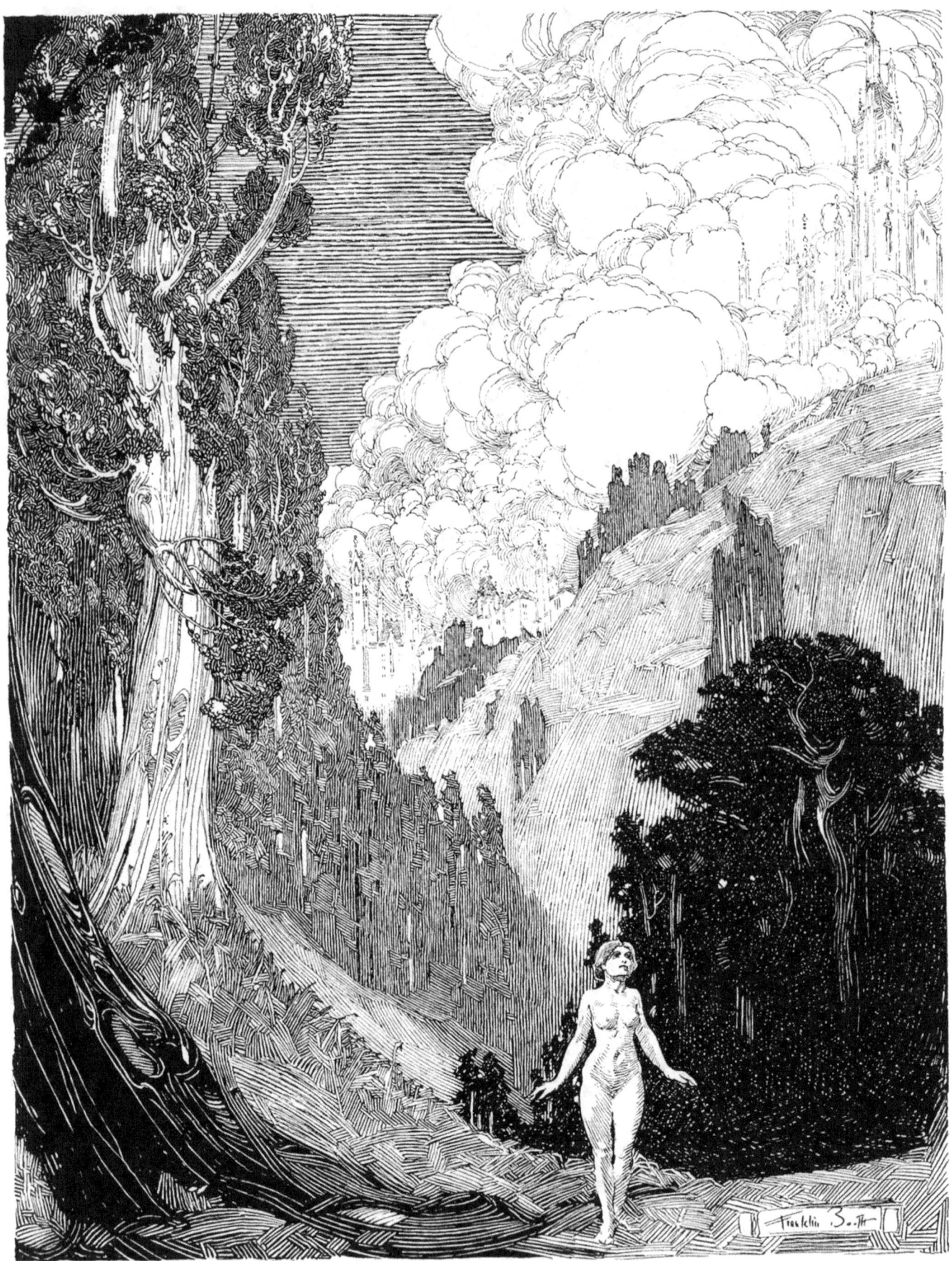

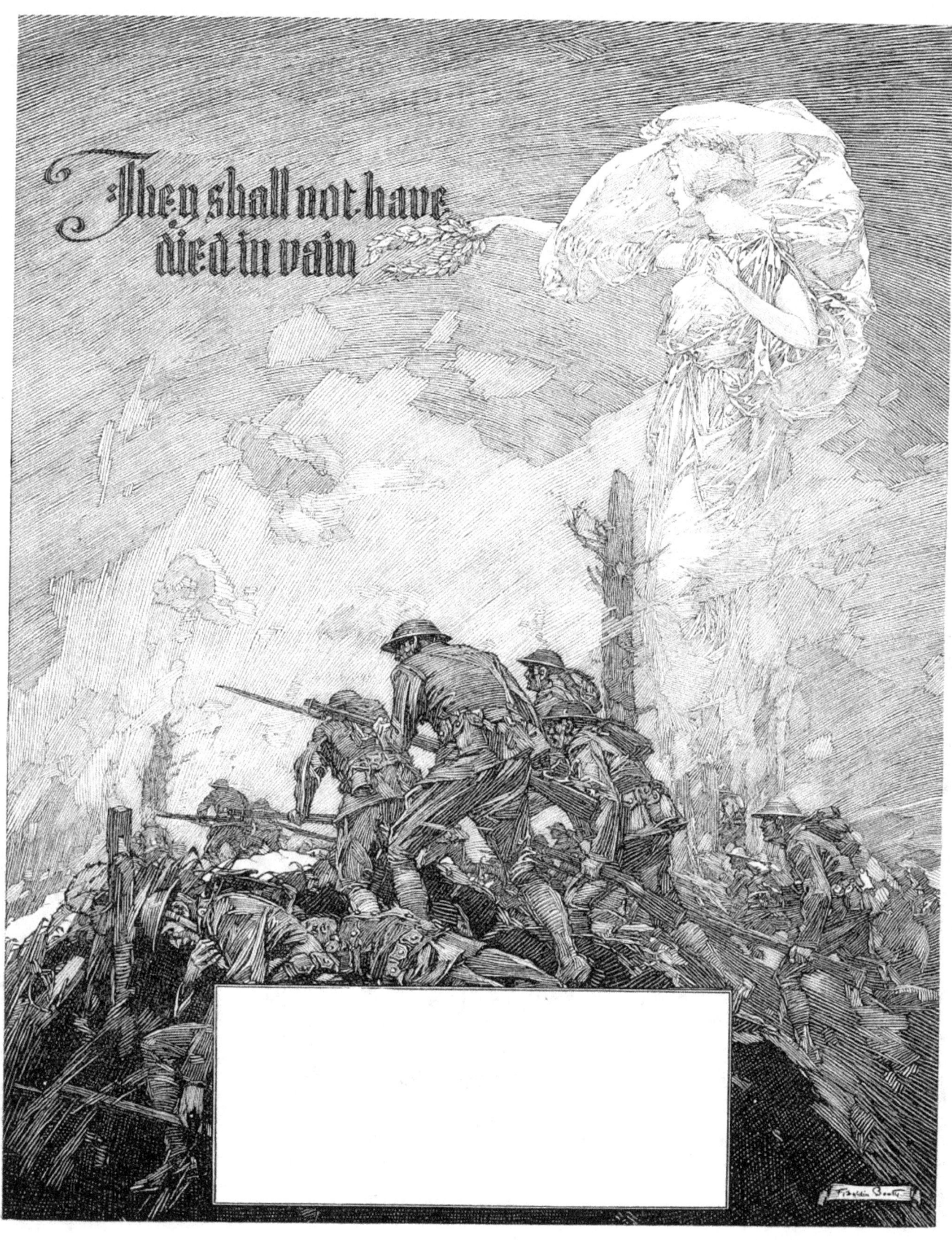

FRANKLIN BOOTH: Left, 'Valley of Silence'. Above, 'Memorial'.

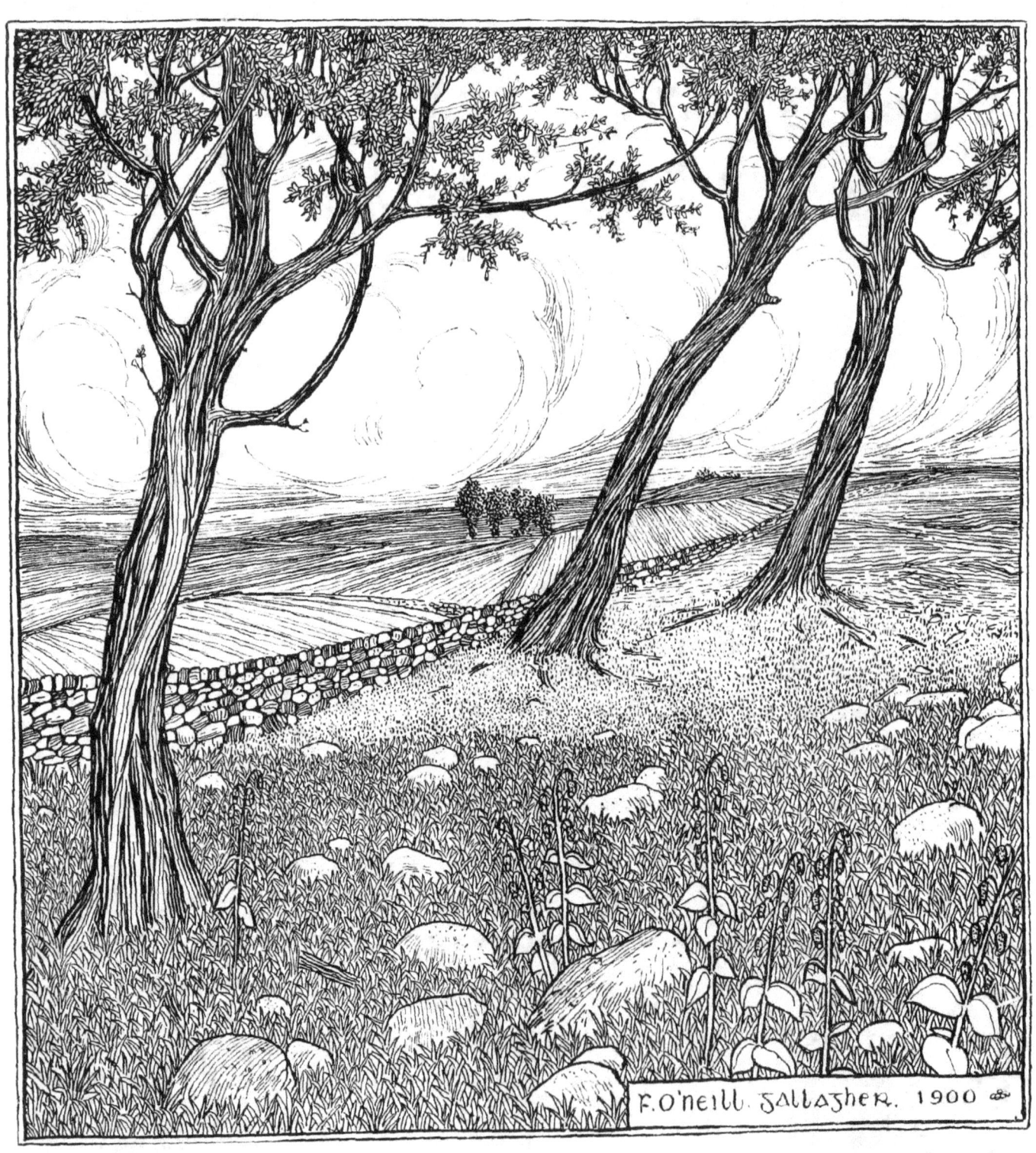

FREDERICK O'NEILL GALLAGHER: Landscape from 'Modern Pen Drawing: European and American'

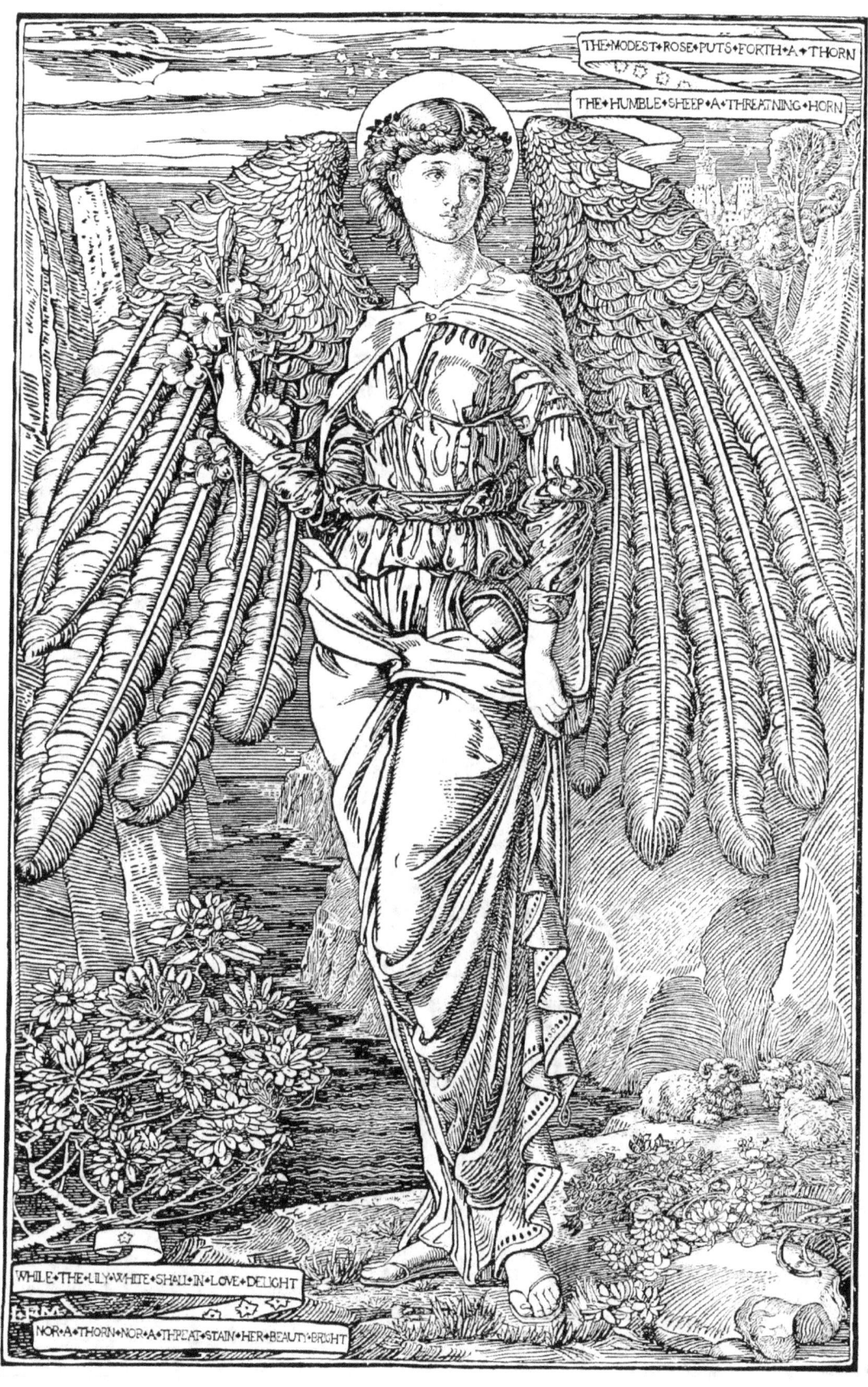

L F MUCKLEY: The modest rose puts forth a thorn. From 'Pen Drawing and Pen Draughtsmen'.

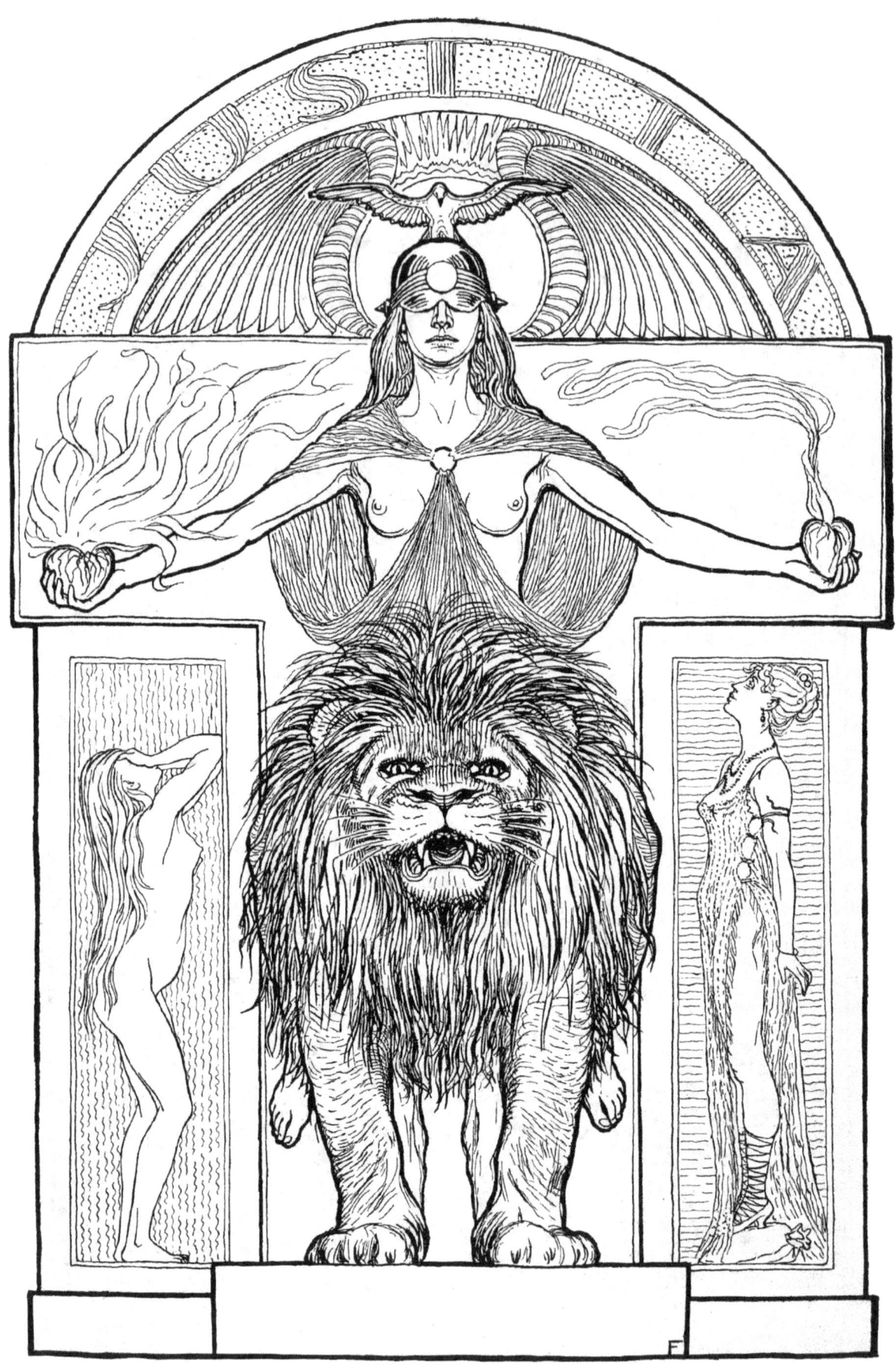

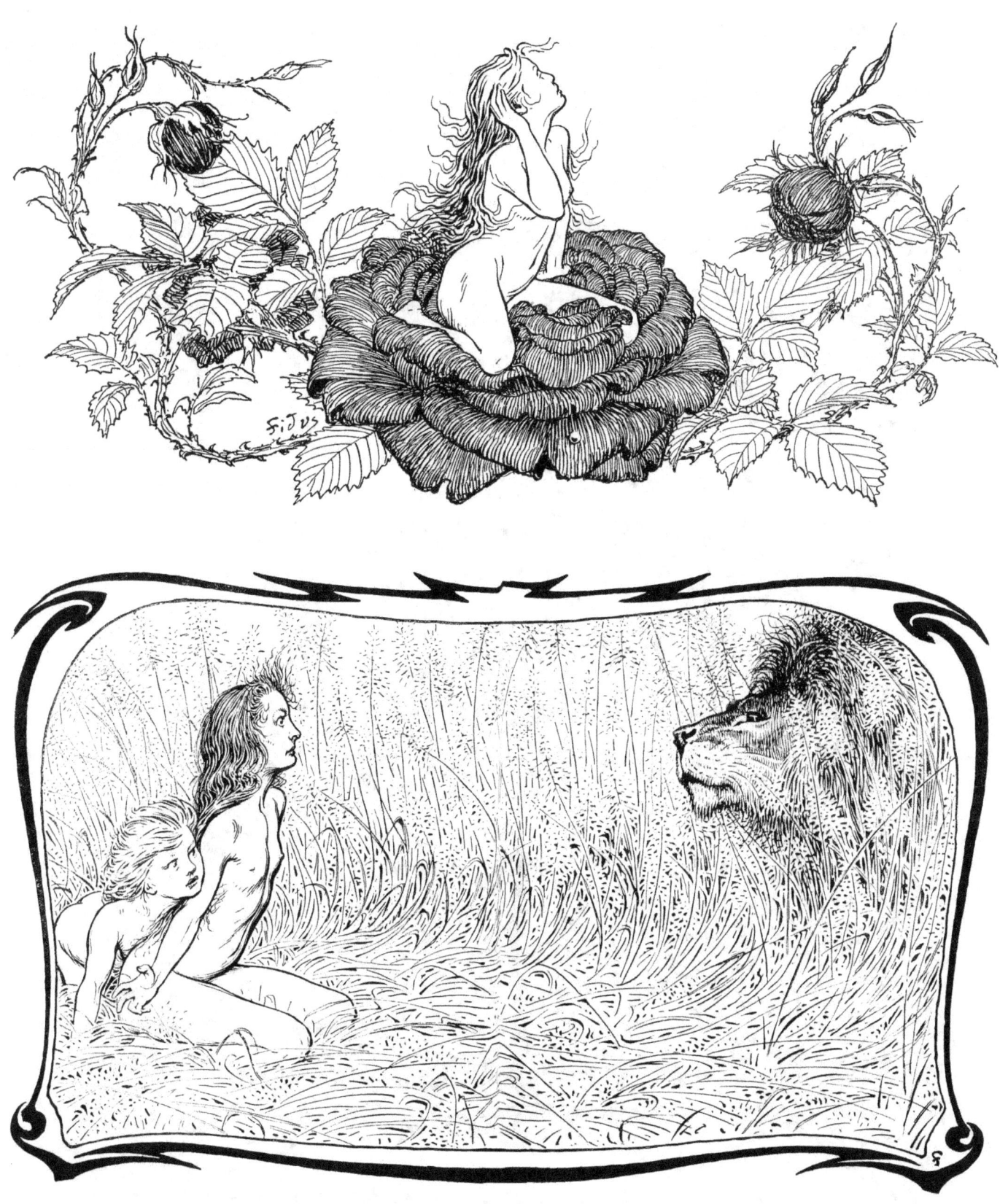

FIDUS (HUGO HOPPENER): Left and above, 'Jugend' magazine illustrations

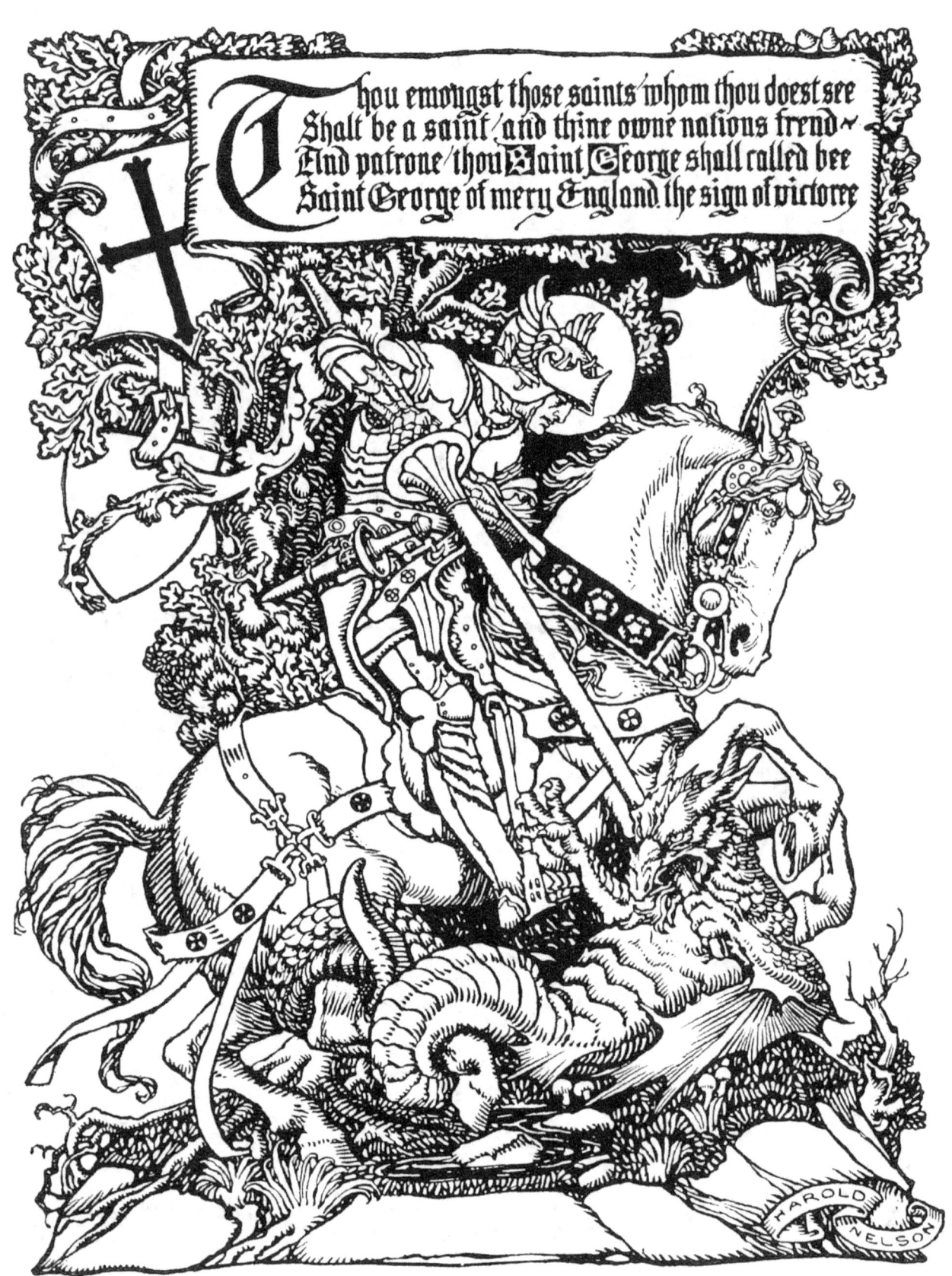

HAROLD NELSON: Saint George Design

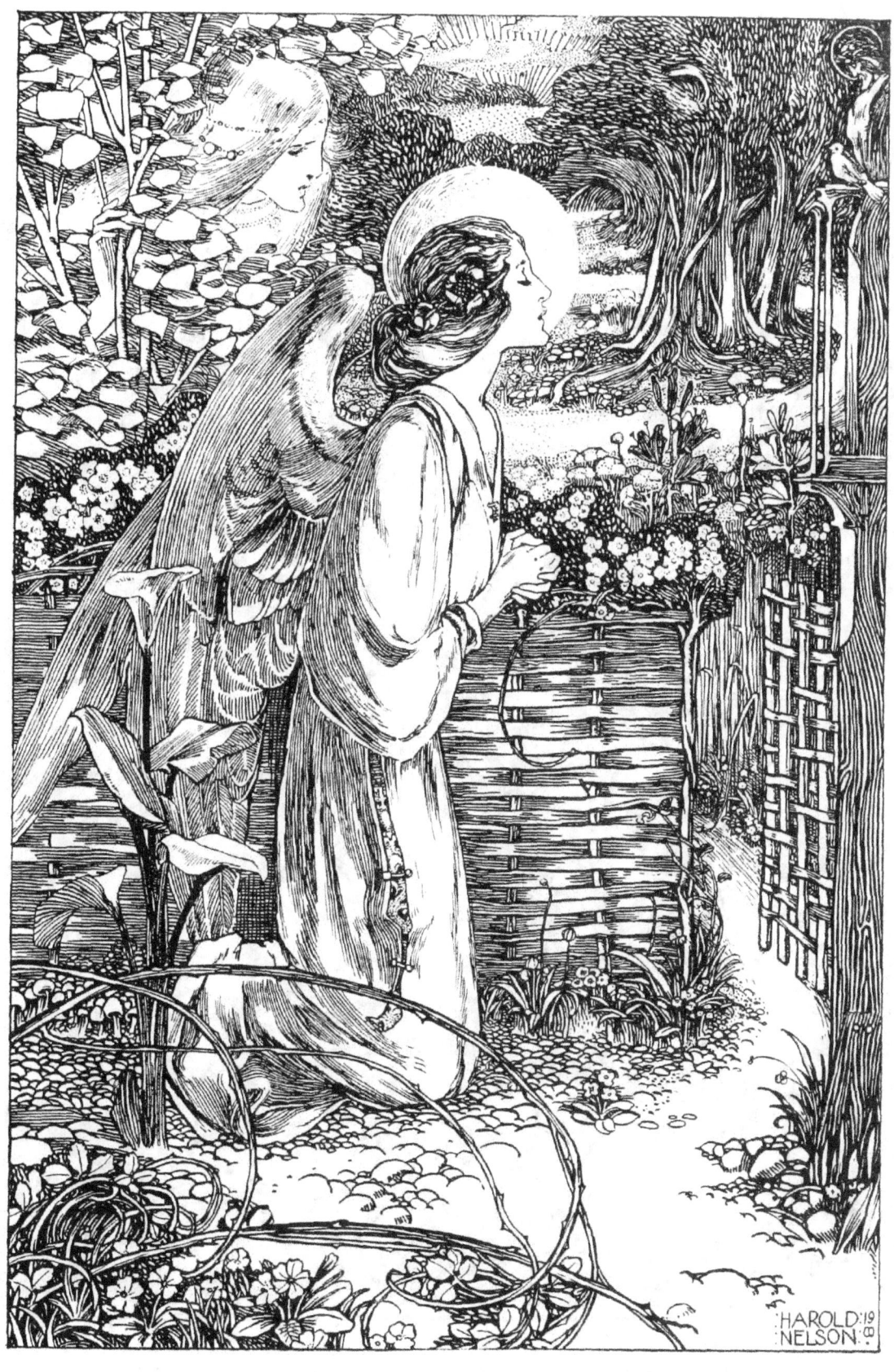

HAROLD NELSON: The Vision of St. Agatha.
From 'Modern Pen Drawing: European and American'

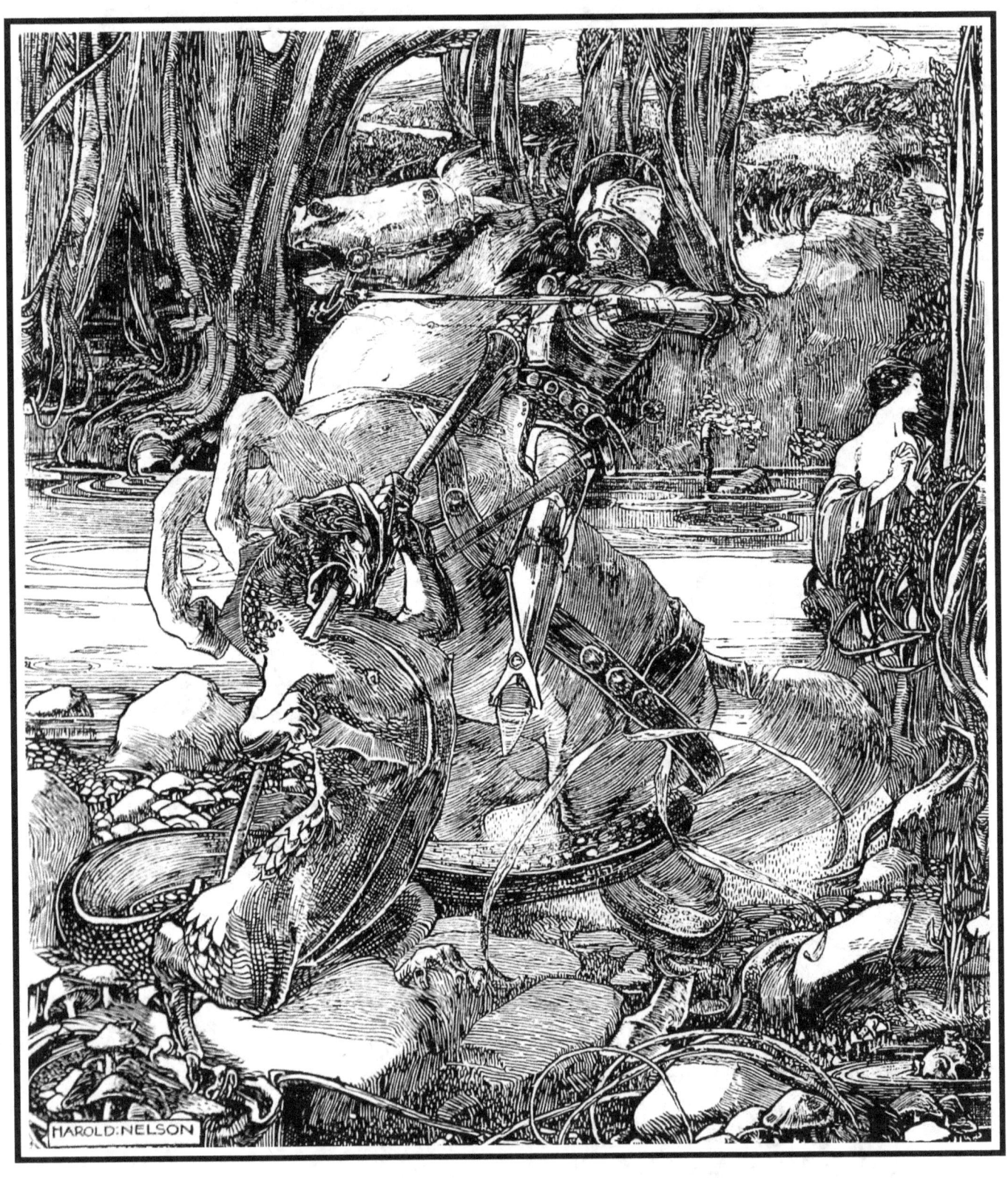

HAROLD NELSON: Saint George. From 'The Magazine of Art' Volume 24

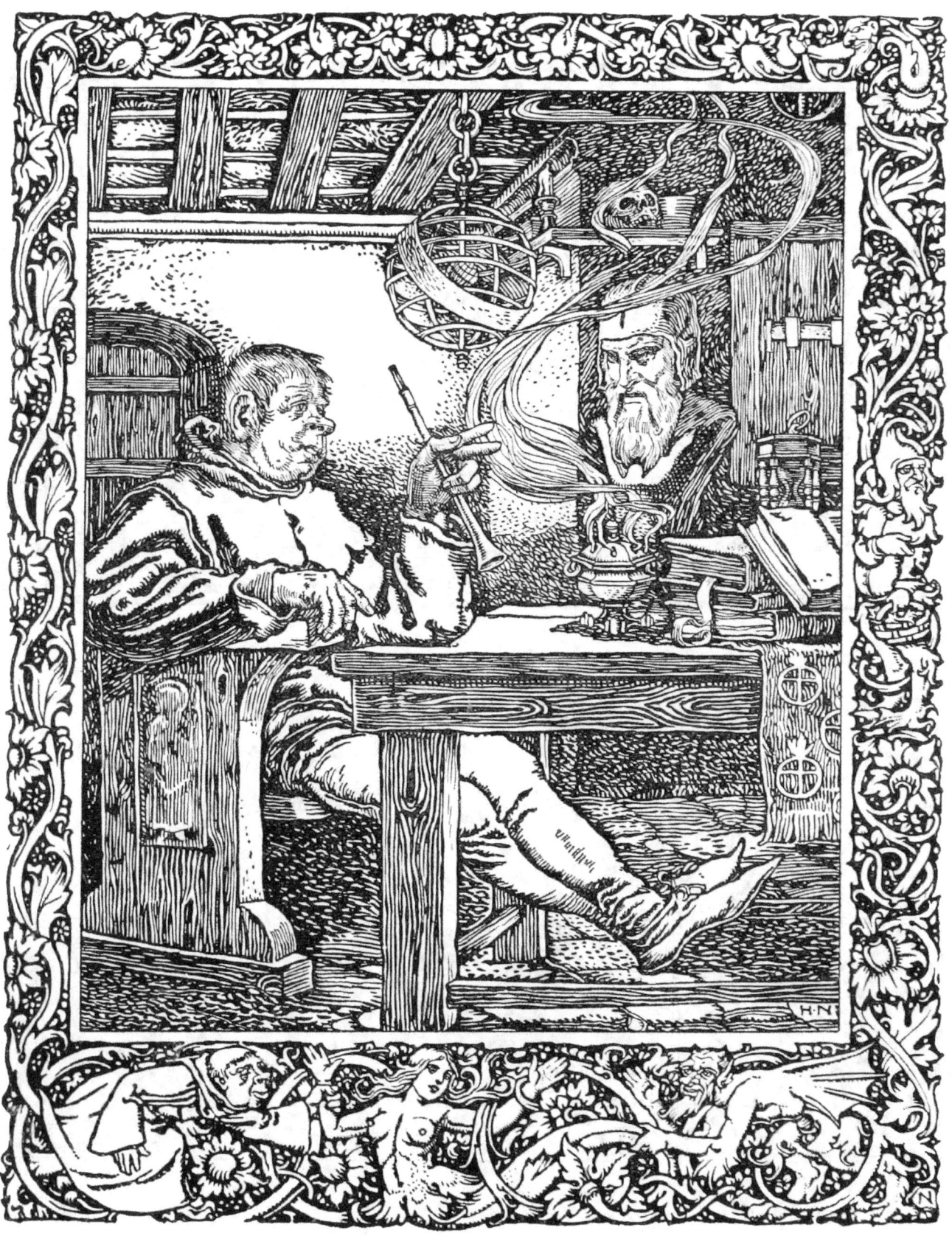

HAROLD NELSON: "Miles, to keepe him (self) from sleeping, got a tabor and pipe, and being merry disposed, sung this song..." From 'Early English Prose Romances'

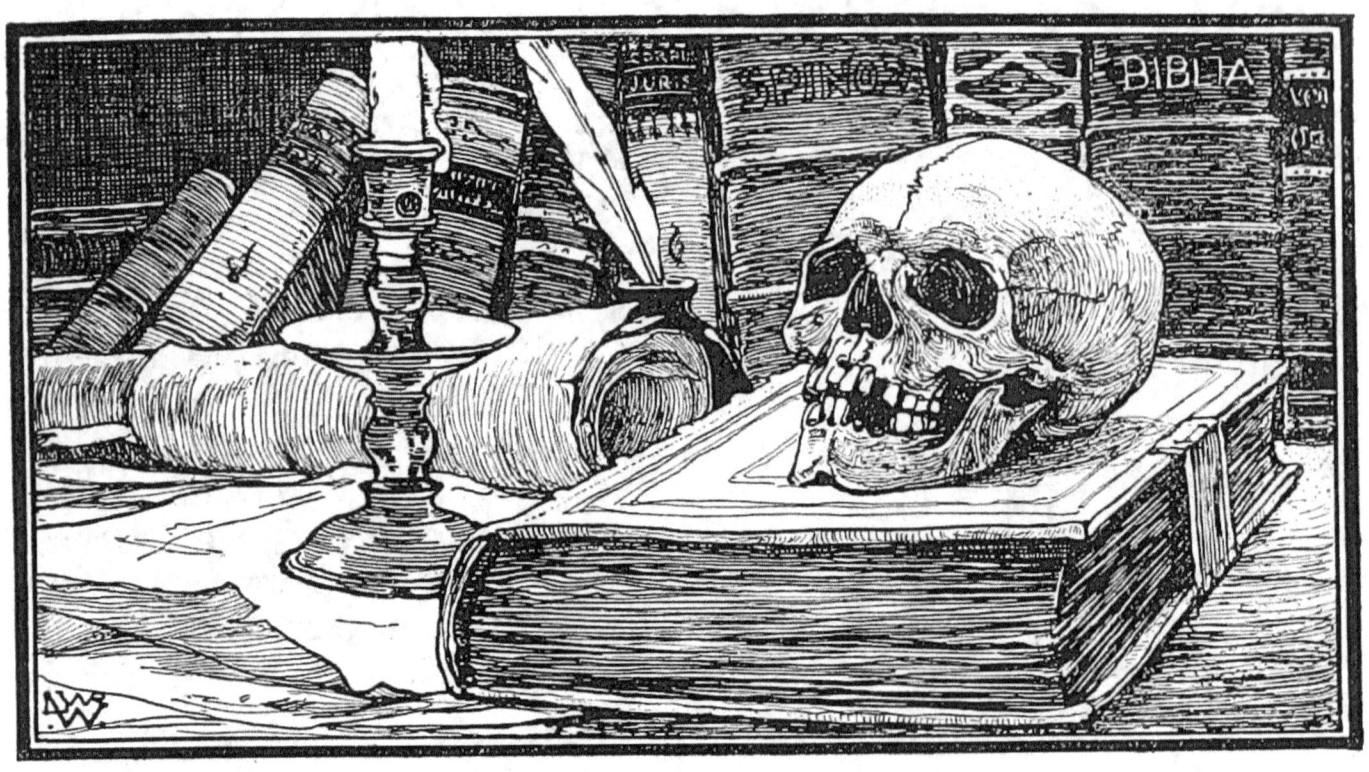

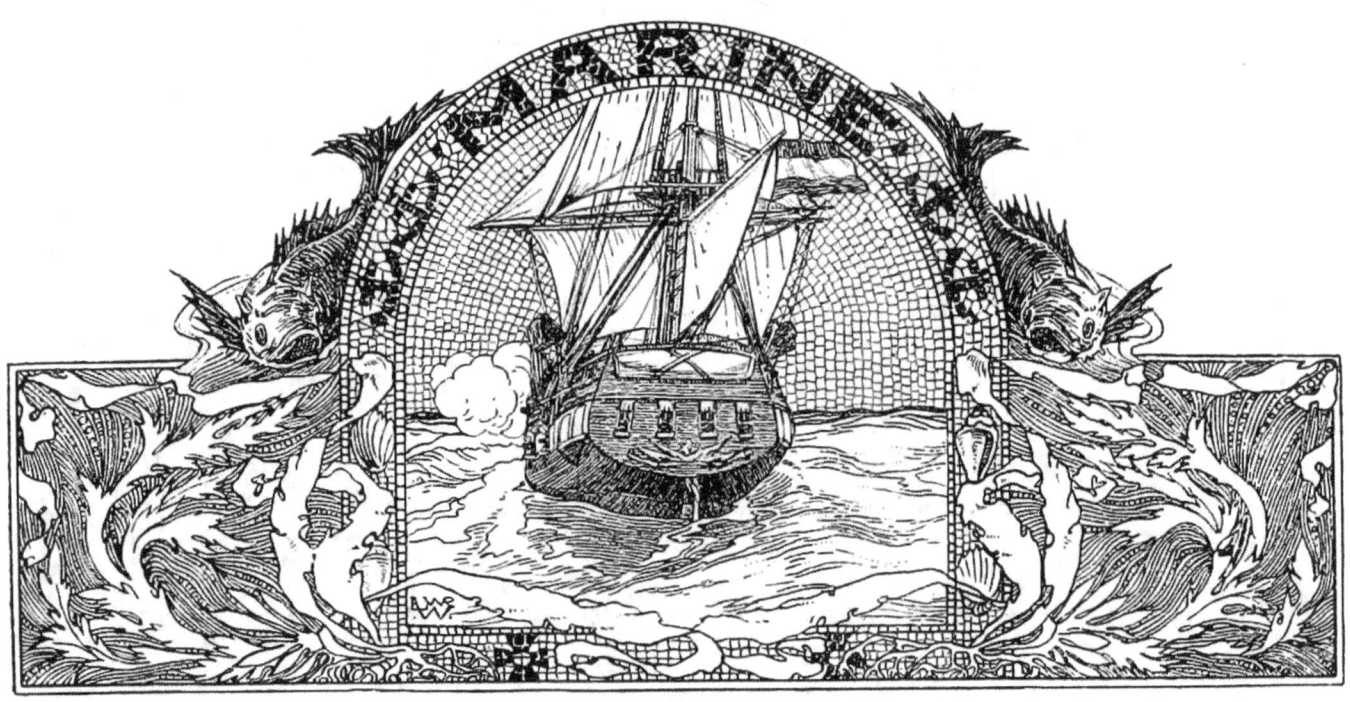

W. R. WENCKEBACH: Above, Two chapter headings from 'Eene halve Eeuw (Half a Century), 1848-1898'.
Right, Drawing of an old street in Amsterdam.

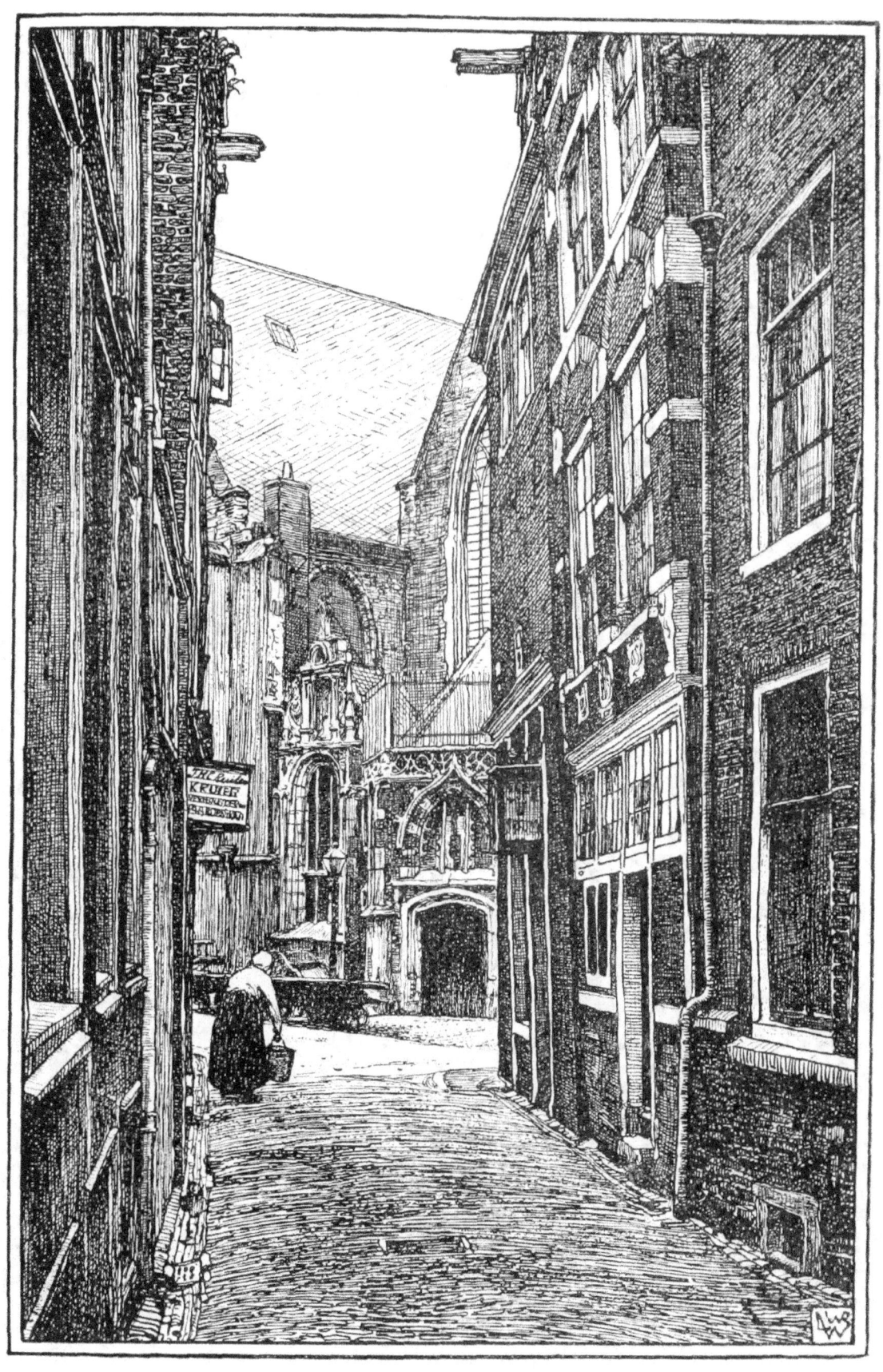

·ENGE·KERKSTEEG·

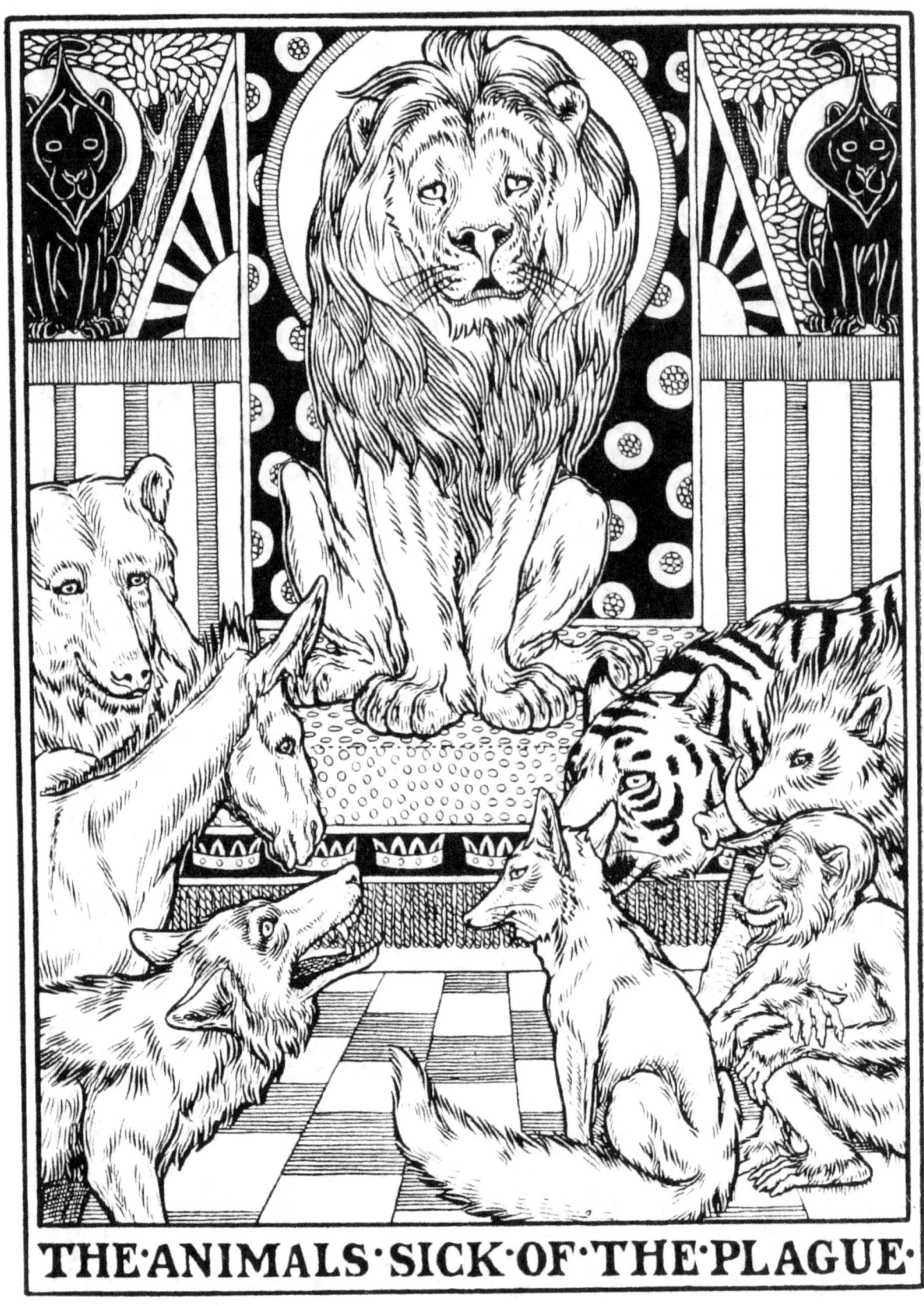

PERCY J BILLINGHURST: From 'A Hundred Fables of La Fontaine'.

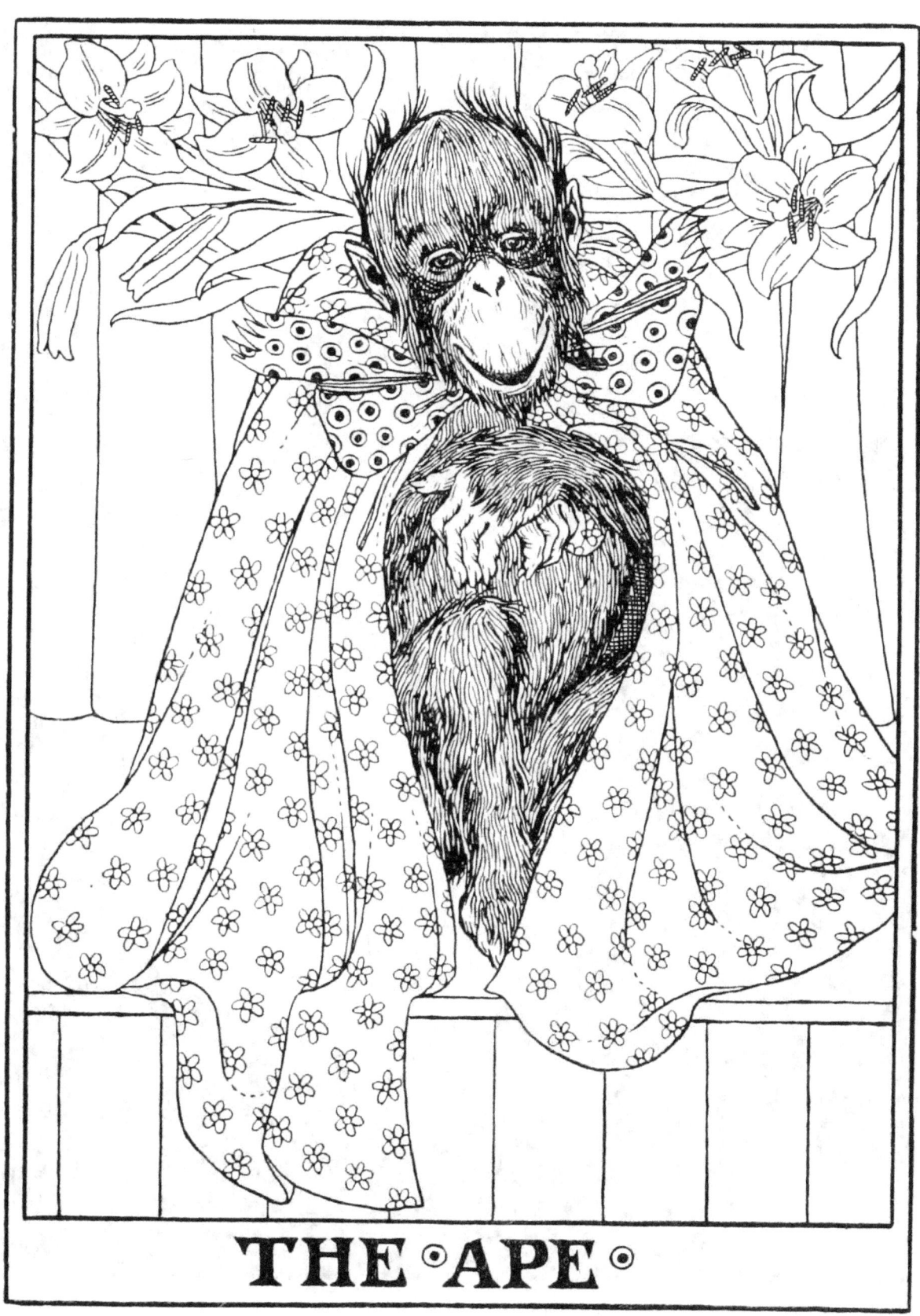

PERCY J BILLINGHURST: From 'A Hundred Fables of La Fontaine'.

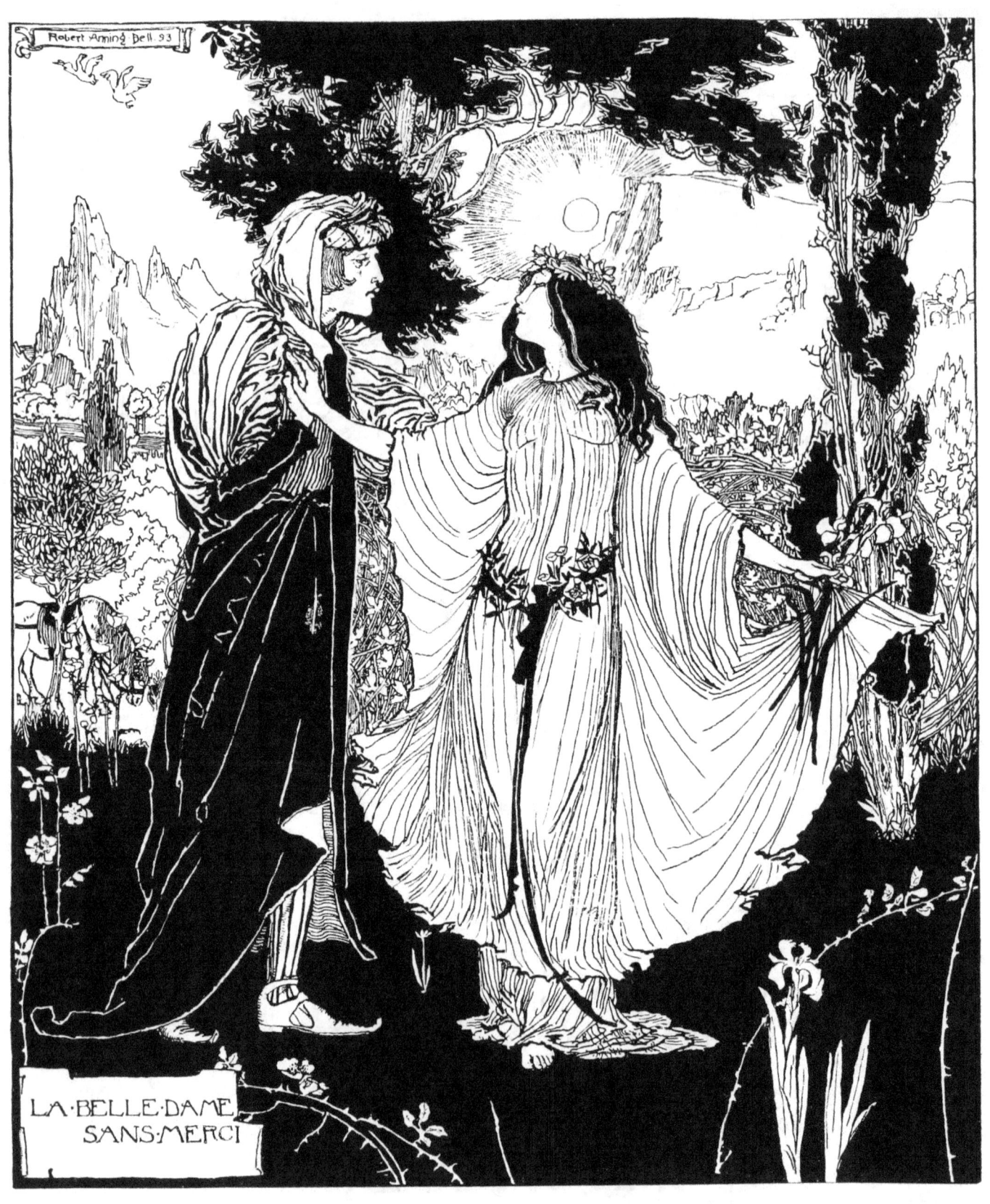

ROBERT ANNING BELL: Above, 'La Belle Dame sans Merci'. From 'The Poetical Works of John Keats'. Right, Design for a Book-plate.

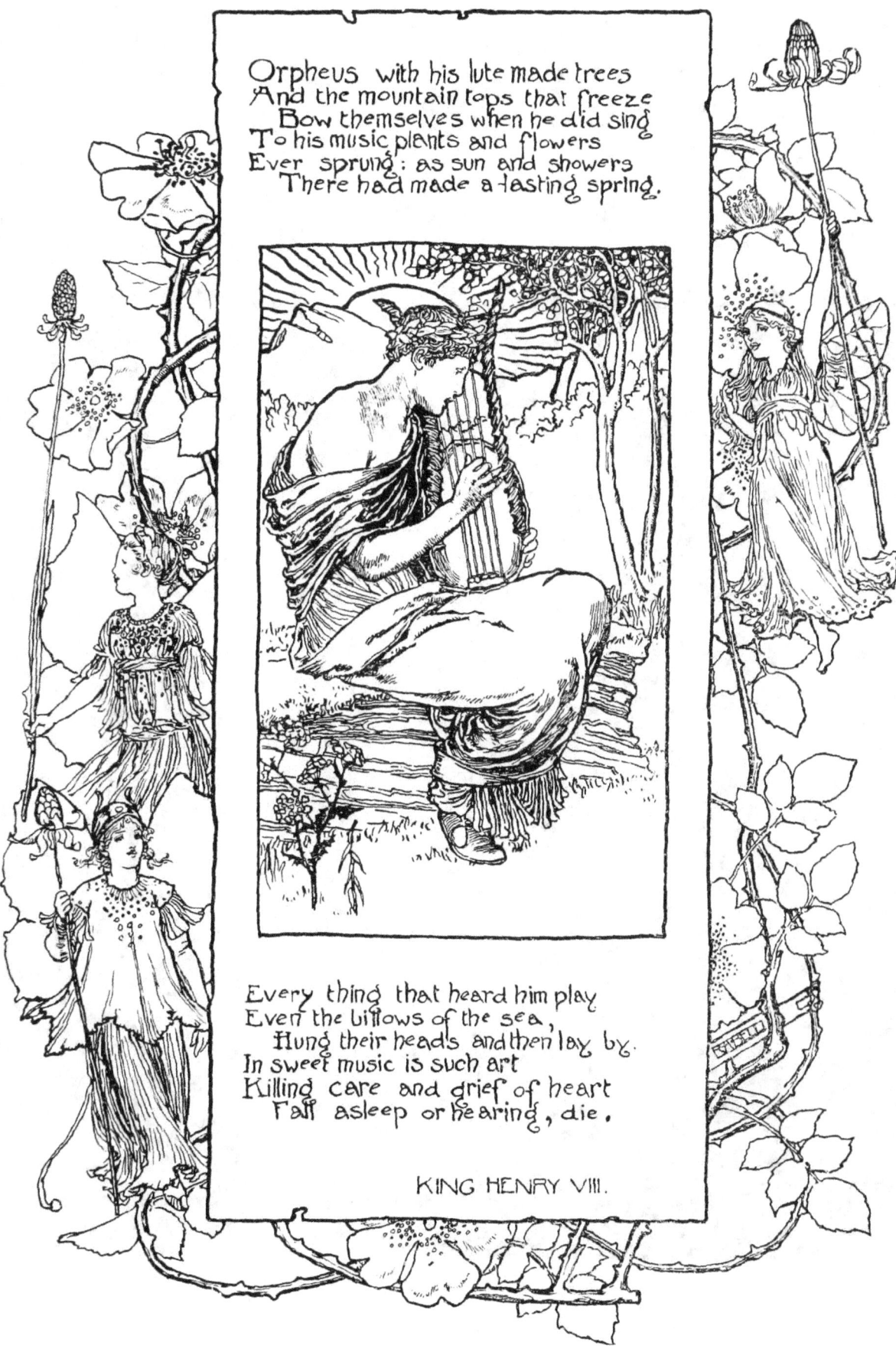

Orpheus with his lute made trees
And the mountain tops that freeze
  Bow themselves when he did sing
To his music plants and flowers
Ever sprung: as sun and showers
  There had made a lasting spring.

Every thing that heard him play
Even the billows of the sea,
  Hung their heads and then lay by.
In sweet music is such art
Killing care and grief of heart
  Fall asleep or hearing, die.

KING HENRY VIII.

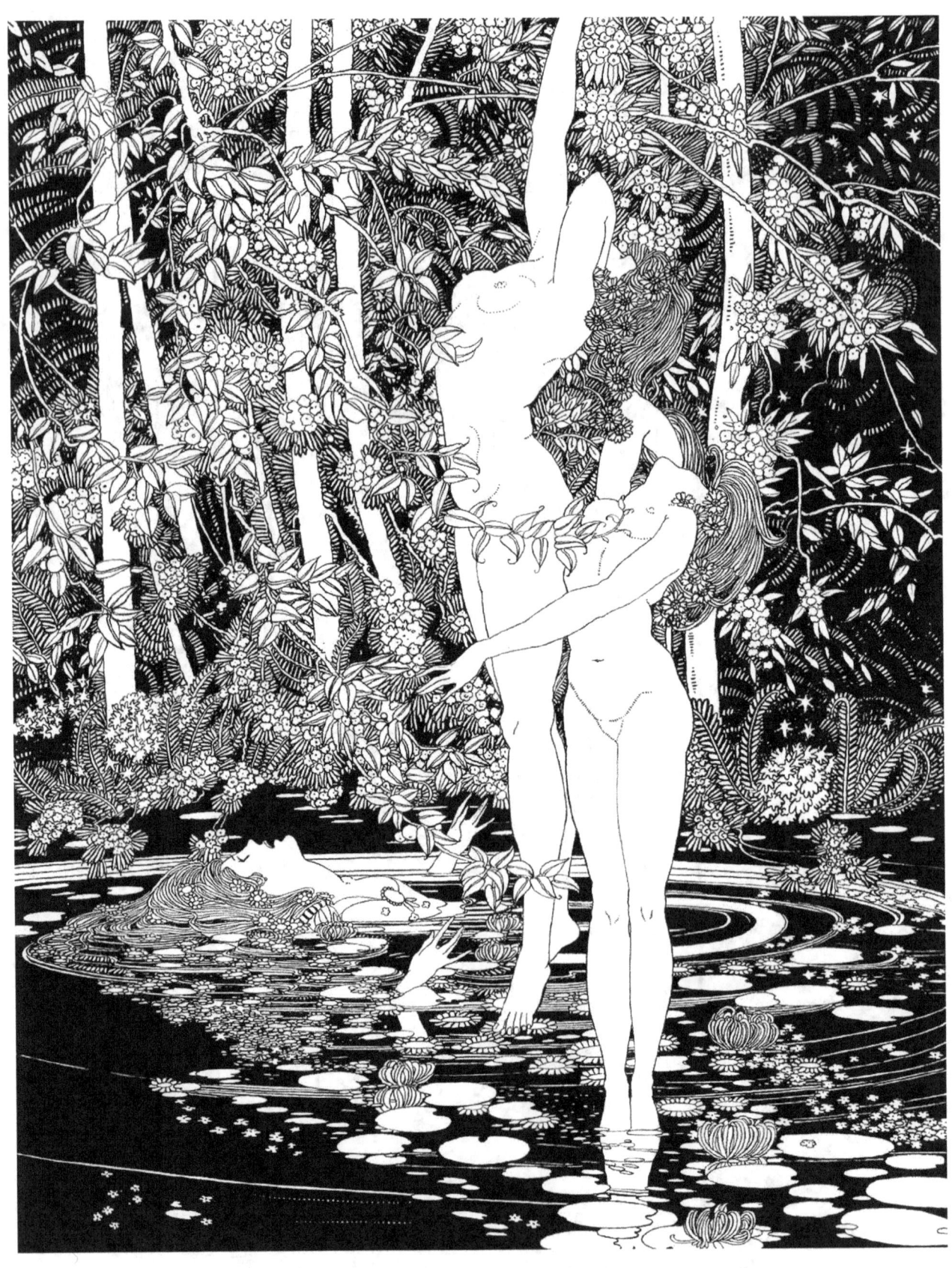

JOHN AUSTIN: Illustration from Shakespeare's 'Hamlet'

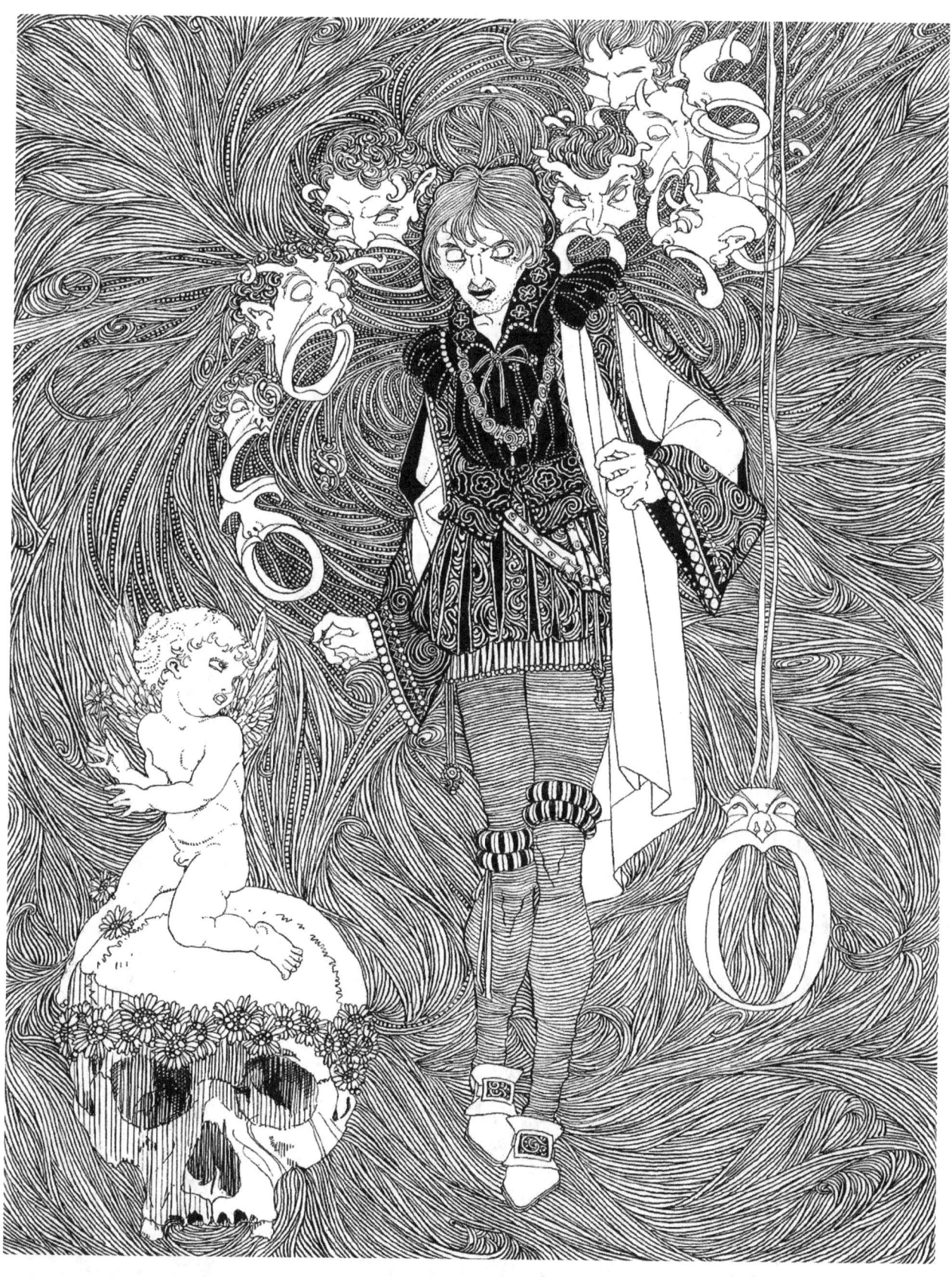

JOHN AUSTIN: Illustration from Shakespeare's 'Hamlet'

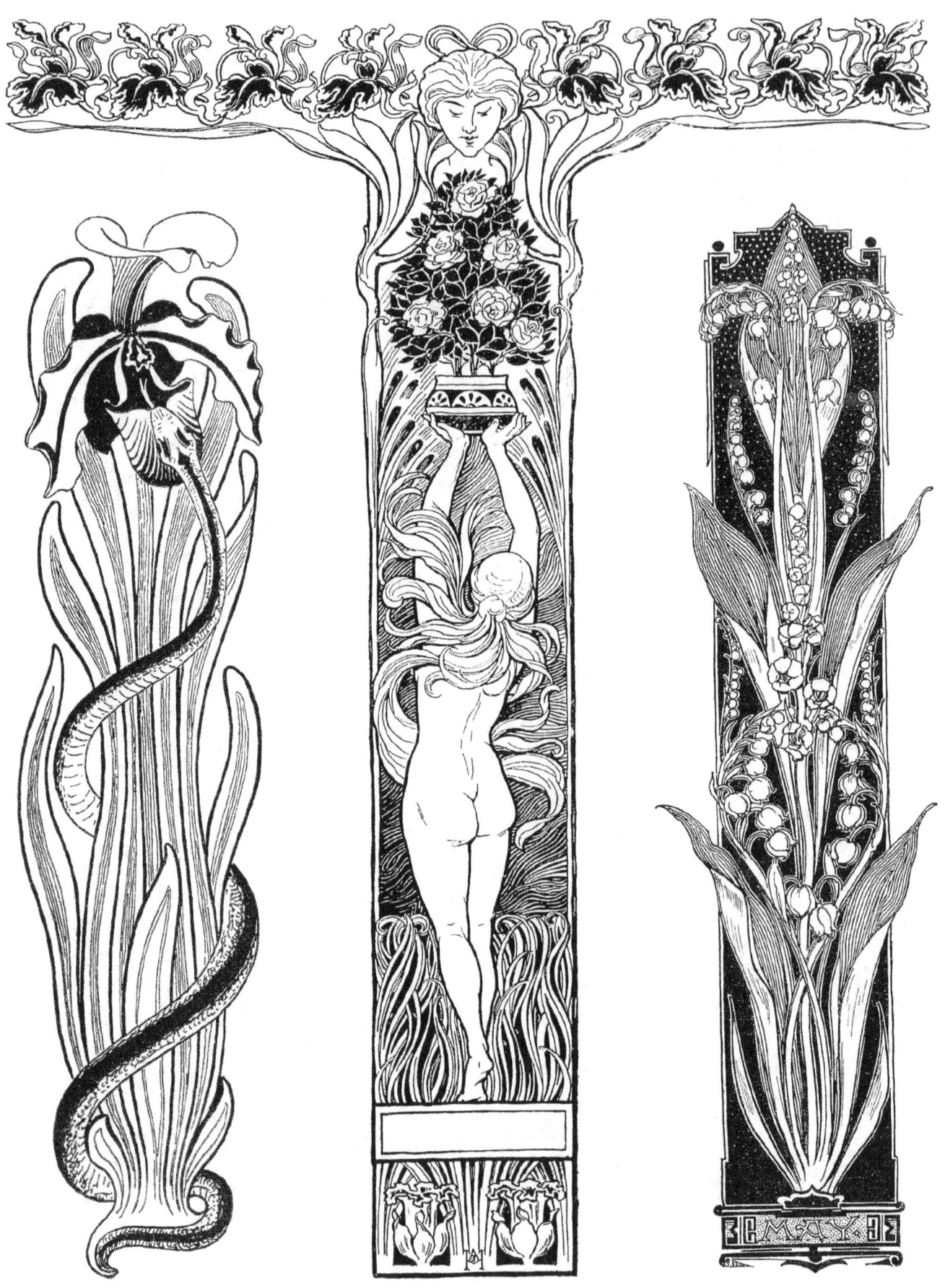

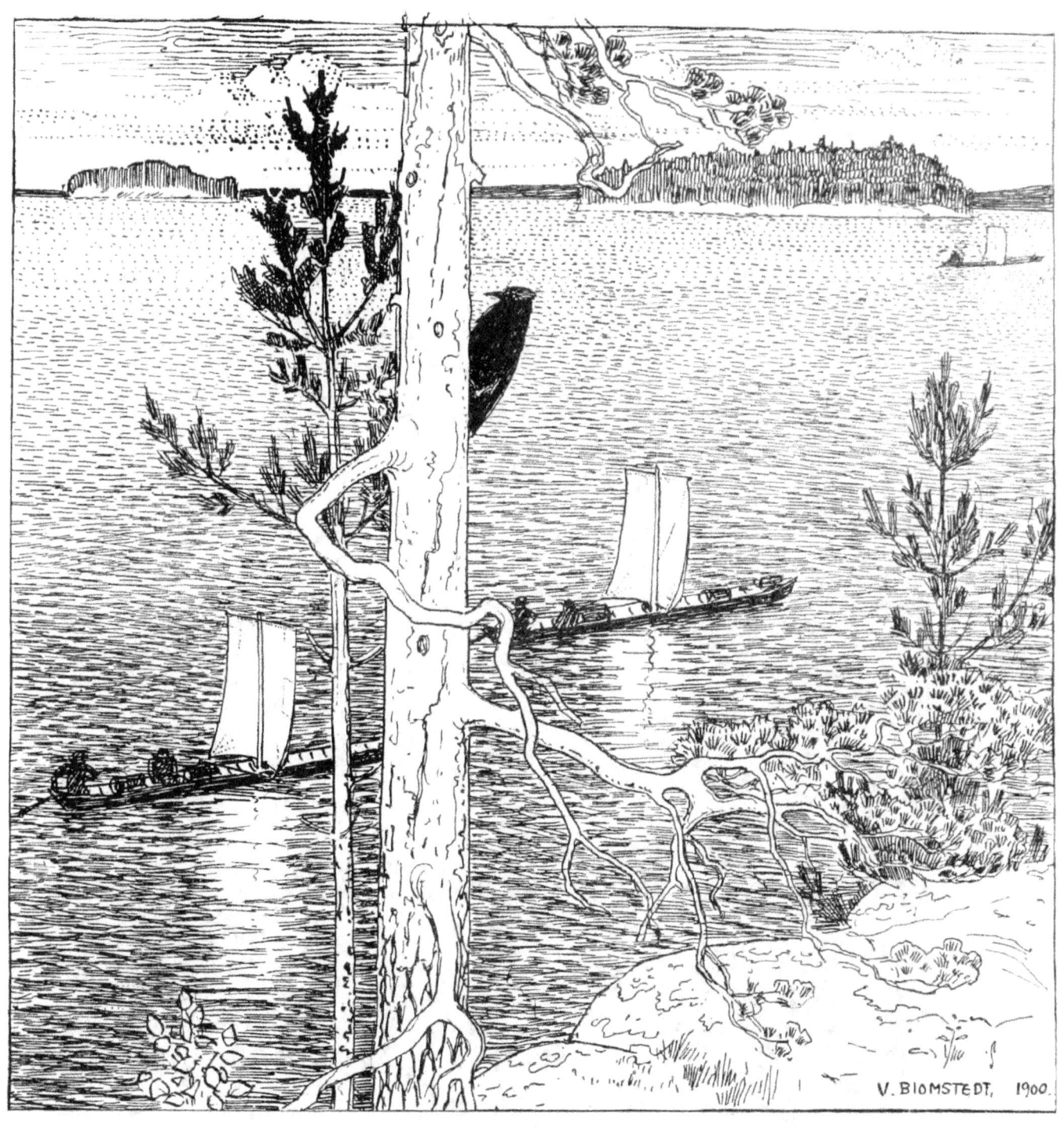

VAINO BLOMSTEDT: Landscape drawing from 'Modern Pen Drawing, European and American'. (Above)

Various unkown artists magazine decorations. (Left)

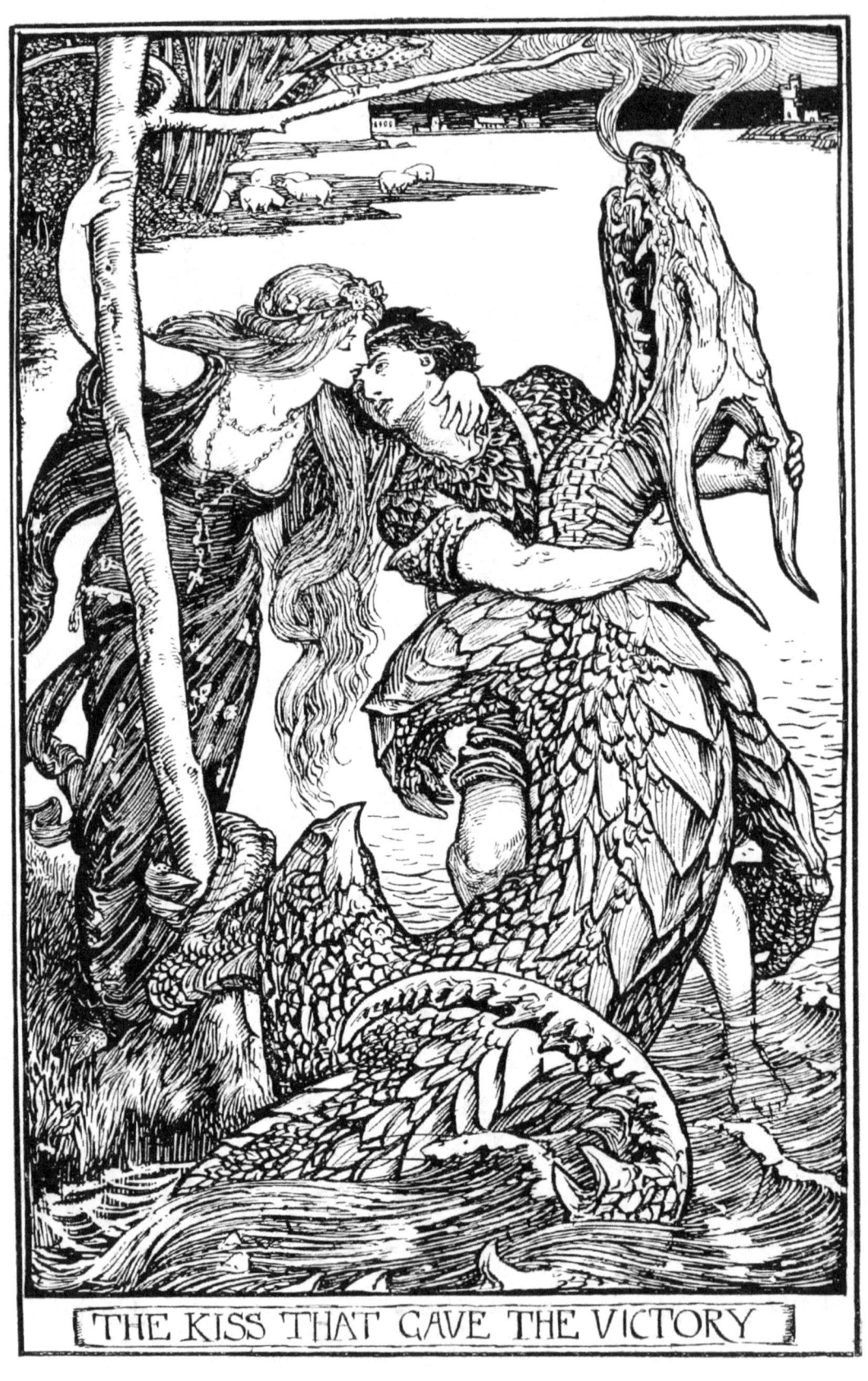

THE KISS THAT GAVE THE VICTORY

HENRY J FORD: Above, Illustration from 'Andrew Lang's Crimson Fairy Book'
Right, Illustration from 'Andrew Lang's Brown Fairy Book'

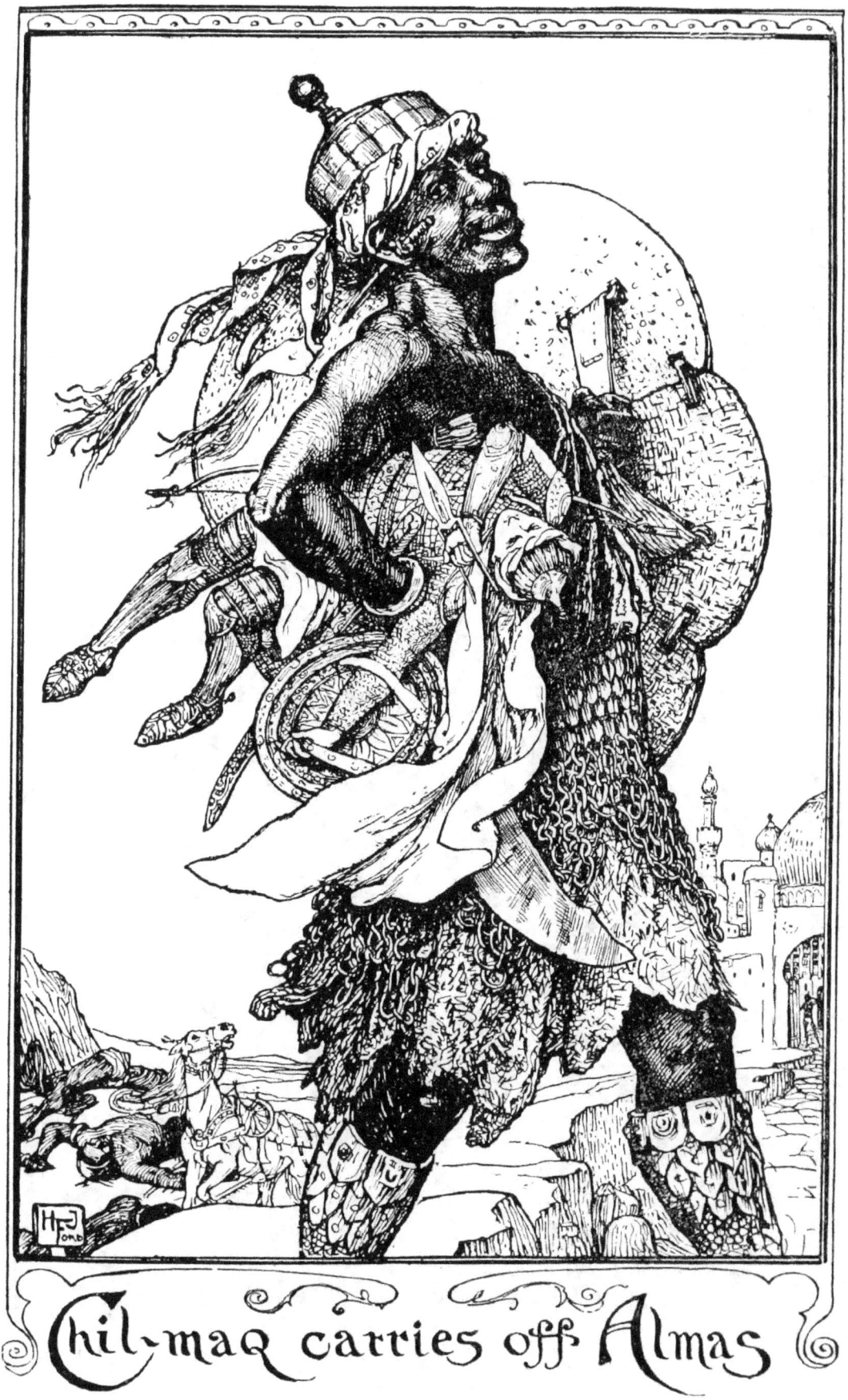
Chil-maq carries off Almas

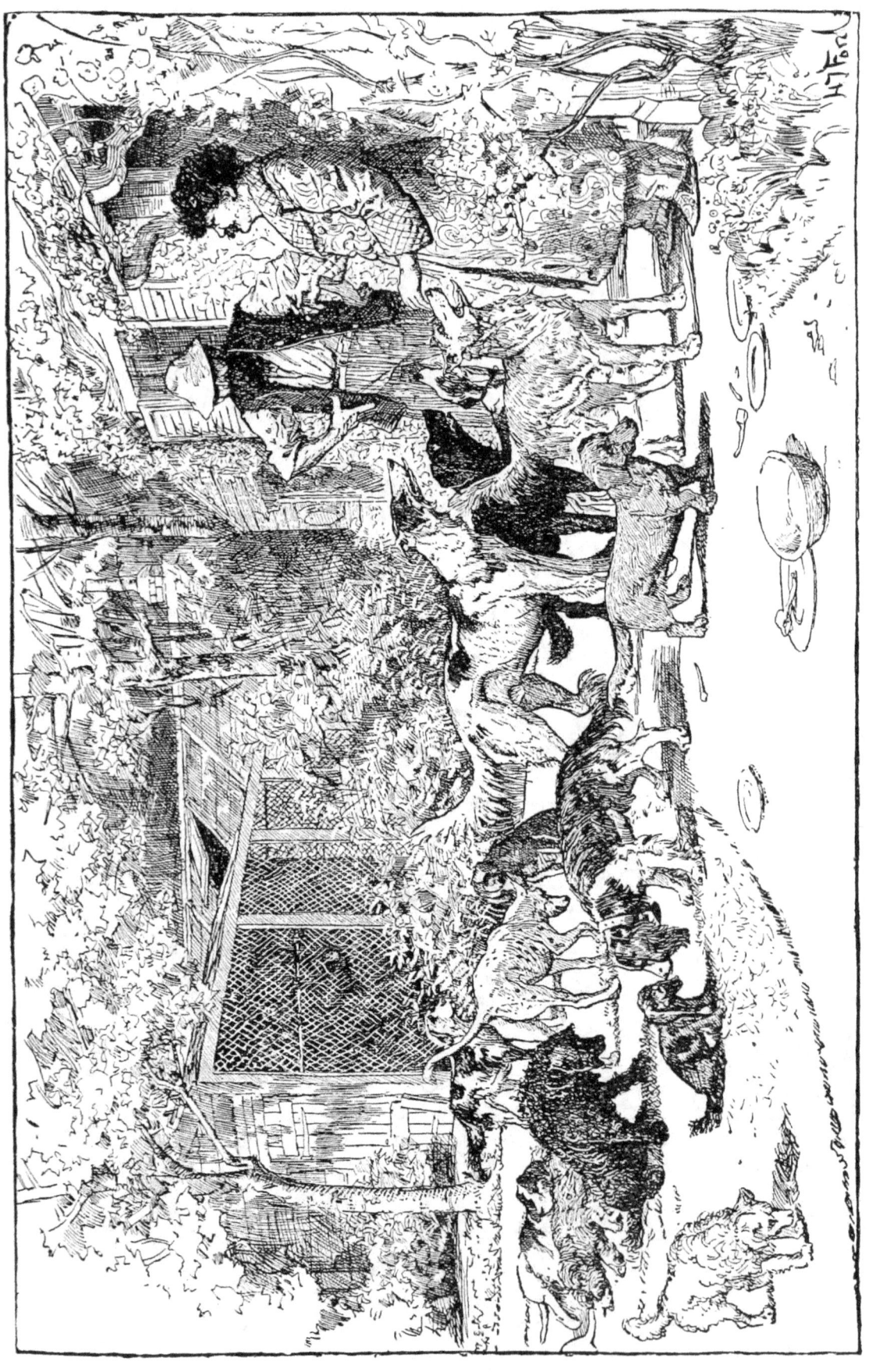

HENRY J FORD: "It's a regular kennel". From 'Andrew Lang's Animal Story Book'

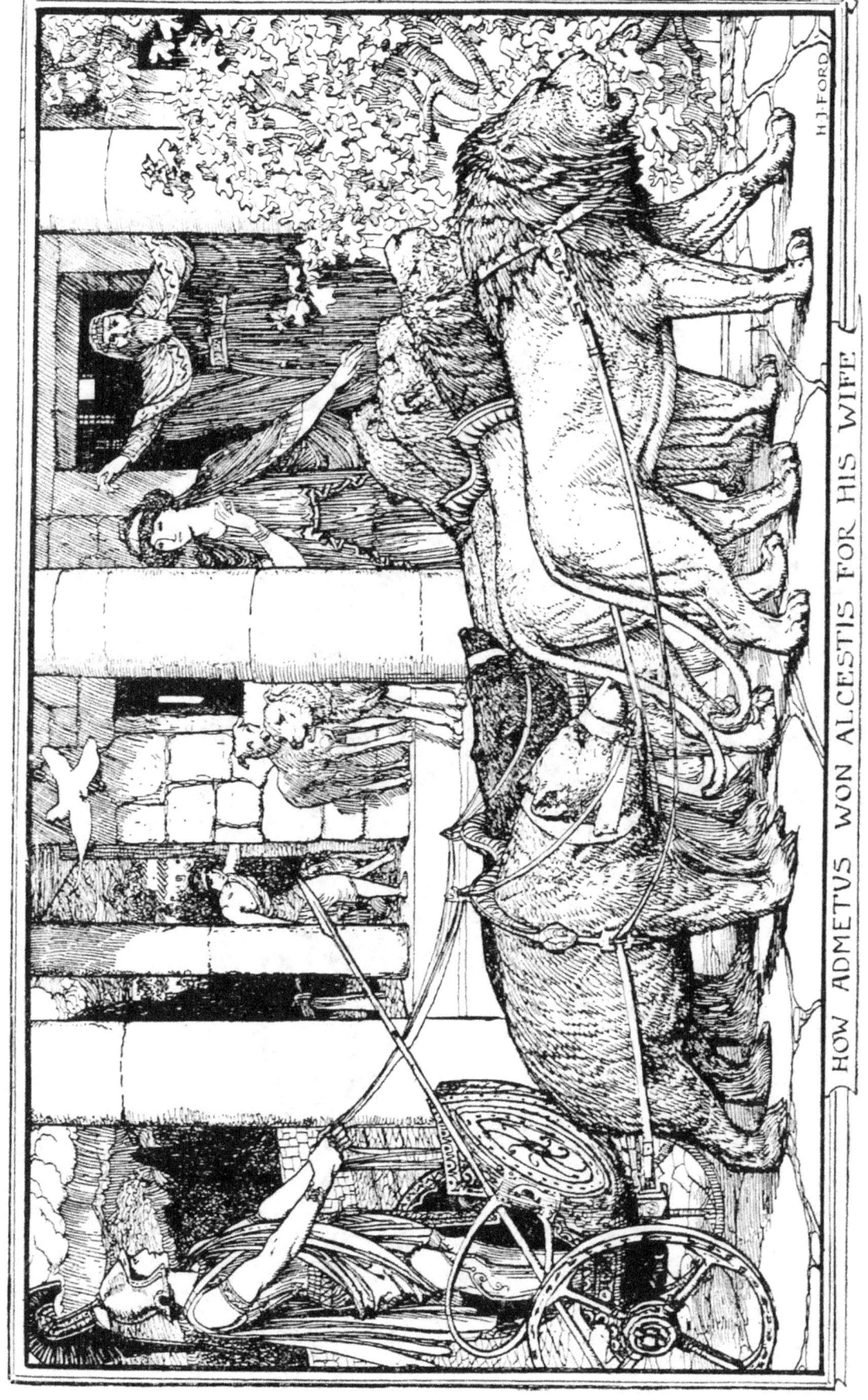

HENRY J FORD: Illustration from 'Andrew Lang's All Sorts of Stories Book'

HOW ADMETUS WON ALCESTIS FOR HIS WIFE

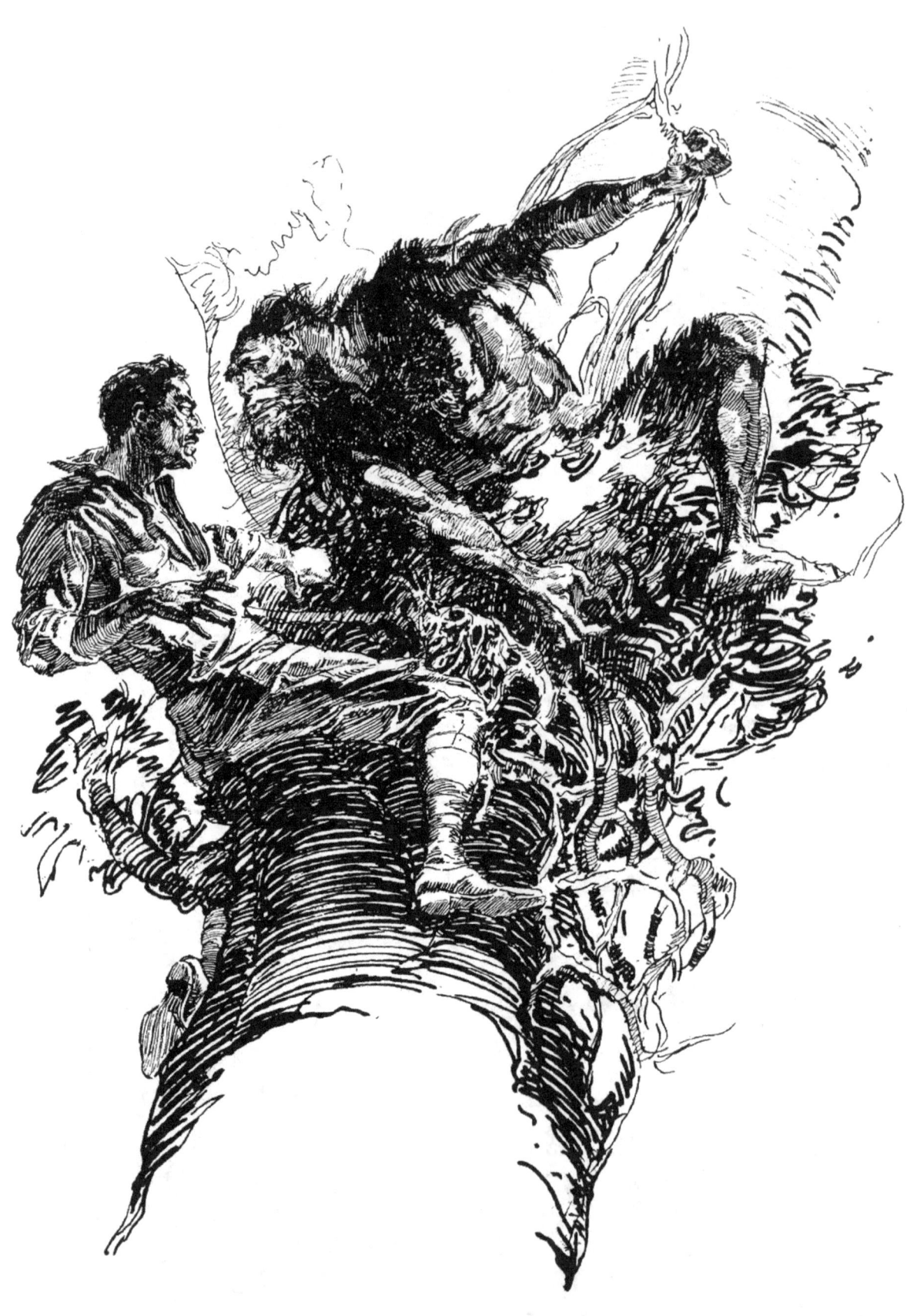

JOSEPH CLEMENT COLL: I read hatred and menace in the evil eyes. From 'The Lost World'

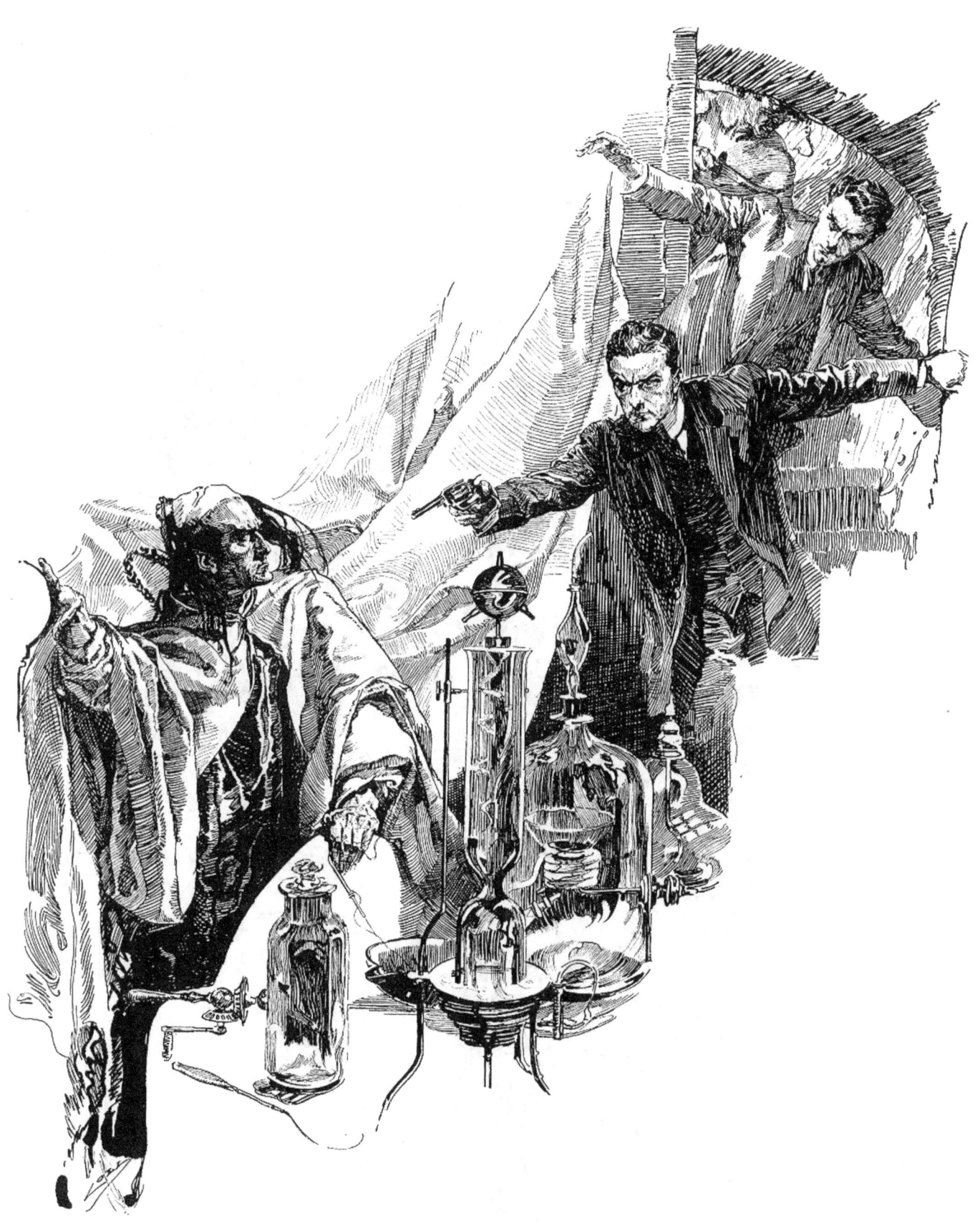

JOSEPH CLEMENT COLL: Story illustration from 'Colliers Magazine' April 1913

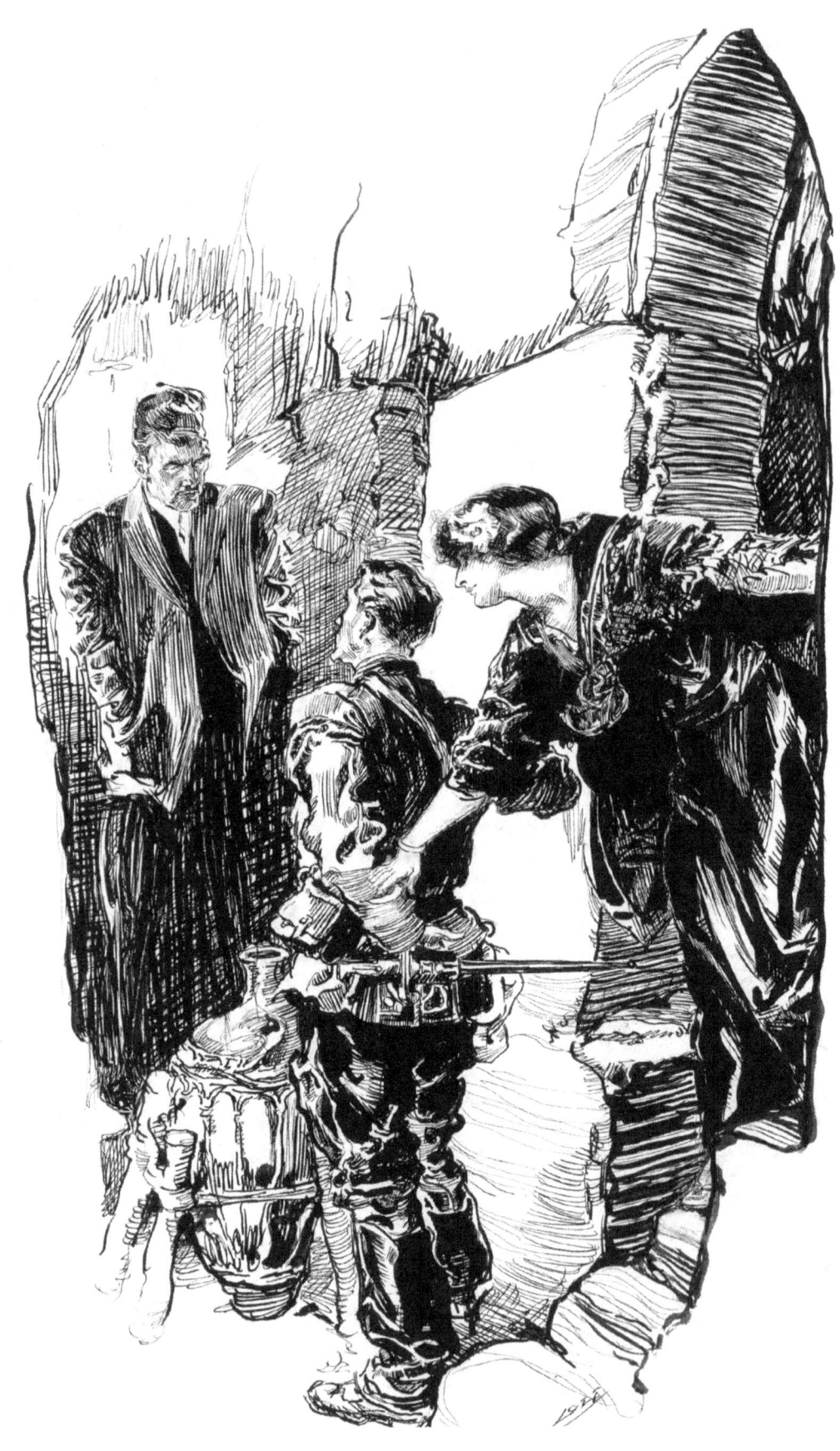

JOSEPH CLEMENT COLL: 'The Confrontation.'

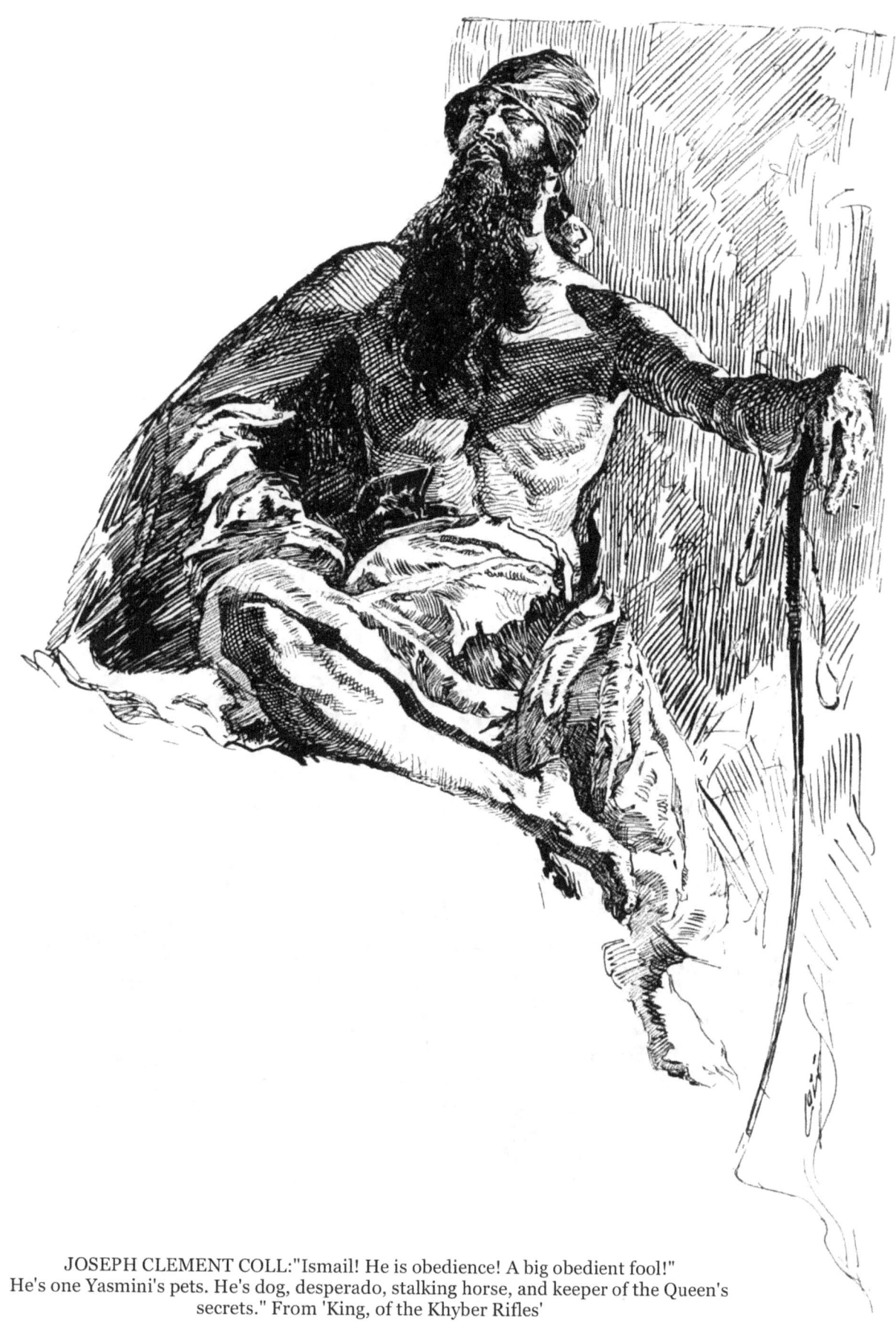

JOSEPH CLEMENT COLL:"Ismail! He is obedience! A big obedient fool!"
He's one Yasmini's pets. He's dog, desperado, stalking horse, and keeper of the Queen's secrets." From 'King, of the Khyber Rifles'

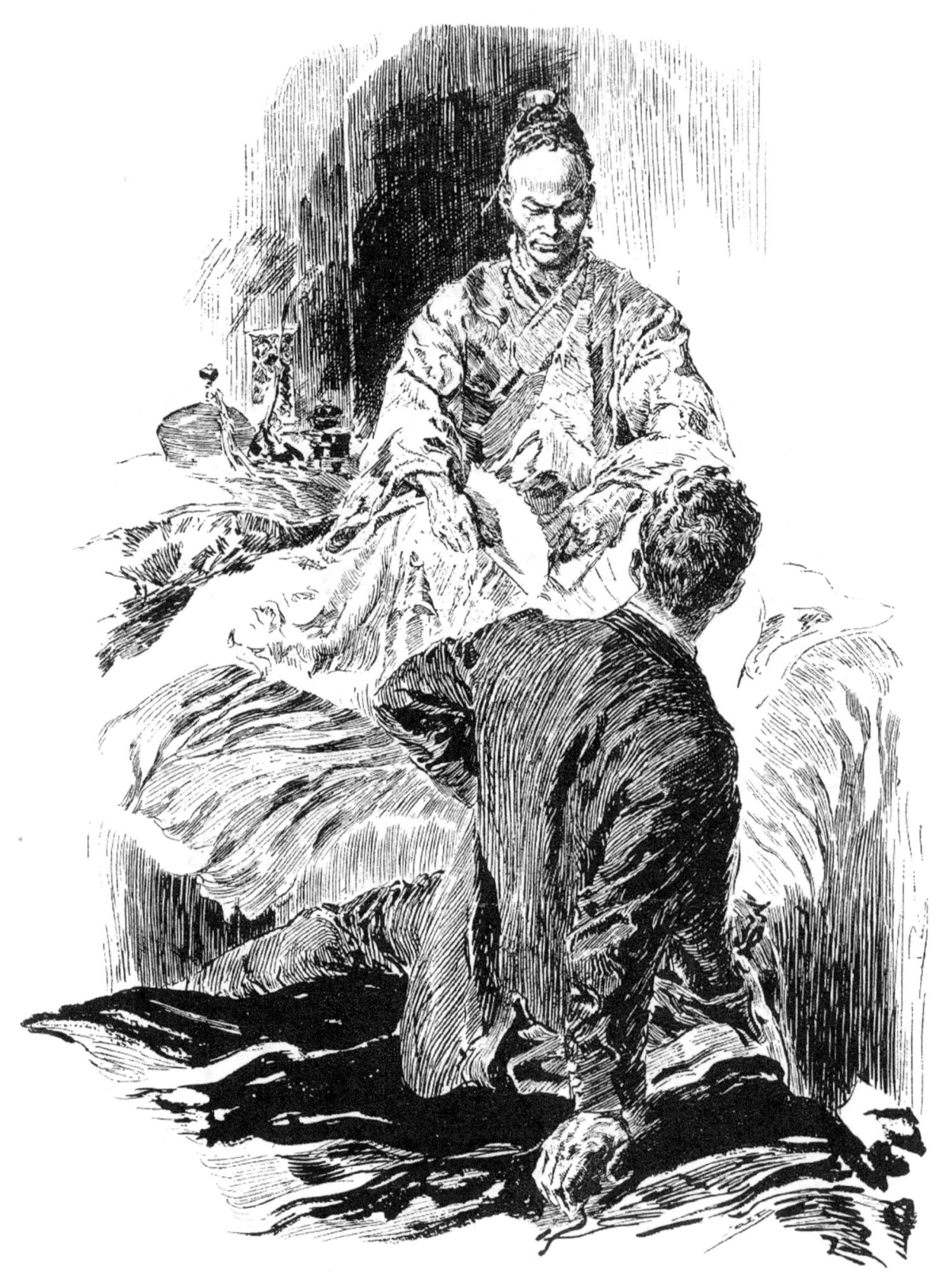

JOSEPH CLEMENT COLL: 'Colliers Magazine' March 1917

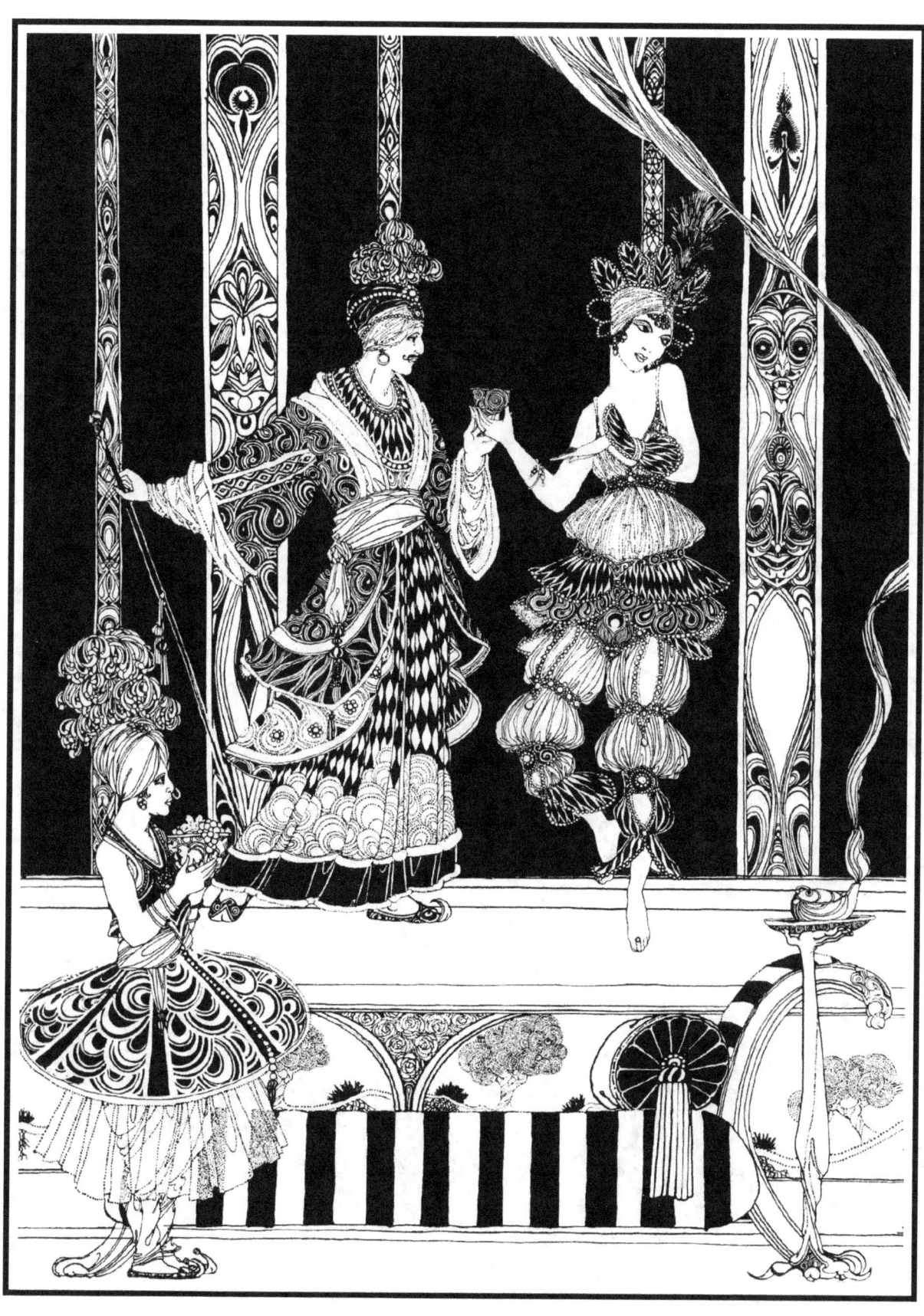

RONALD BALFOUR: Illustration for 'Rubáiyát of Omar Khayyám'

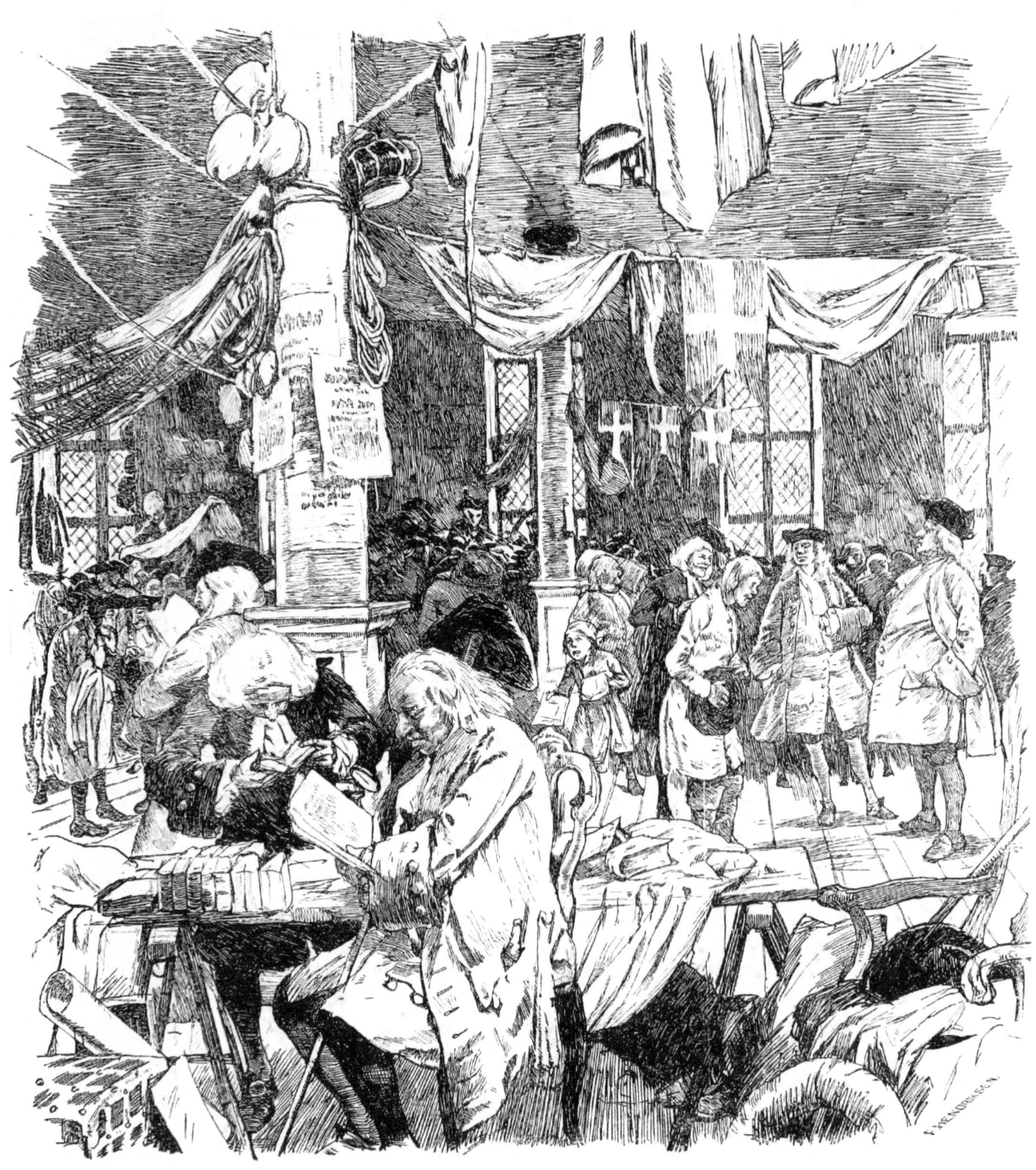

HANS TEGNER: Illustraion from 'Pen Drawing and Pen Draughtsmen'.

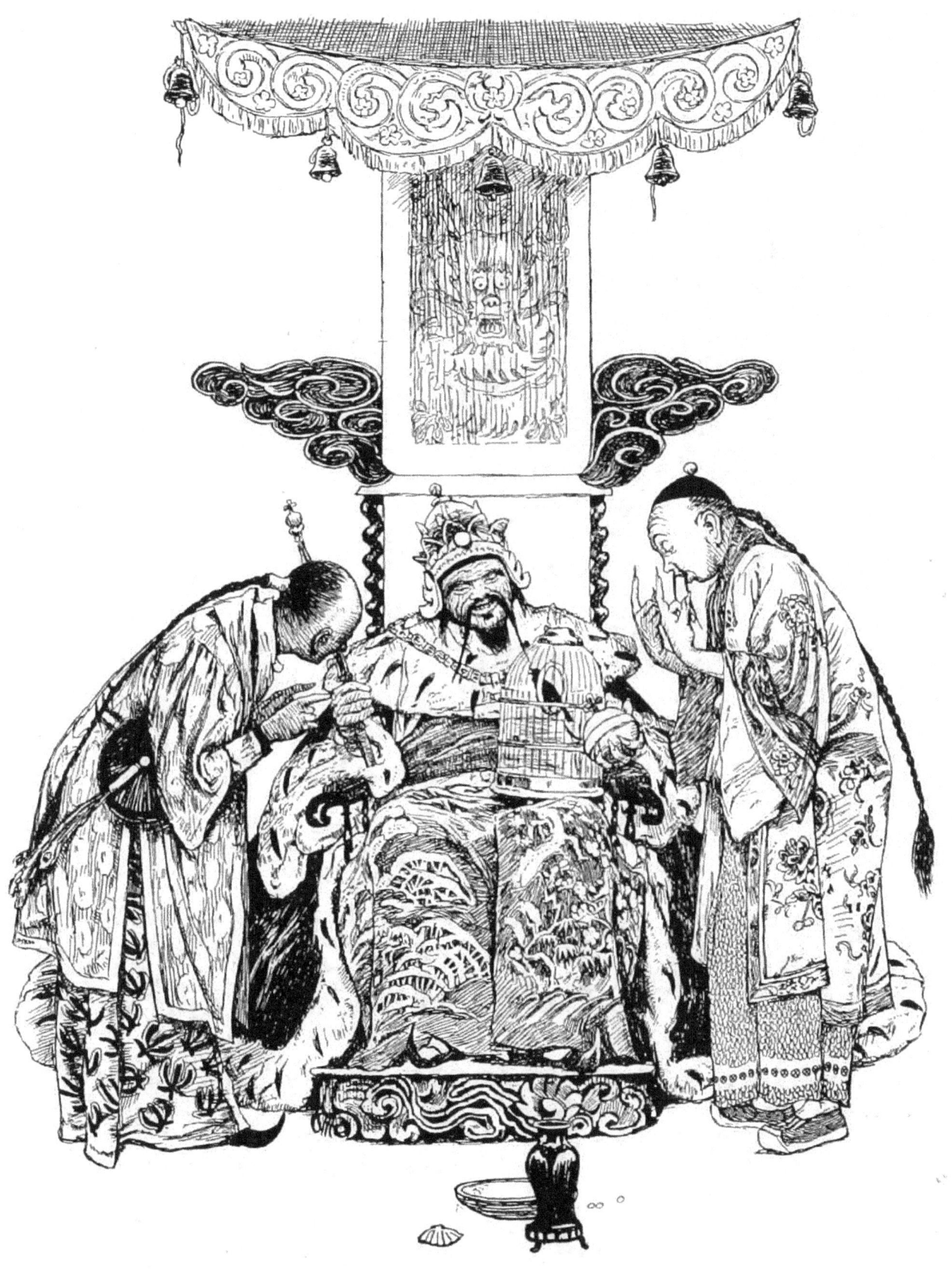

HANS TEGNER: The nightingale was indeed a great success. From 'Fairy Tales and Stories'.

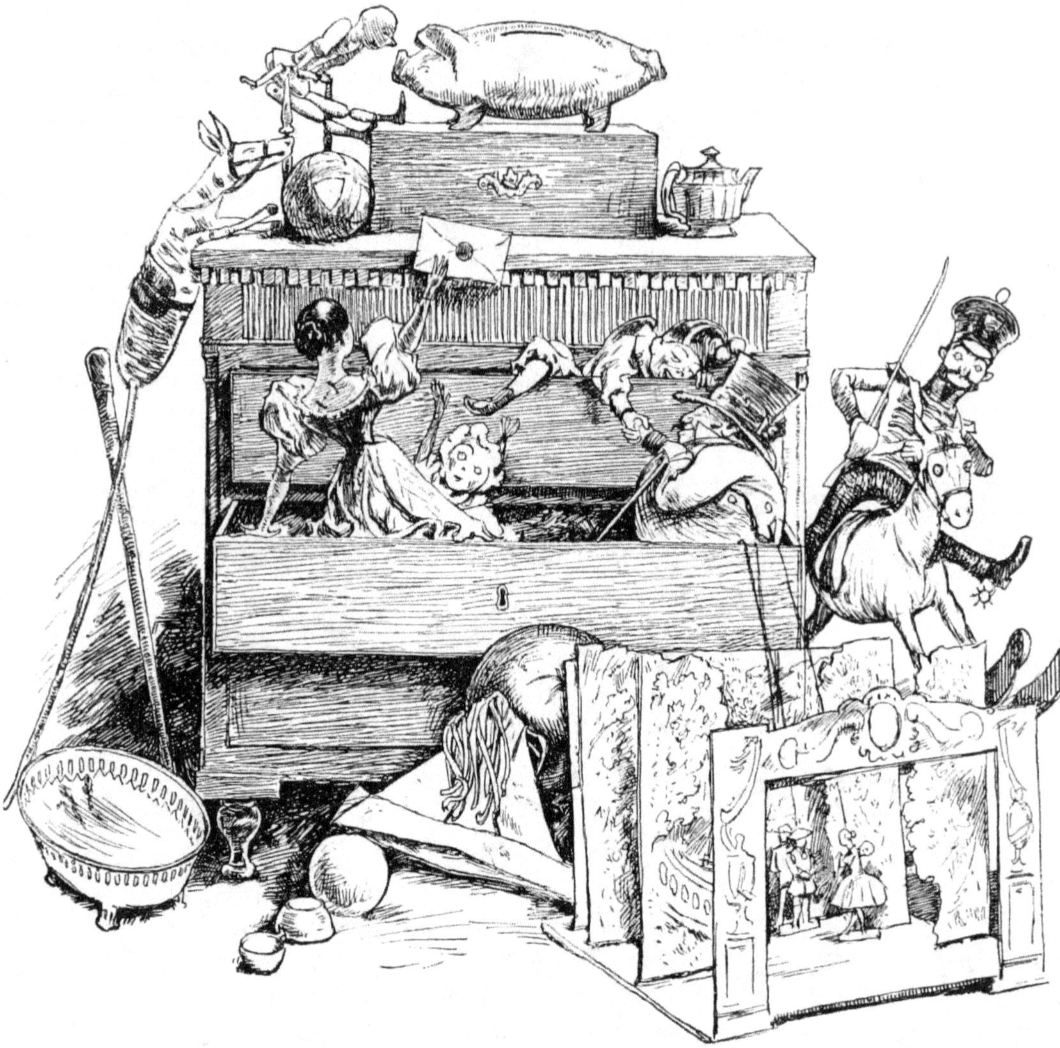

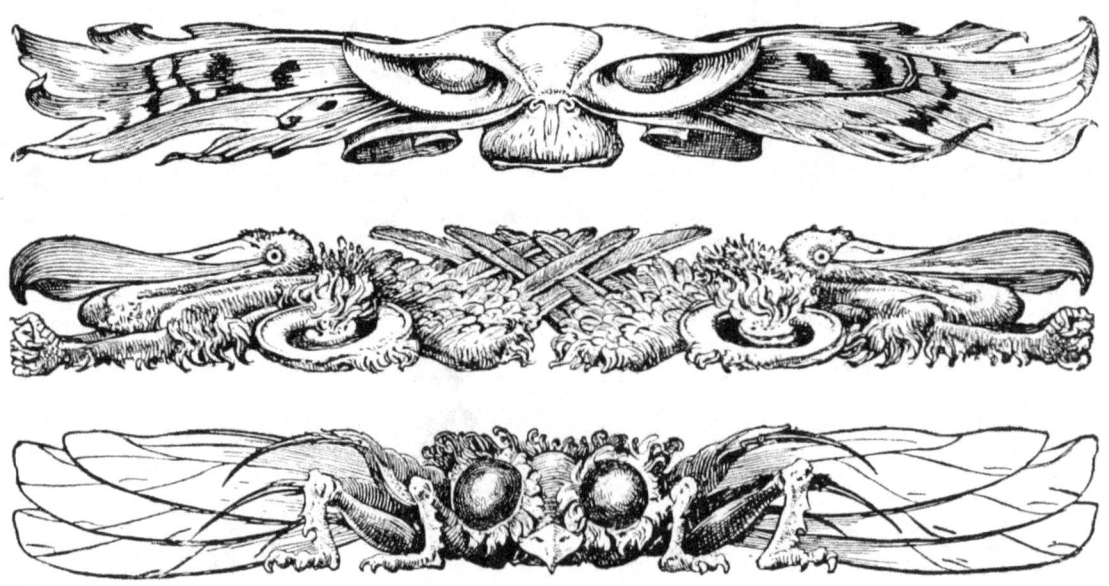

HANS TEGNER: In-text embellishments from 'Fairy Tales and Stories'.

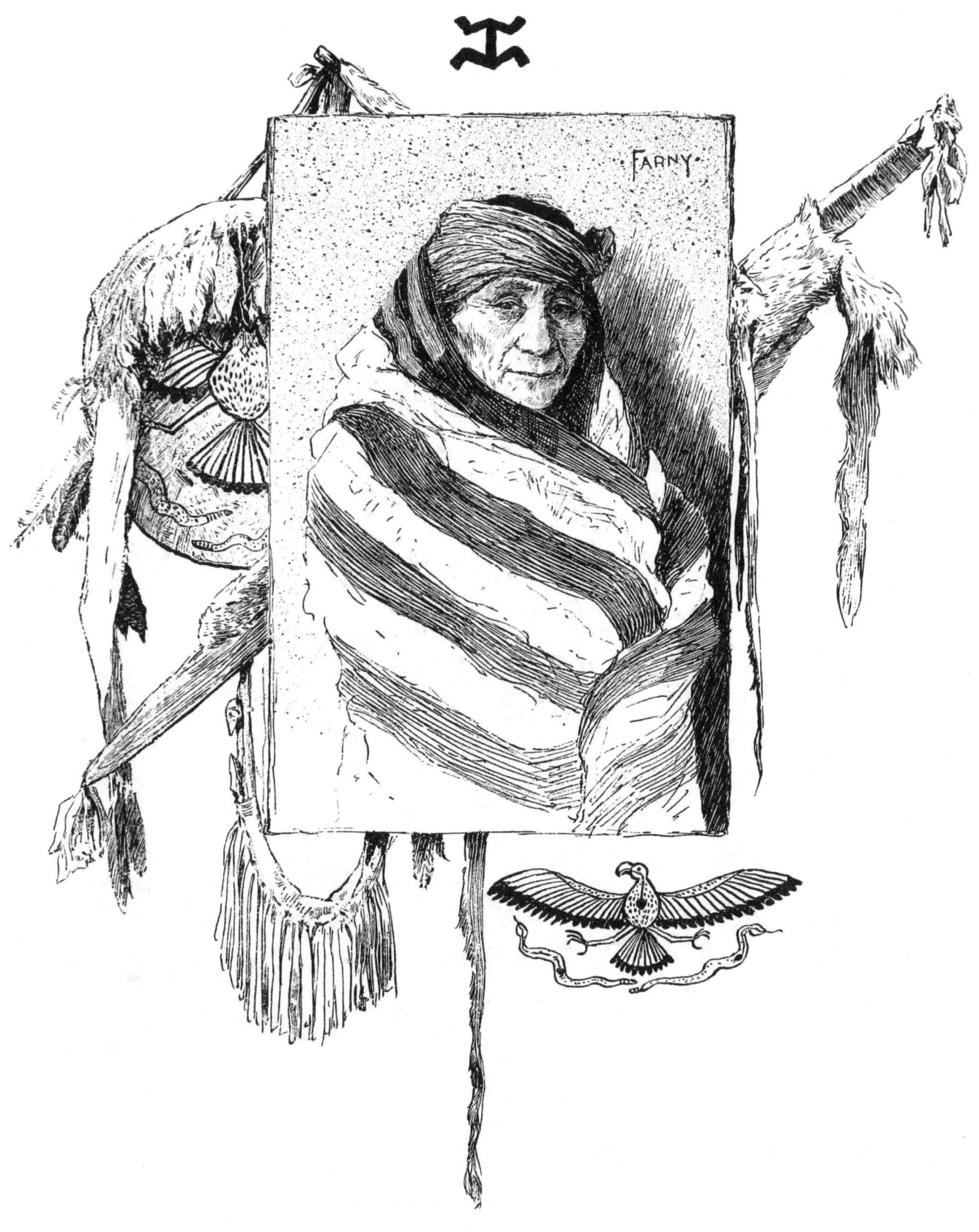

HENRY F FARNY: Native American illustration from 'Pen Drawing and Pen Draughtsmen'.

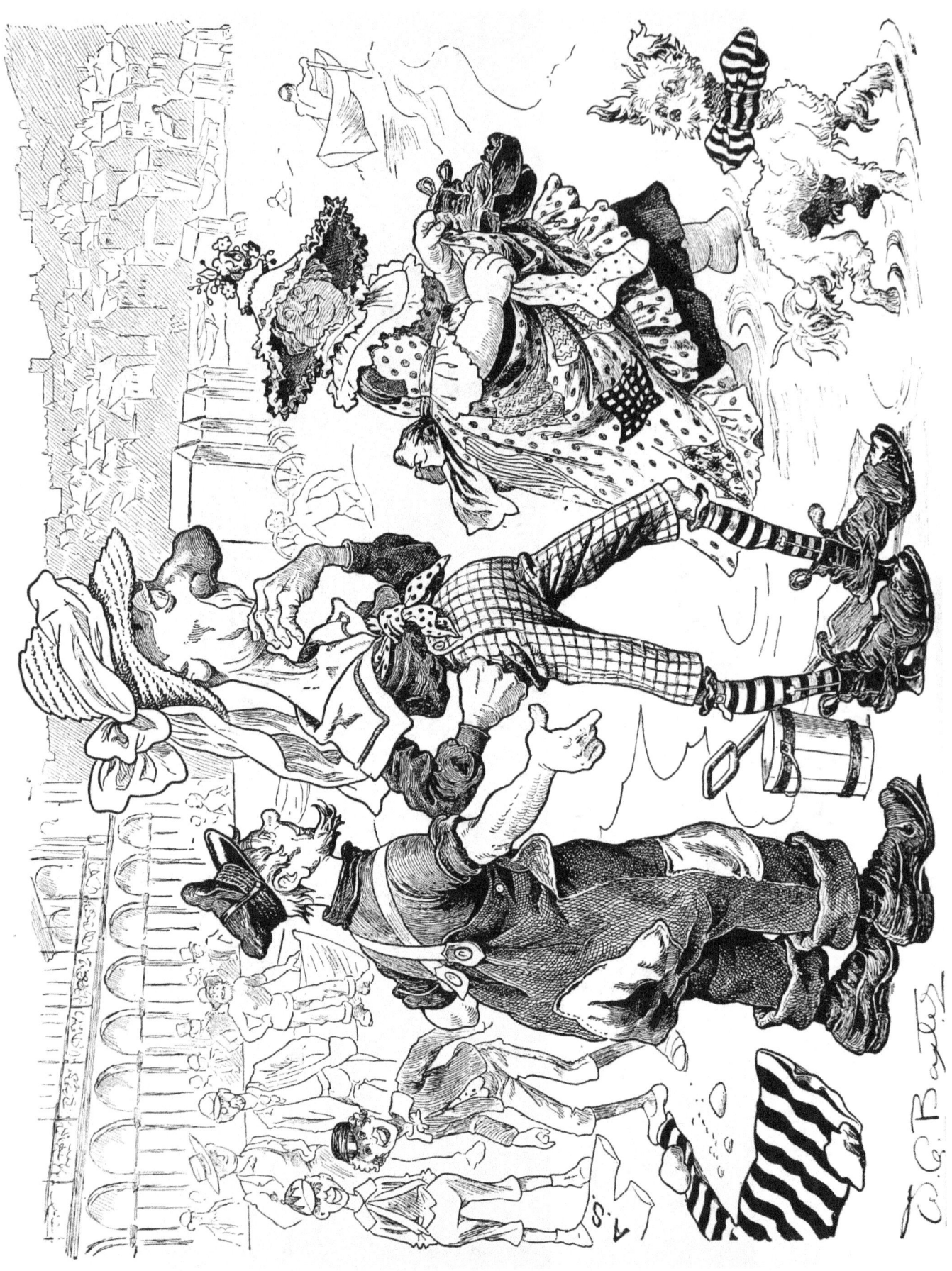

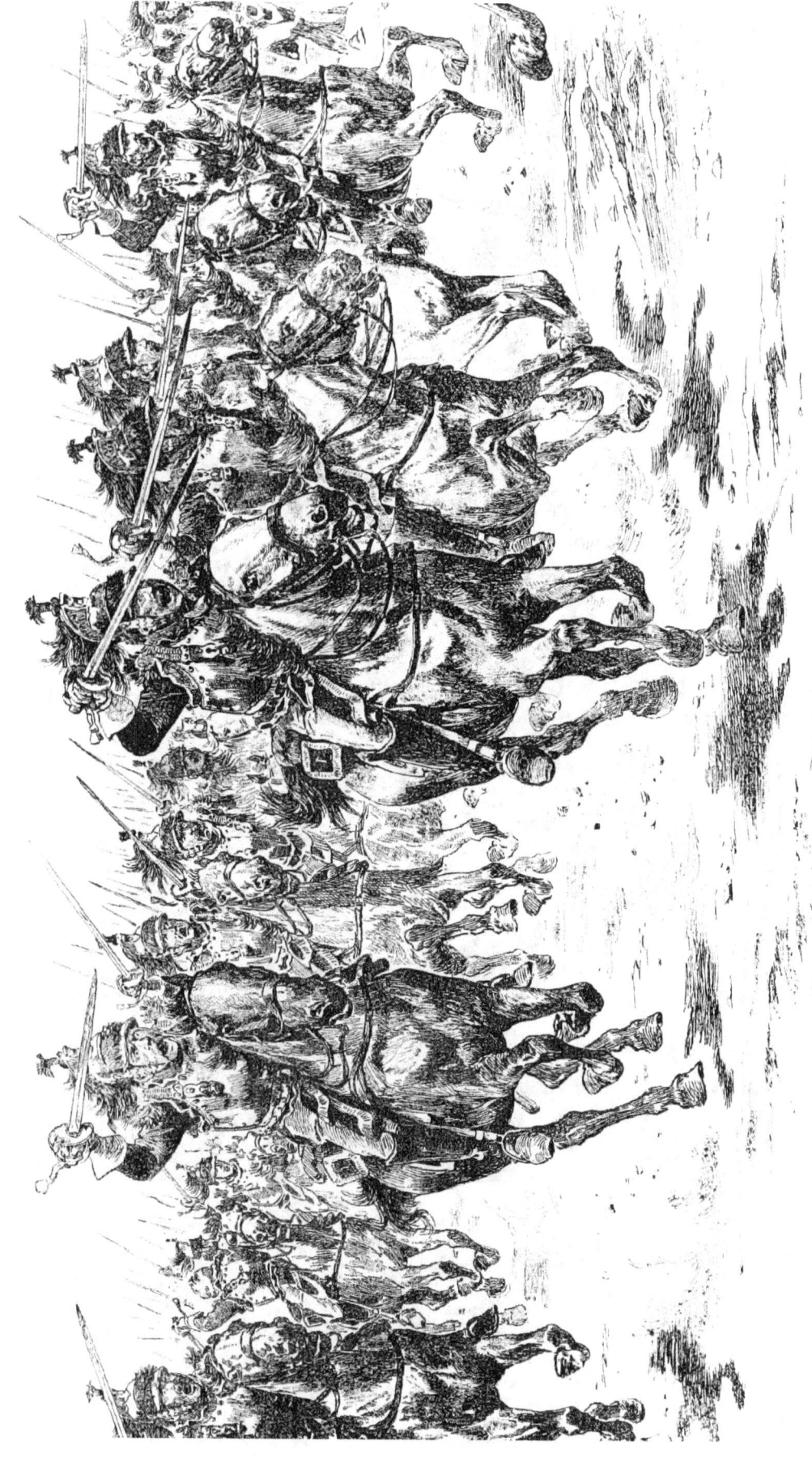

JACQUES ONFROY BREVILLE (aka JOB): Napoleonic French Cavalry Charge (Above)

W. G. BAXTER: Illustration for 'Ally Soper's Half-Holiday'. From 'Pen Drawing and Pen Draughtsmen' (Previous Page)

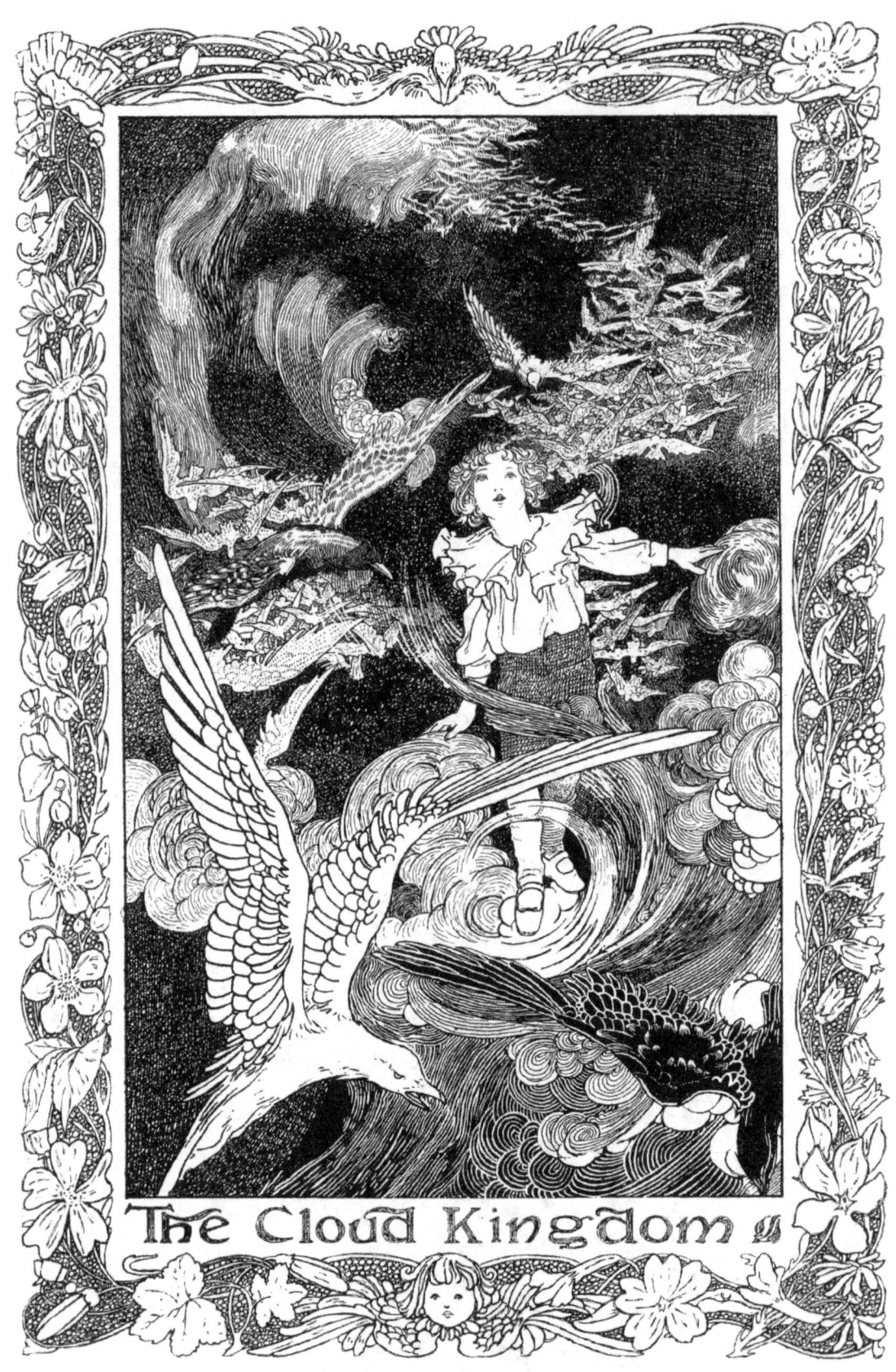

CHARLES ROBINSON: Frontispiece from 'The Cloud Kingdom'

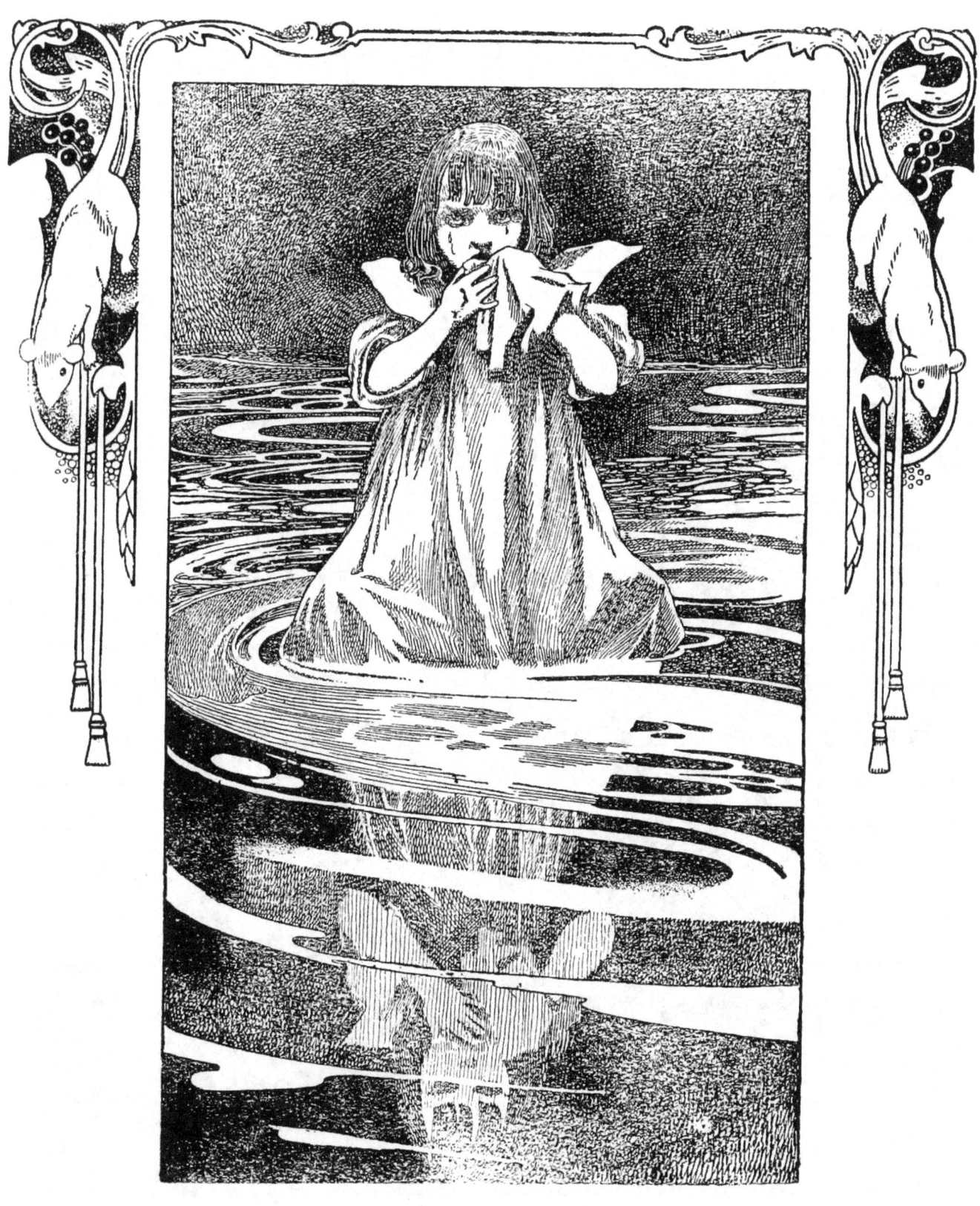

CHARLES ROBINSON: There was a large pool all around her about four inches deep and reaching half down the hall.
From 'Alice's Adventures in Wonderland'

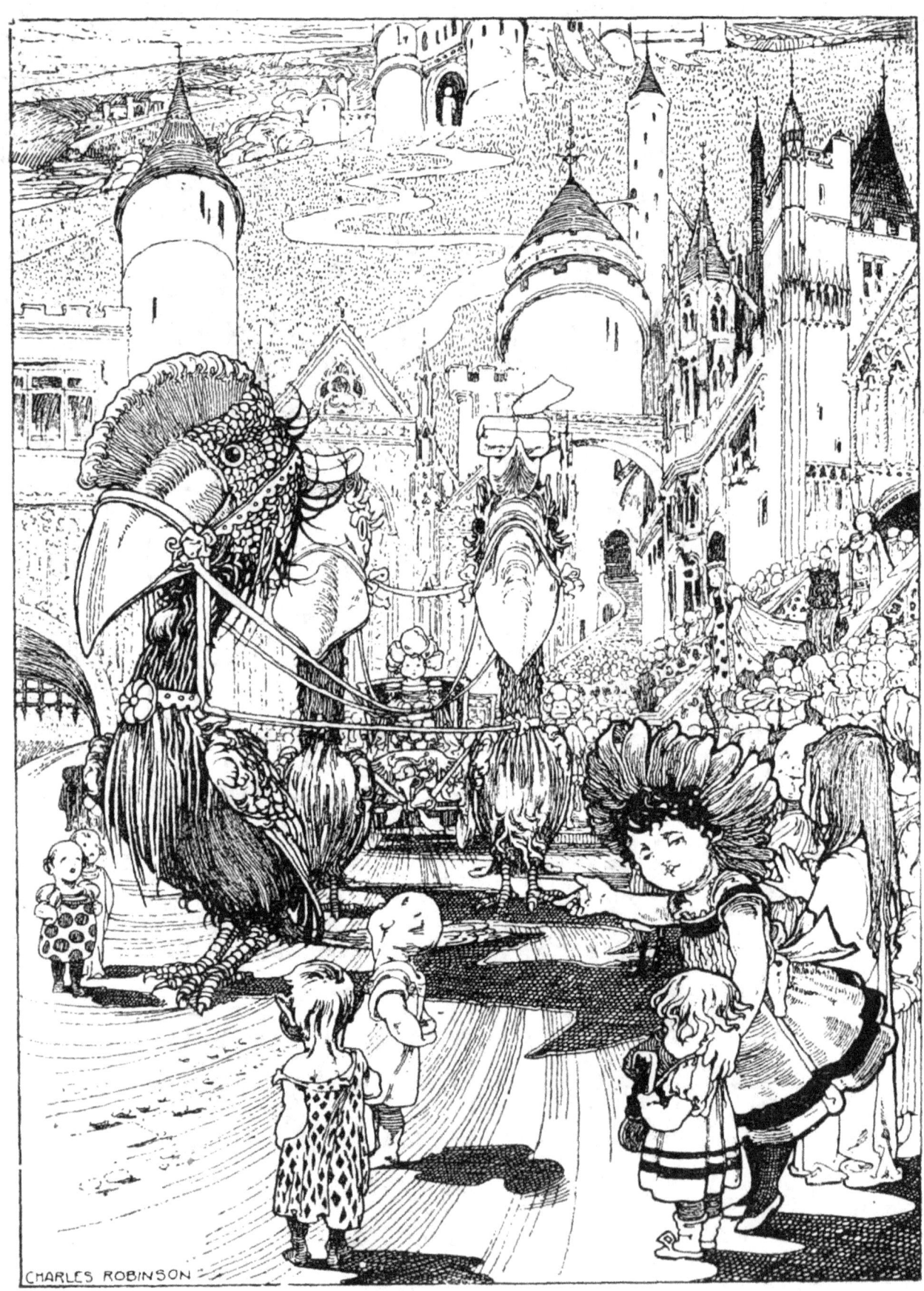

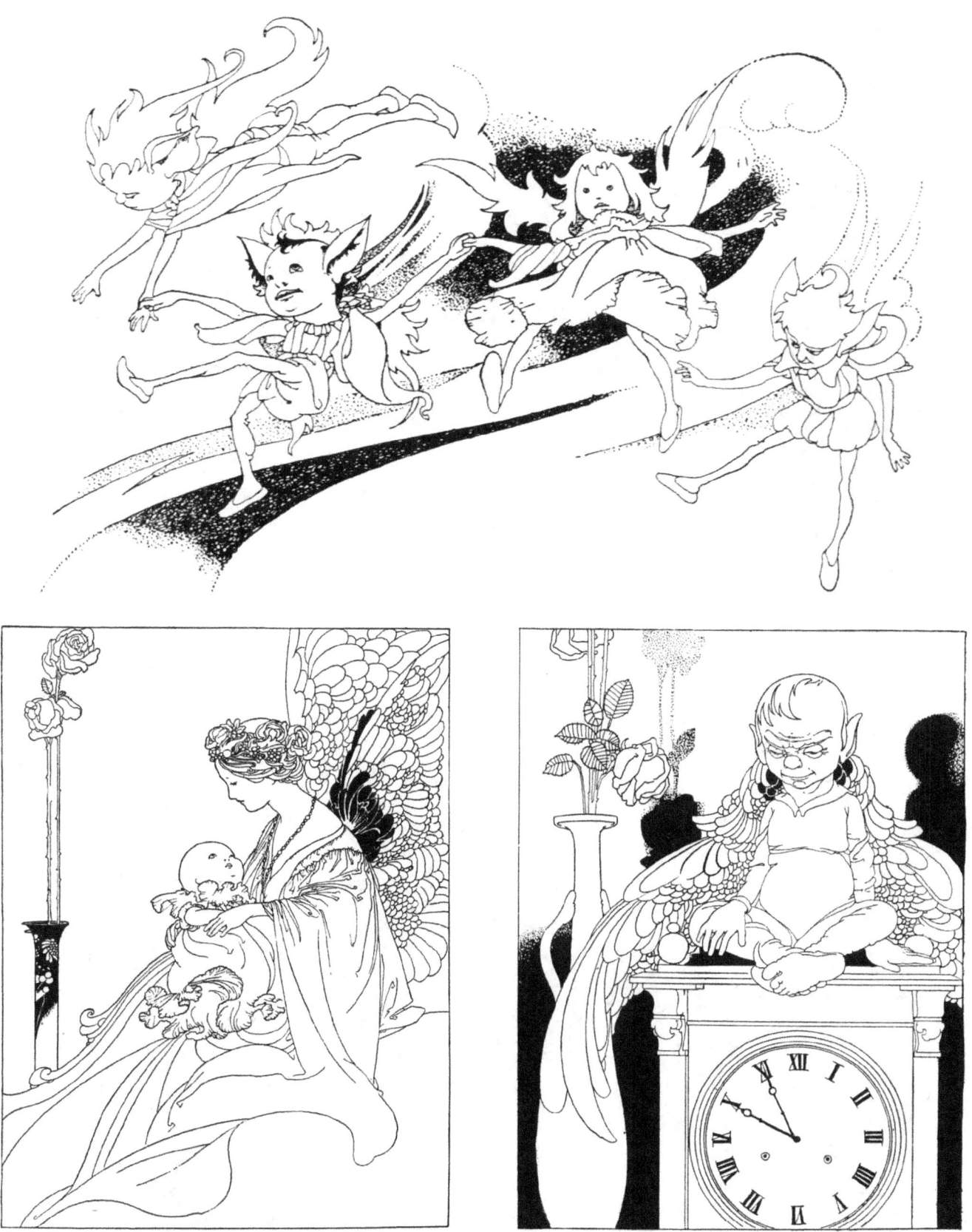

CHARLES ROBINSON: Above, In-text embellishments from 'The Story of the Weathercock'.
Left, Illustration from 'Make Believe'.

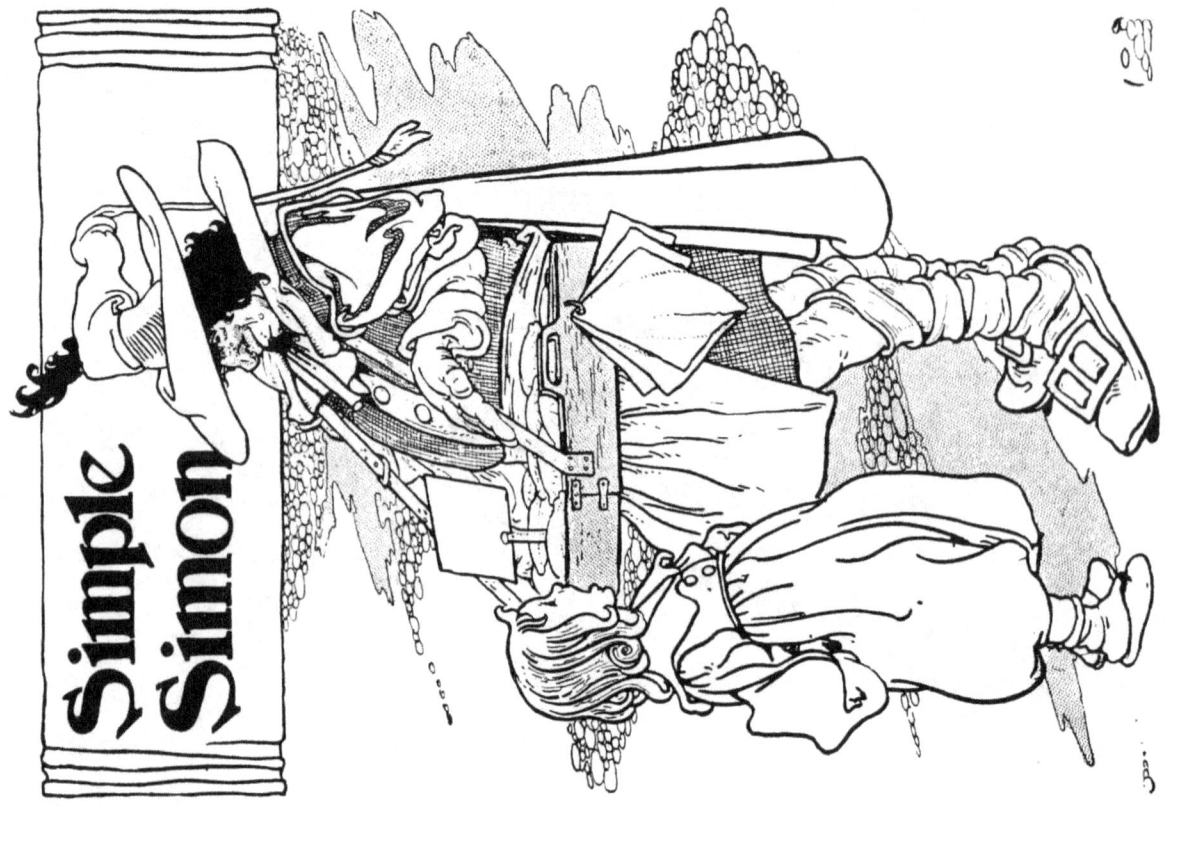
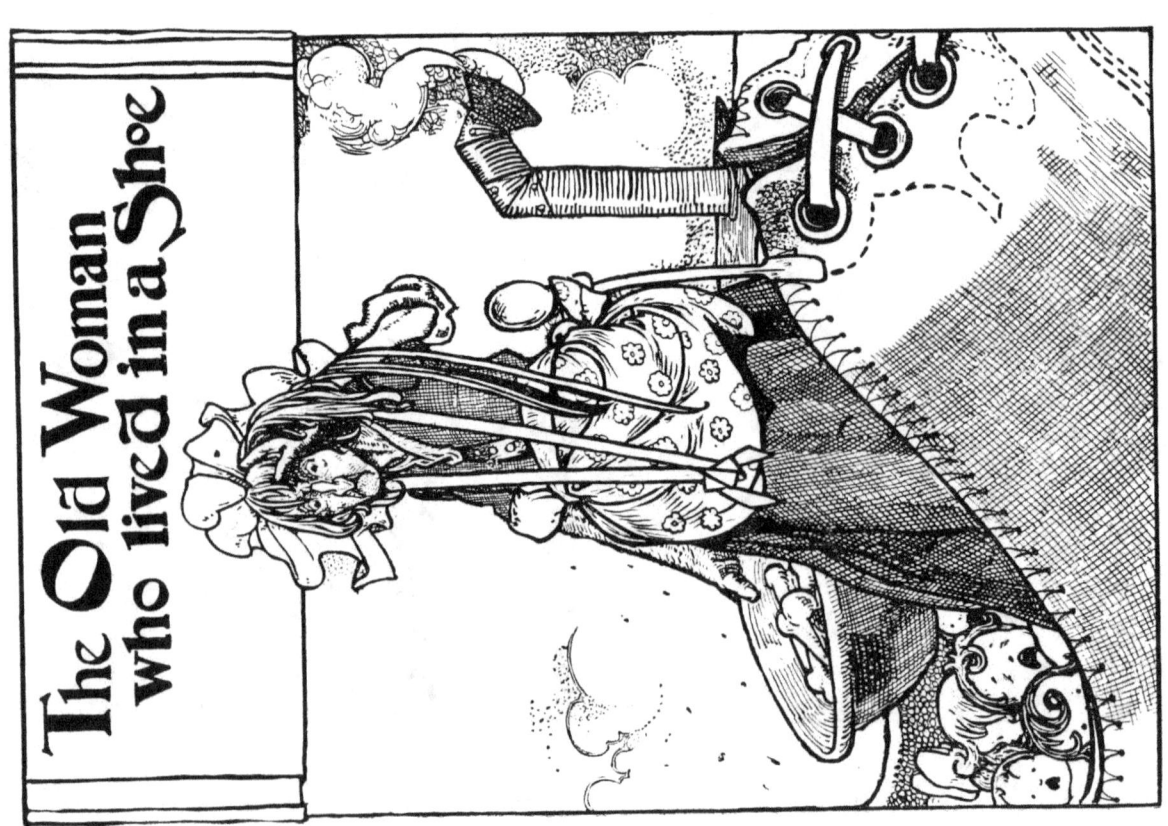

CHARLES ROBINSON: Two story title designs from 'The Big Book of Nursery Rhymes'

FREDERIC REMINGTON: A Question of Brands. From 'Pen Drawing and Pen Draughtsmen'

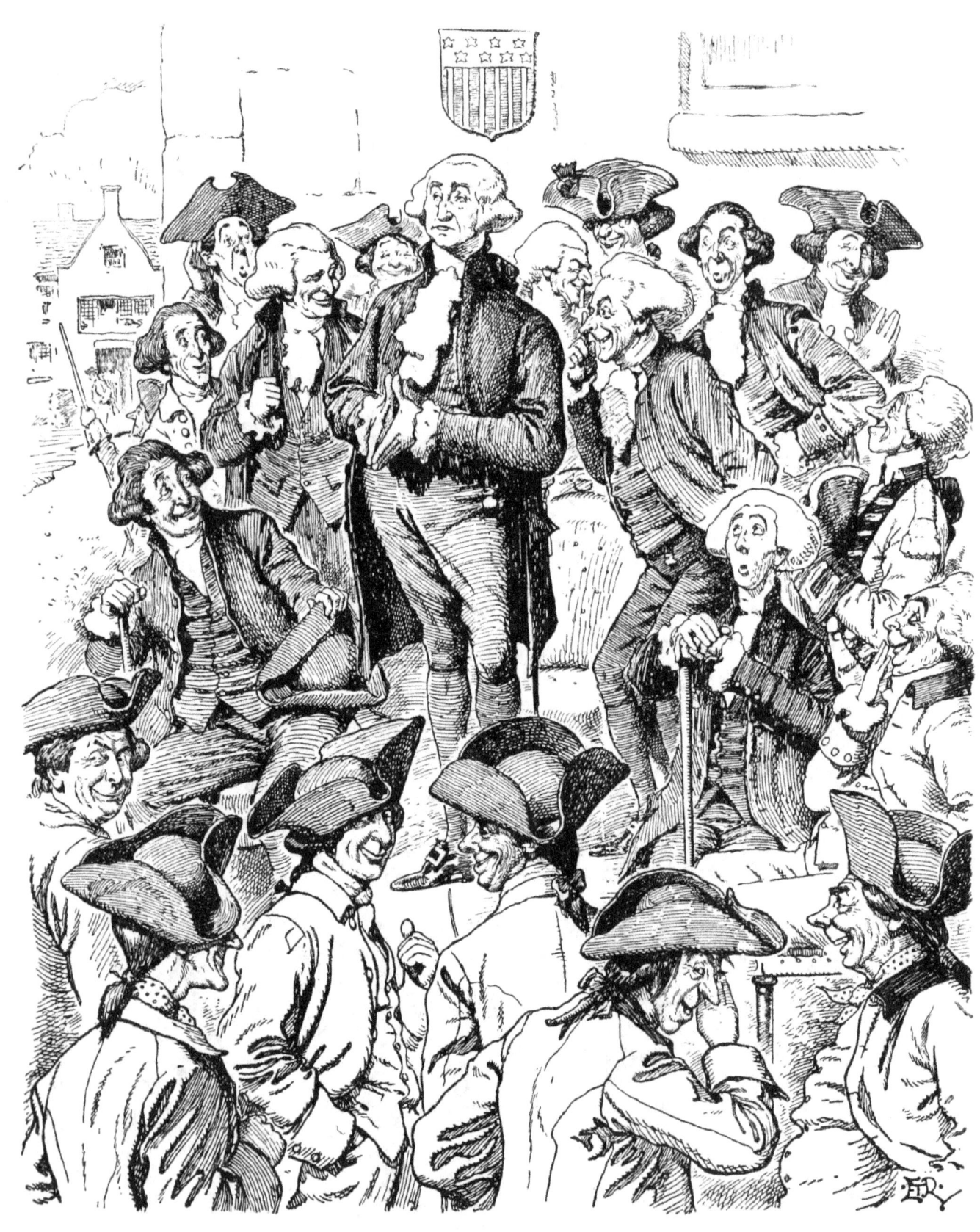

EDWARD T REED: George Washington trying to tell a lie.
From 'Modern Pen Drawing: European and American'

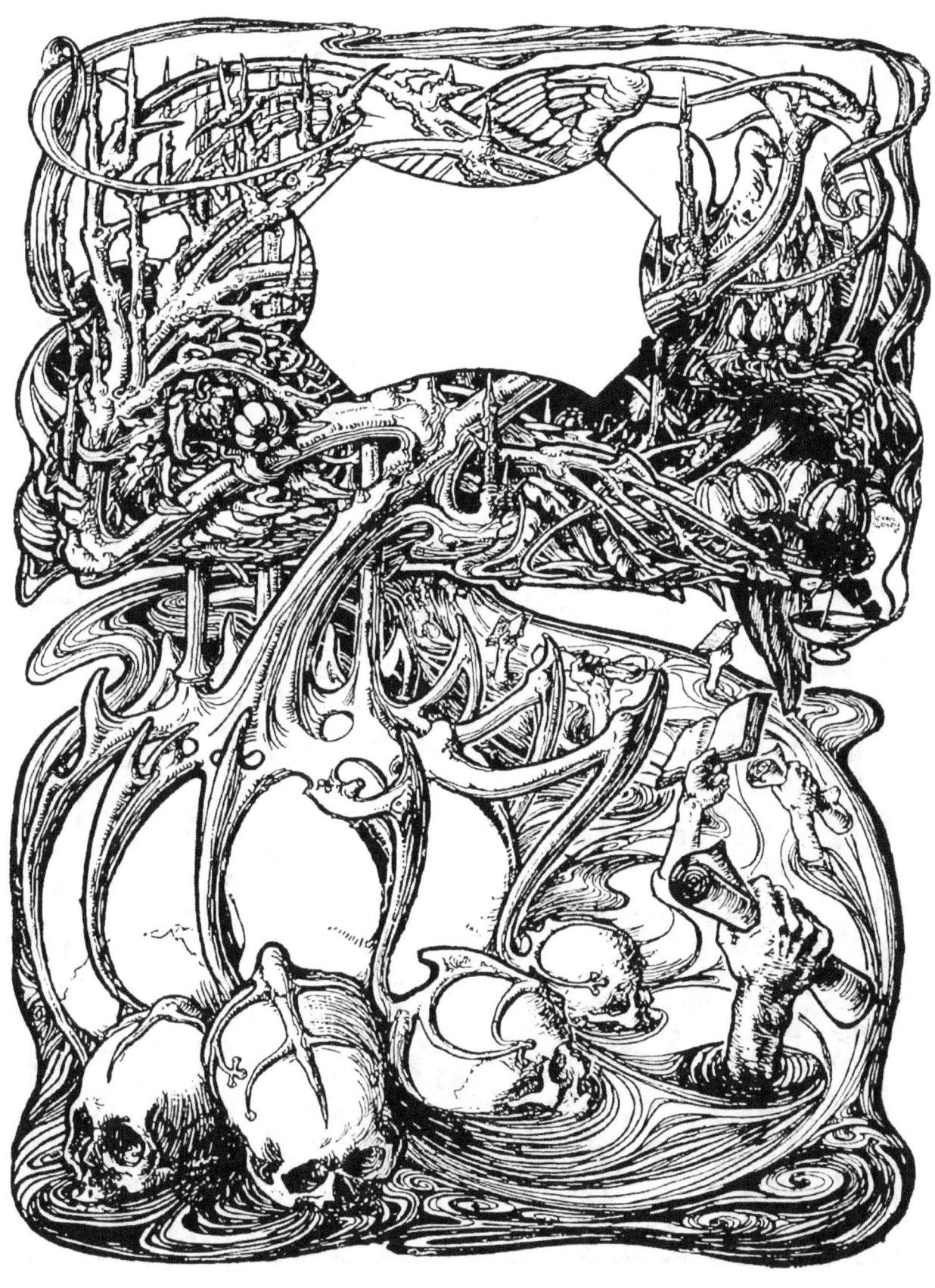

CYRIL GOLDIE: Book-plate illustration from 'The Studio International' magazine 1898

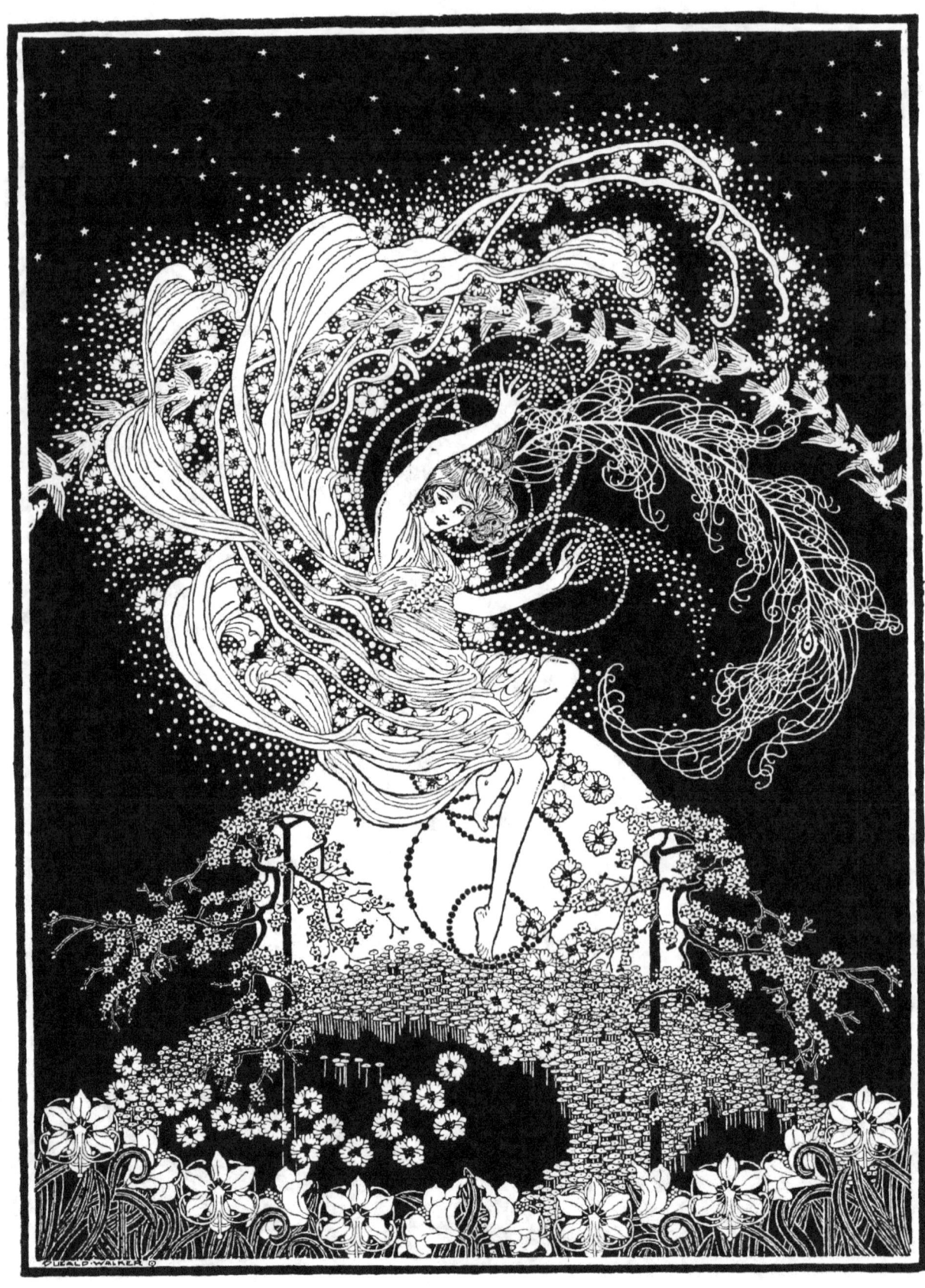

DUGALD S WALKER: "When buds are breaking and birds singing merrily, dance with me".
From 'Dream Boats and Other Stories'

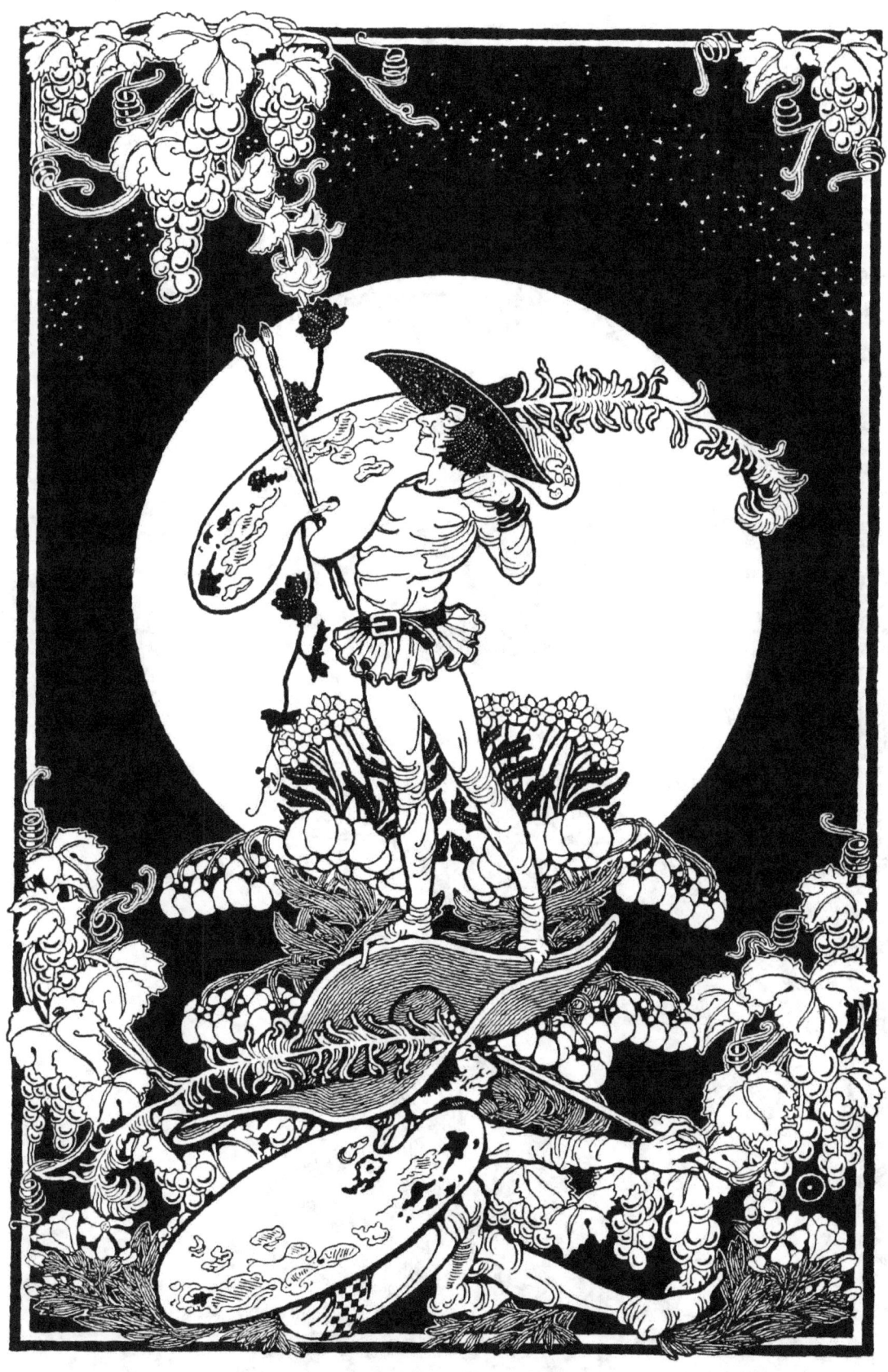

DUGALD S WALKER: "Whence do the elves get all the colour they need with which to paint the flowers, fruits and foliage?" From 'Dream Boats and Other Stories'

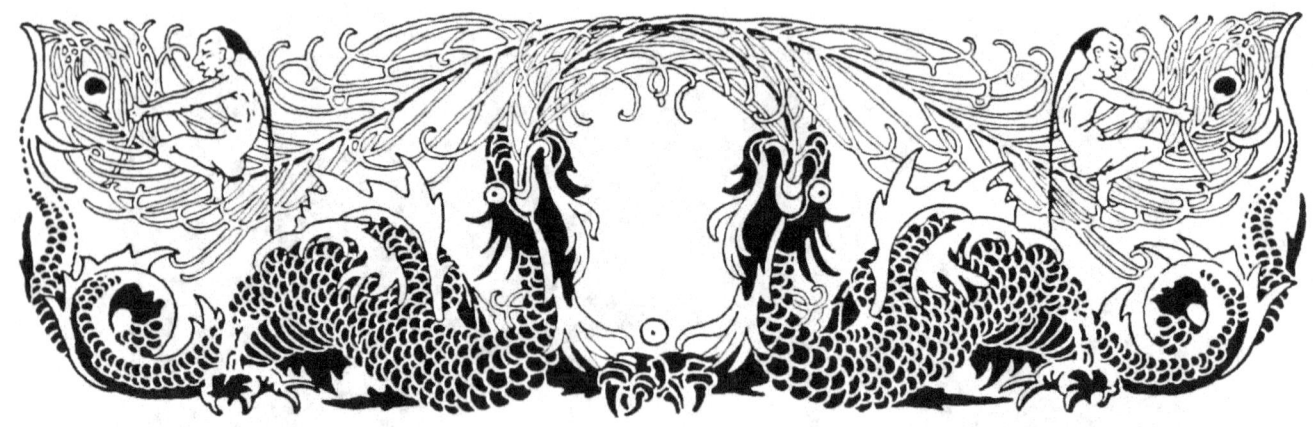

DUGALD S WALKER: Above, Chapter heading. Below, "The oak finds happiness in providing a refreshing drink for migrating fairies" From 'Dream Boats and Other Stories'

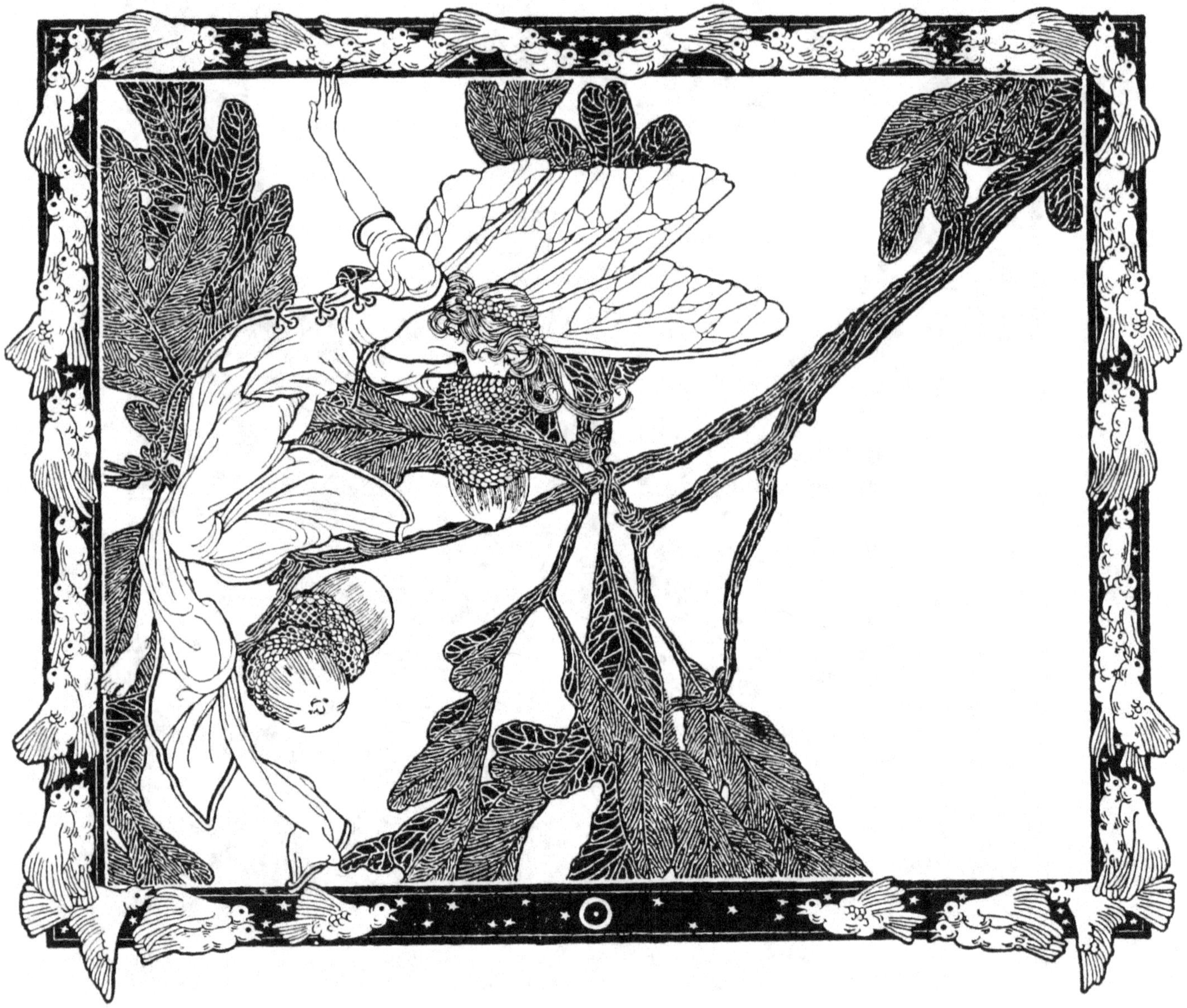

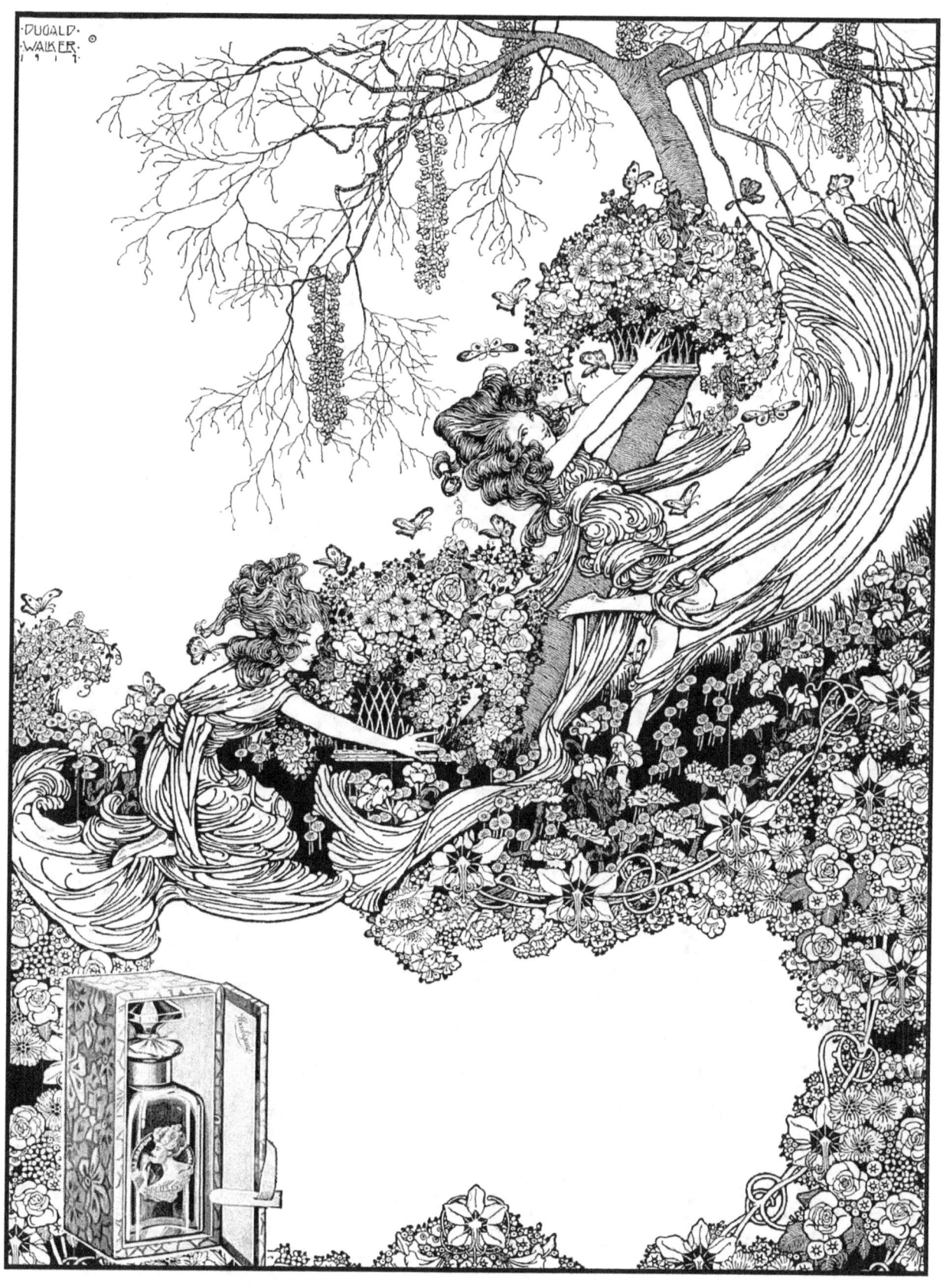

DUGALD S WALKER: Illustration for magazine advert.

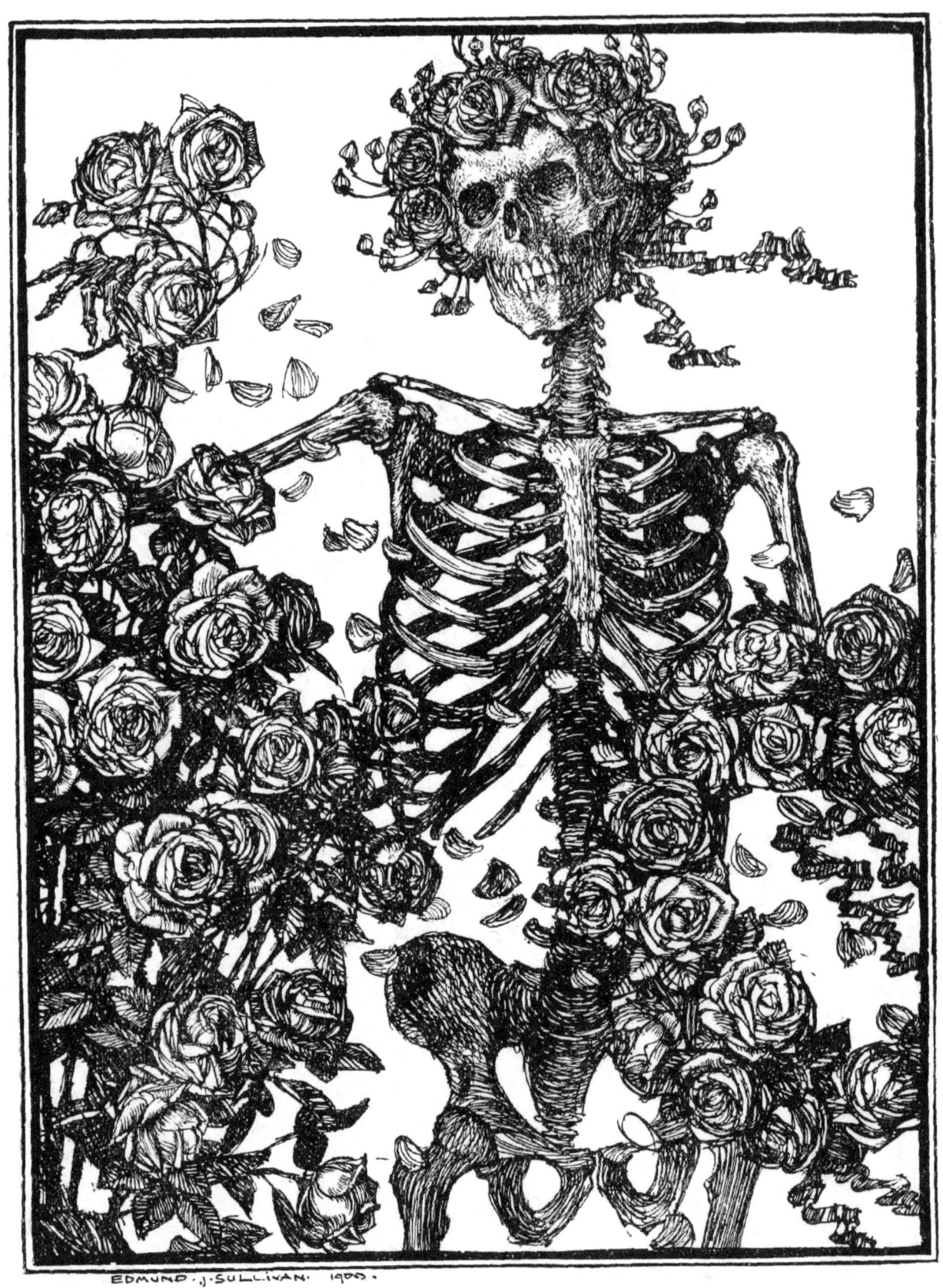

EDMUND J SULLIVAN: Illustration for 'Rubáiyát of Omar Khayyám'

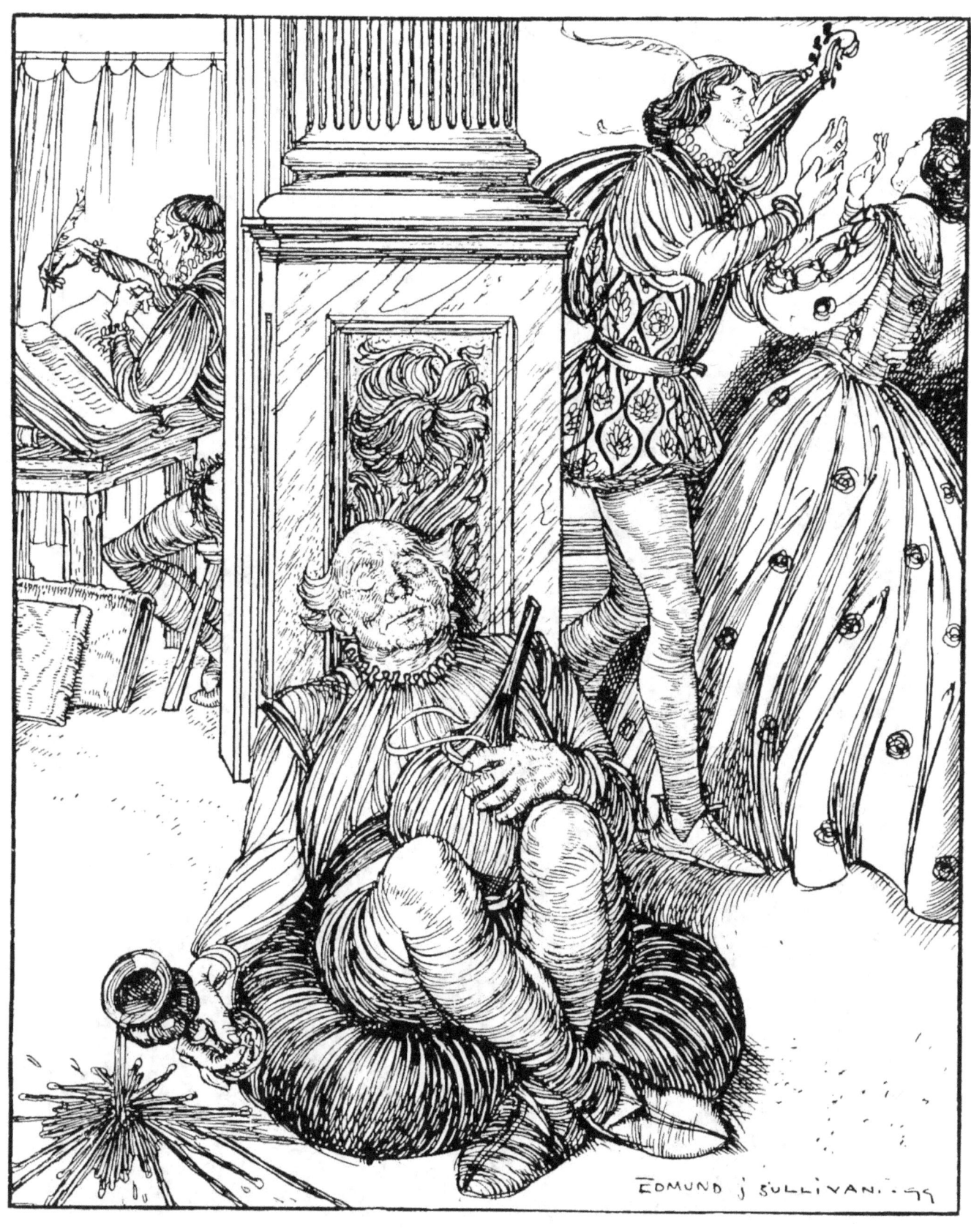

EDMUND J SULLIVAN: The Day Dream. From 'A Dream of Fair Women & Other Poems'

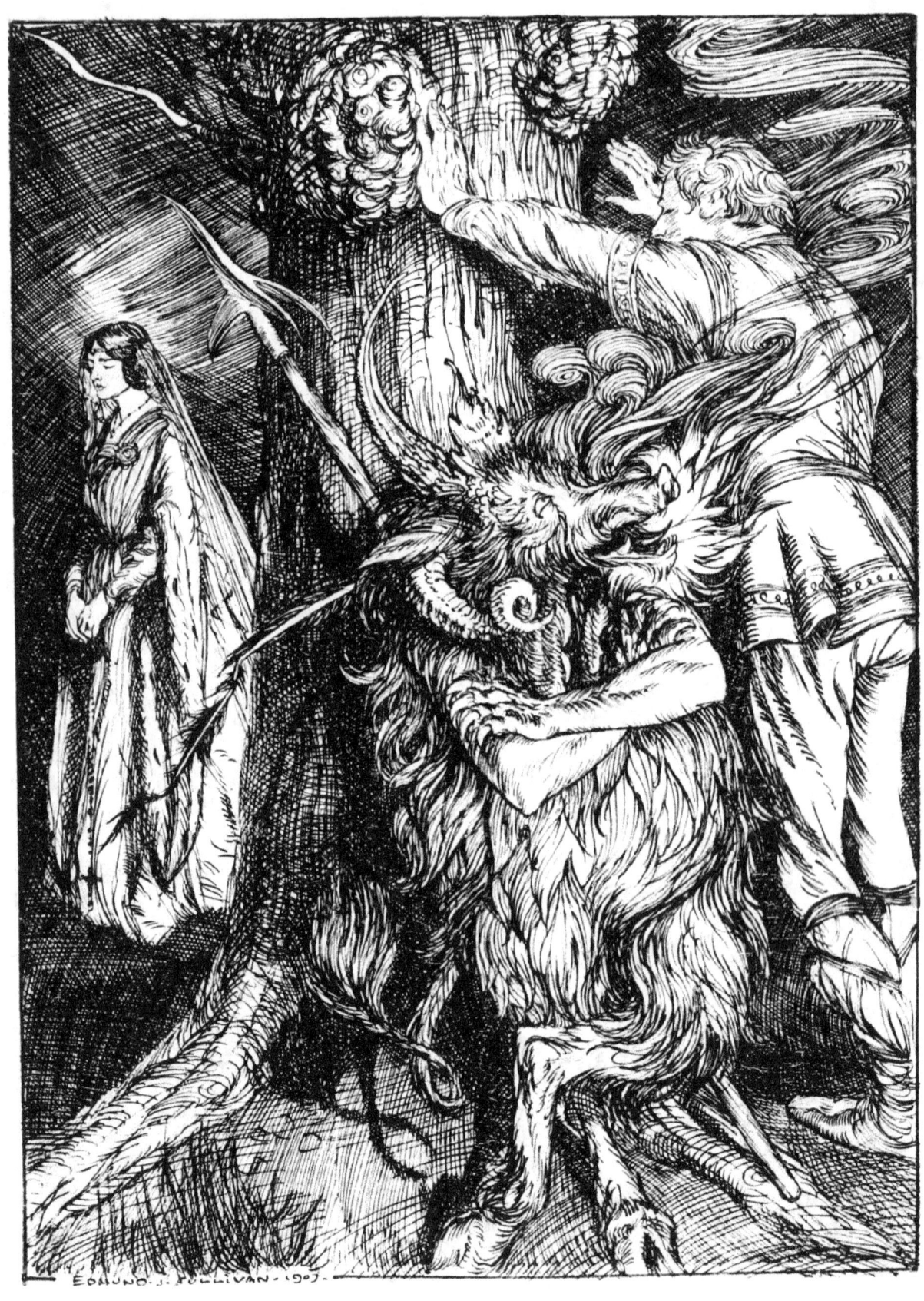

EDMUND J SULLIVAN: Gabriela's very self was seen softly approaching.
From 'Sintram and his Companions'.

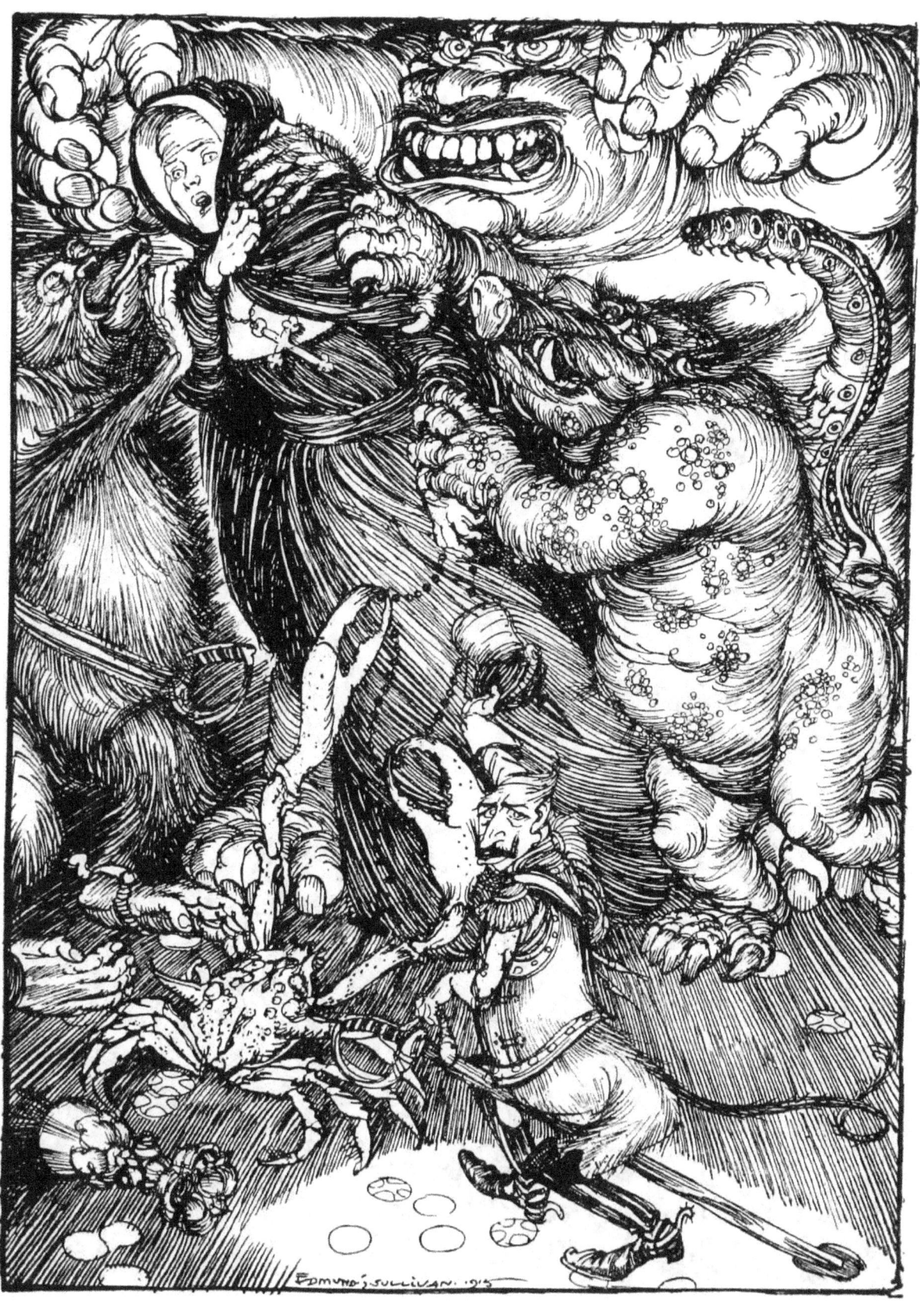

EDMUND J SULLIVAN: A Bride of Christ. From 'The Kaiser's Garland'.

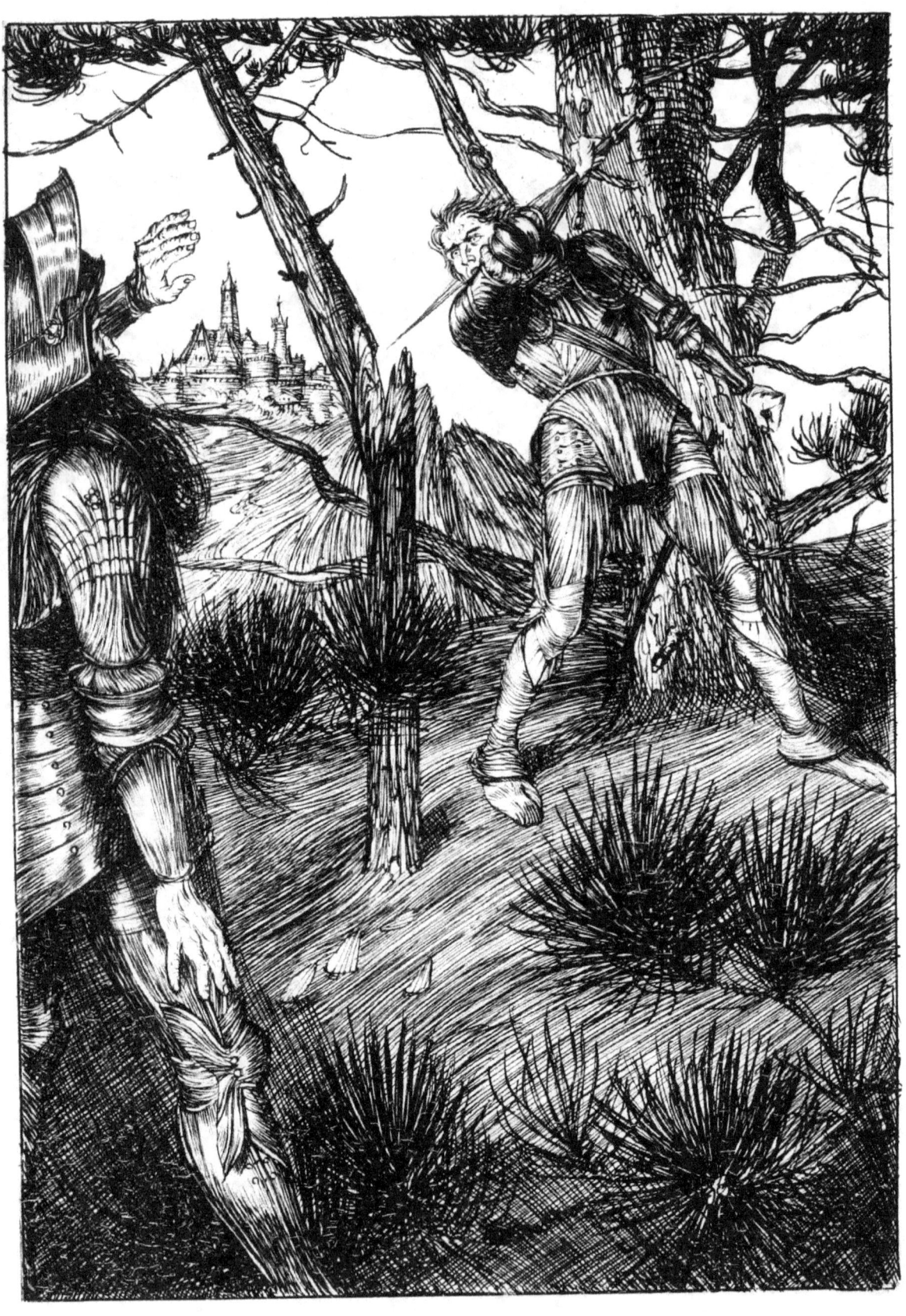

EDMUND J SULLIVAN: Suddenly old Rolf stood before him.
From 'Sintram and his Companions'.

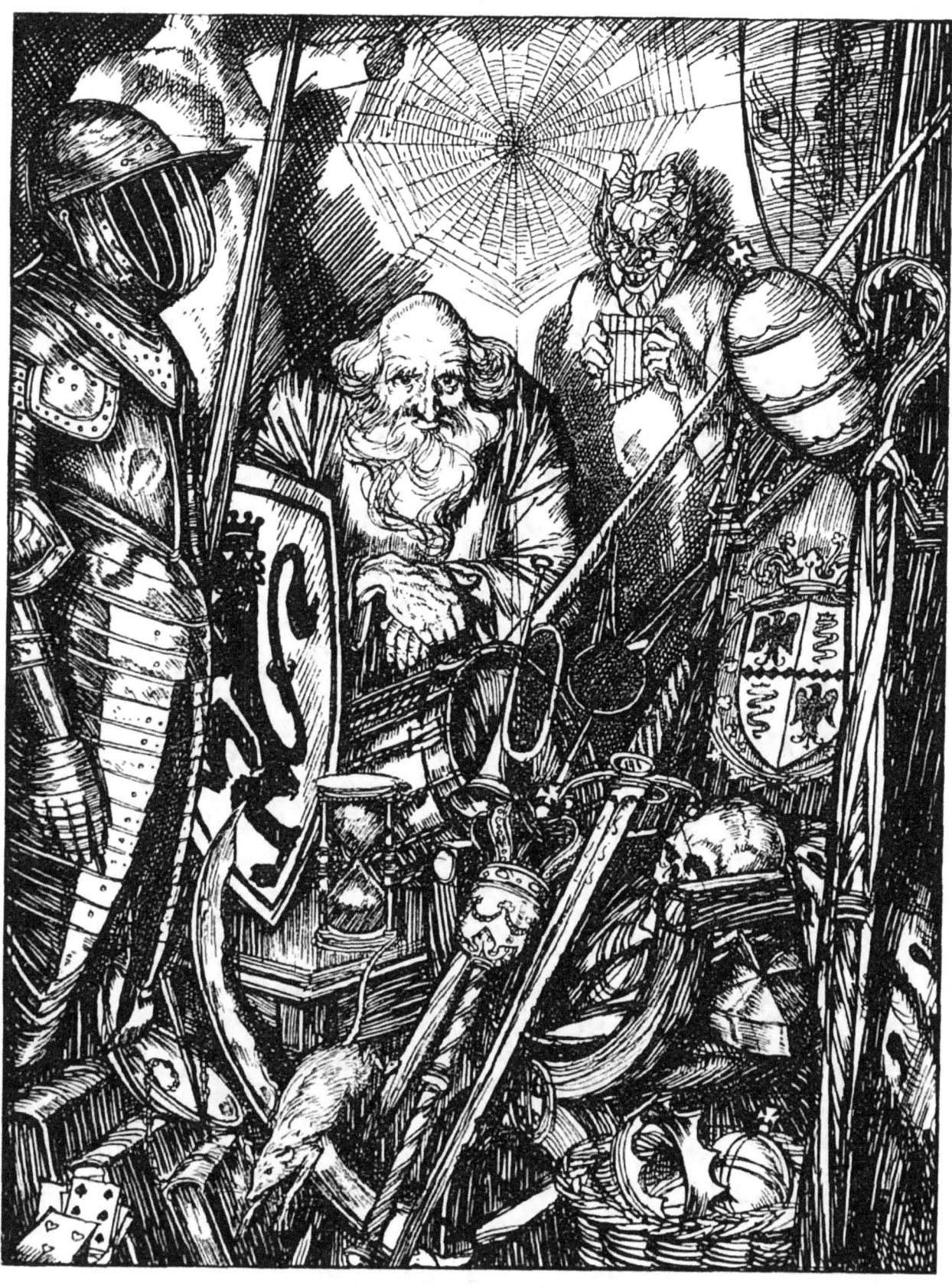

EDMUND J SULLIVAN: The Symbol Shop. From 'Sartor Resartus'.

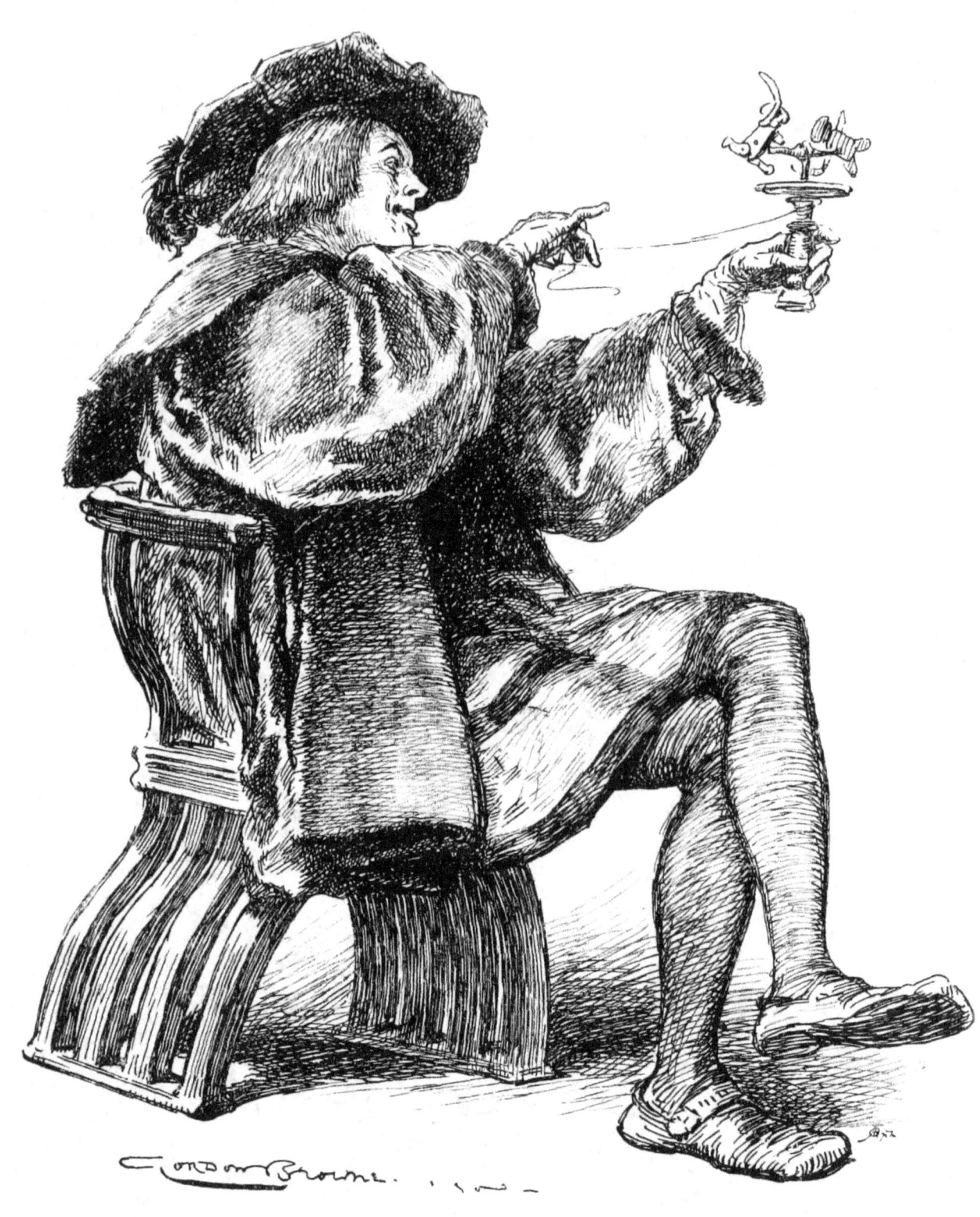

GORDON BROWNE: 'The Puppets'.

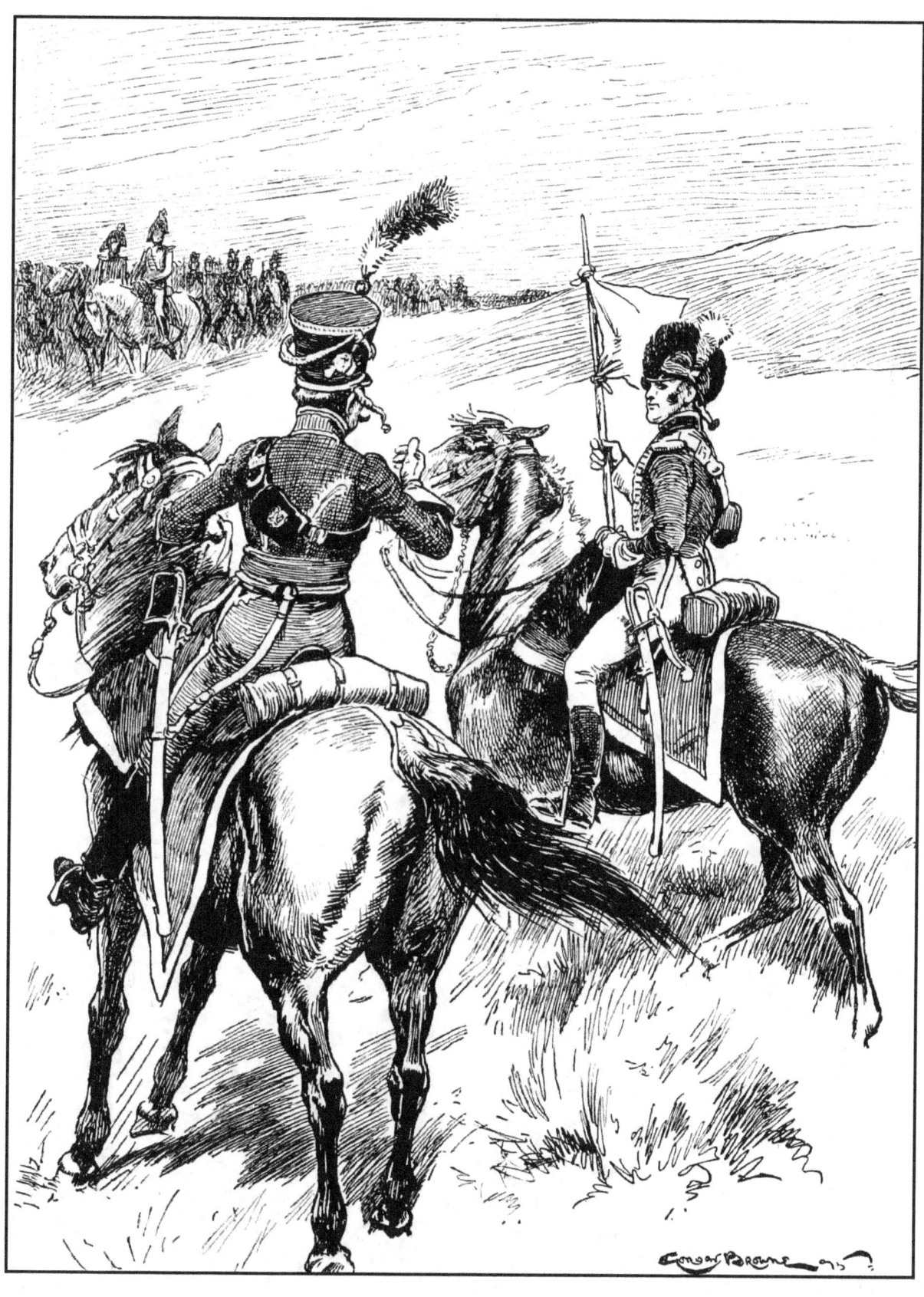

GORDON BROWNE: Suddenly a French officer galloped up to Major Wilson.
From 'Battles of the Nineteeth Century' Vol.II

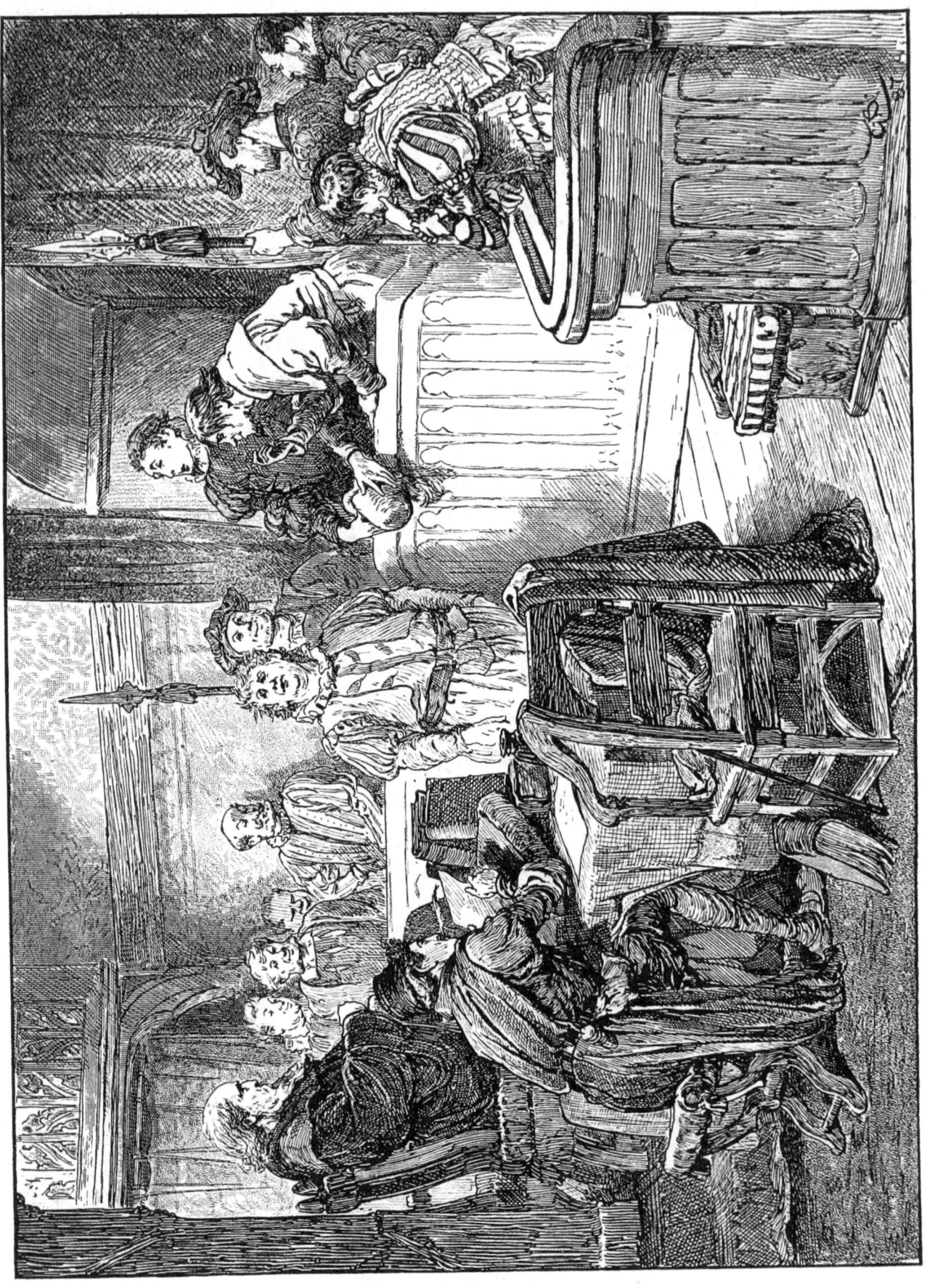

GORDON BROWNE: "Doth your honour see any harm in his face?" From the play 'Measure For Measure'. 'The Works of William Shakespeare'

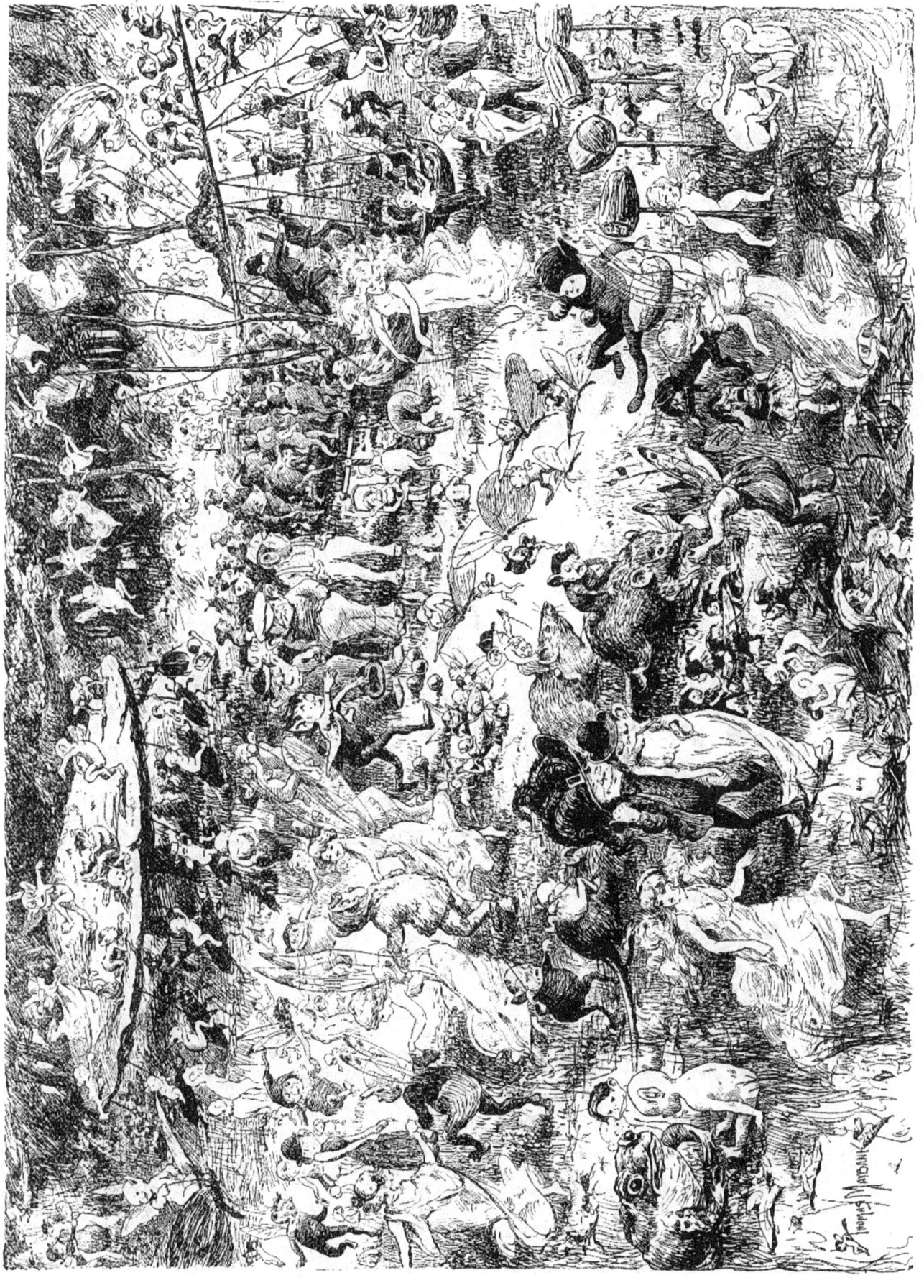

THOMAS MAYBANK: A Bank Holiday in Goblin Land.

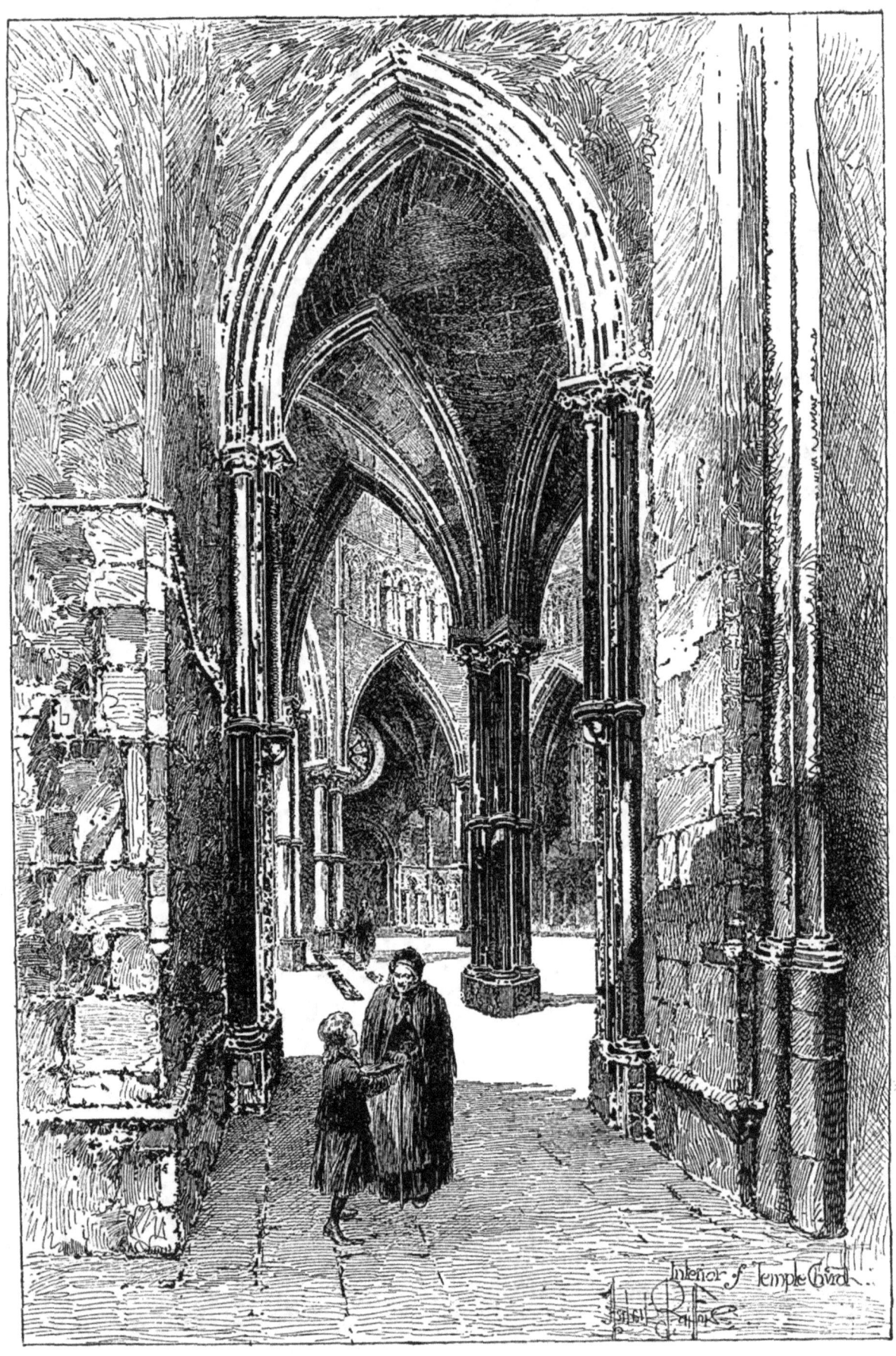

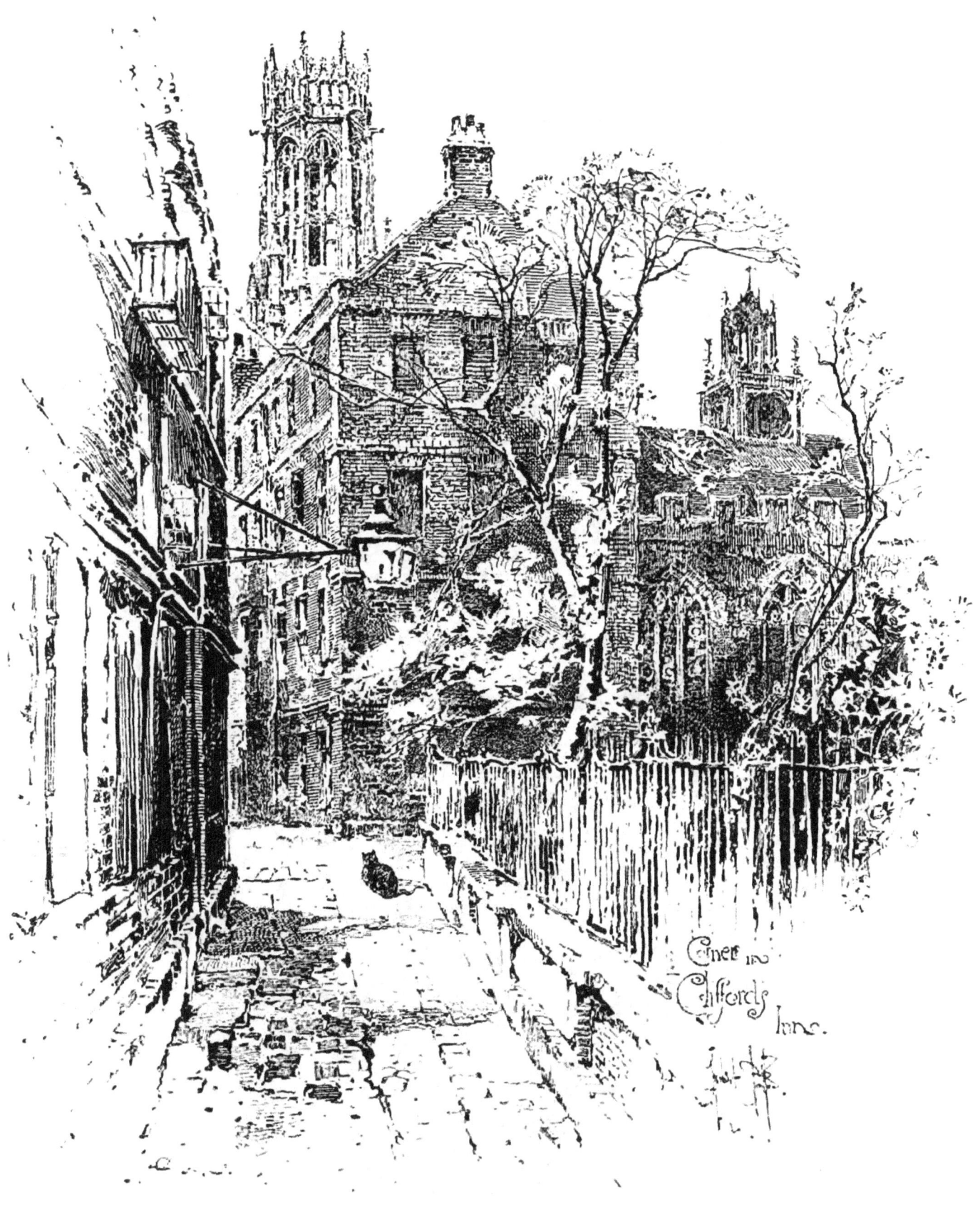

HERBERT RAILTON: Above, Clifford's Inn. Left, Interior of the Temple Church. From 'The Inns of Court & Chancery'.

HERBERT RAILTON: New Hall and Library, from New Square. From 'The Inns of Court & Chancery'

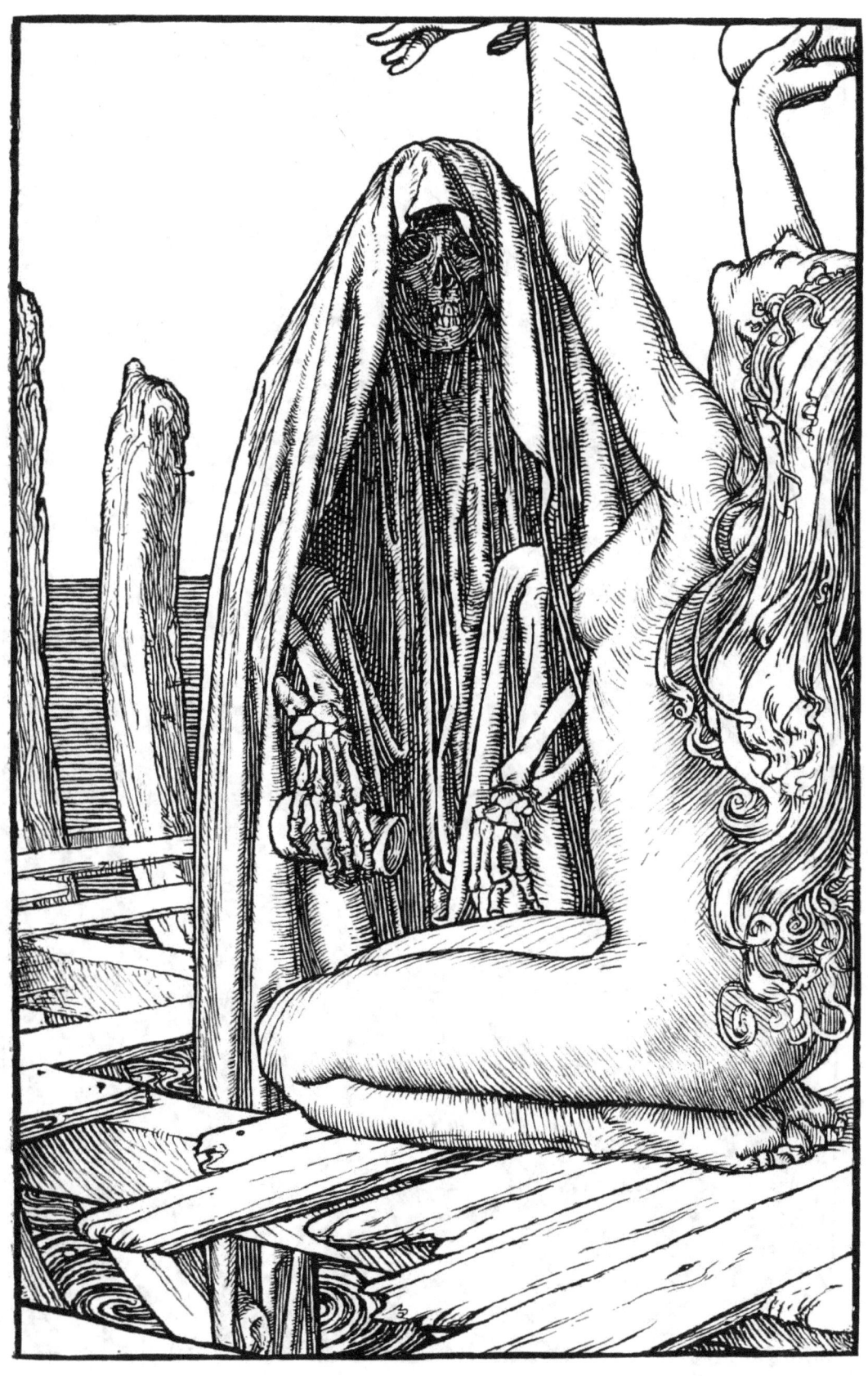

GERALD METCALFE: "The game is done! I've won, I've won!"
From 'The Poems of Coleridge'.

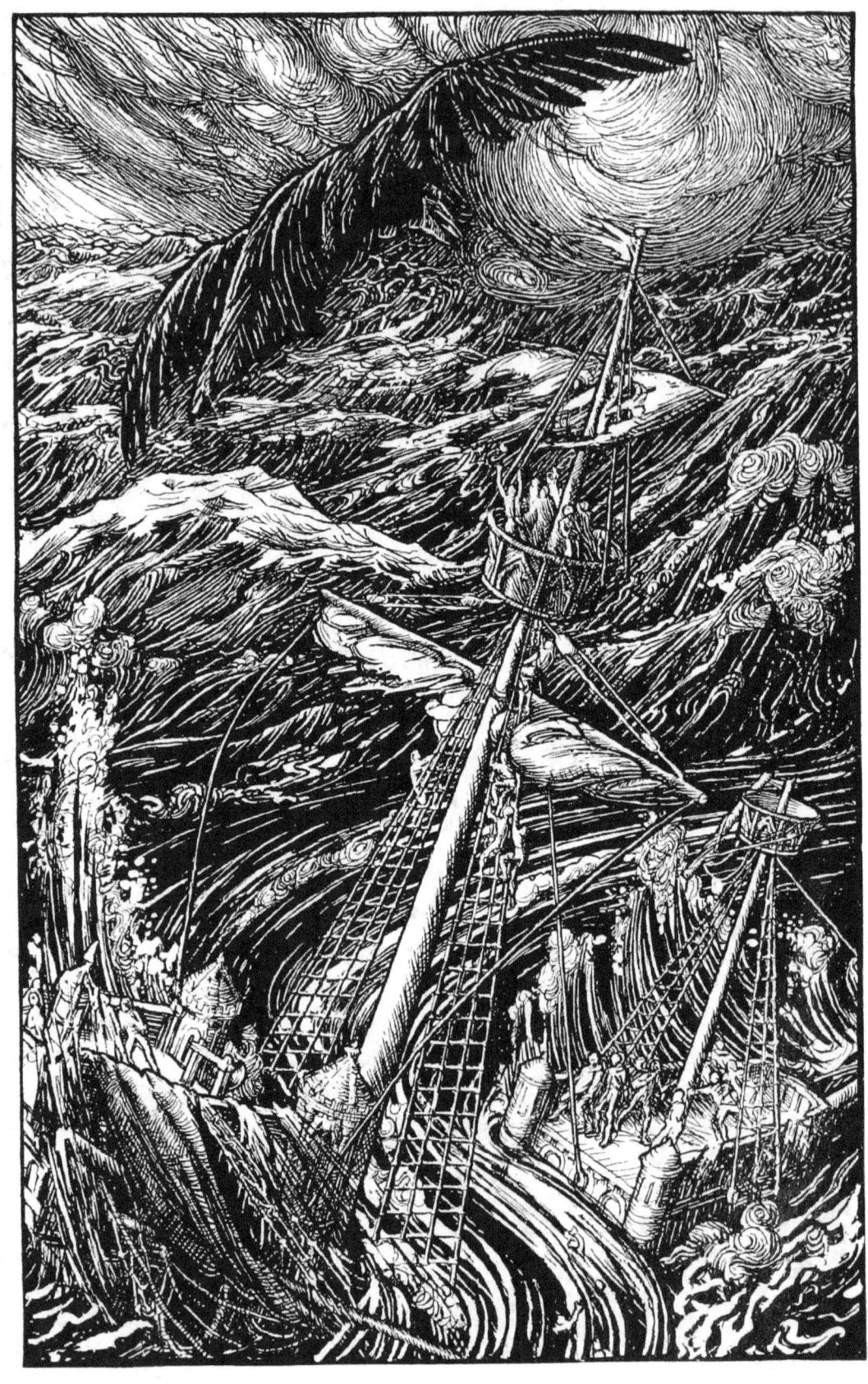

GERALD METCALFE: Round and round flew the raven and cawed to the blast.
From 'The Poems of Coleridge'.

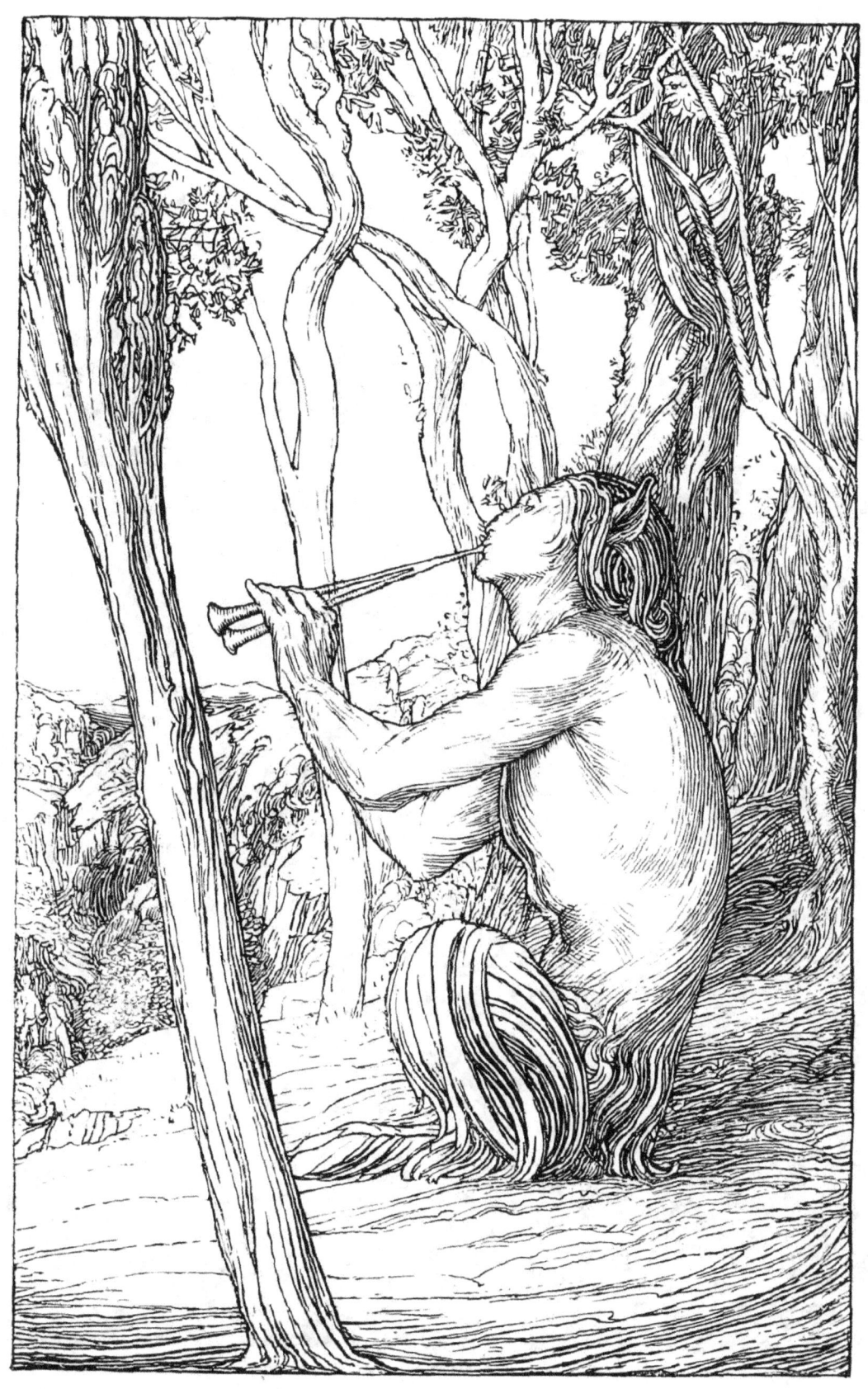

GERALD METCALFE: Boccaccio's garden and its faery.
From 'The Poems of Coleridge'.

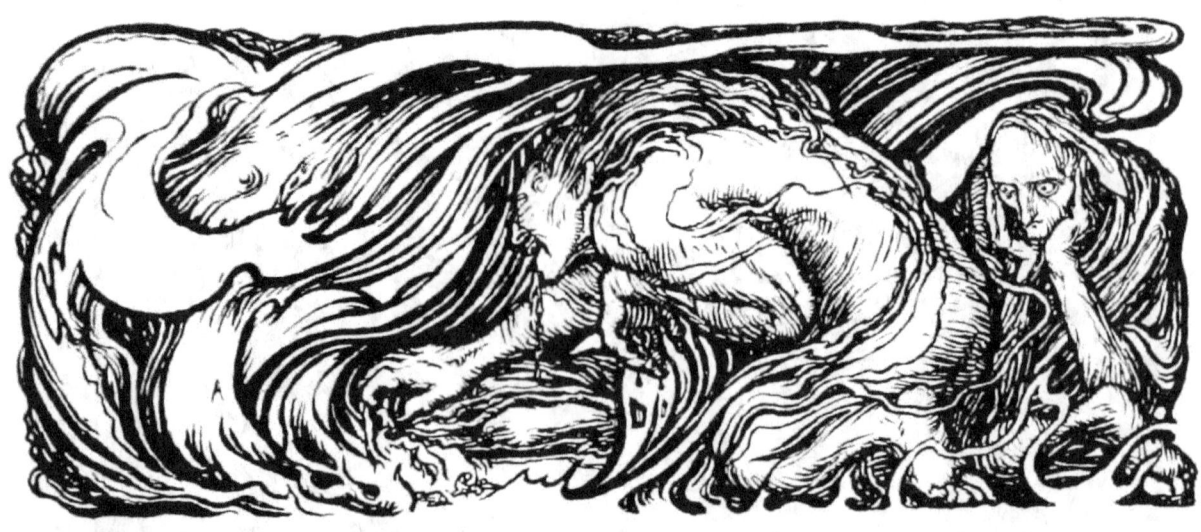

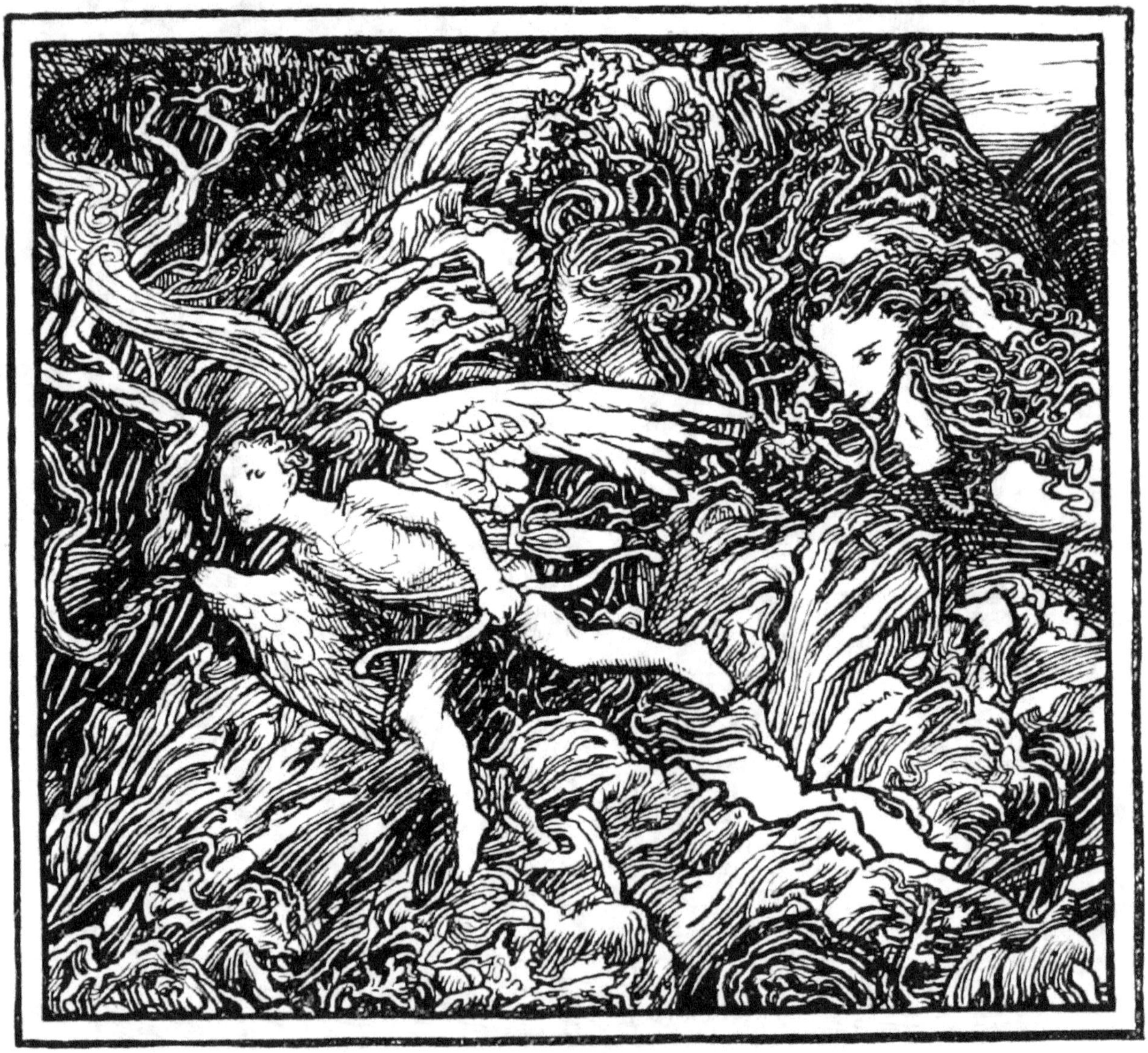

GERALD METCALFE: Two illustrations for poem headings
From 'The Poems of Coleridge'.

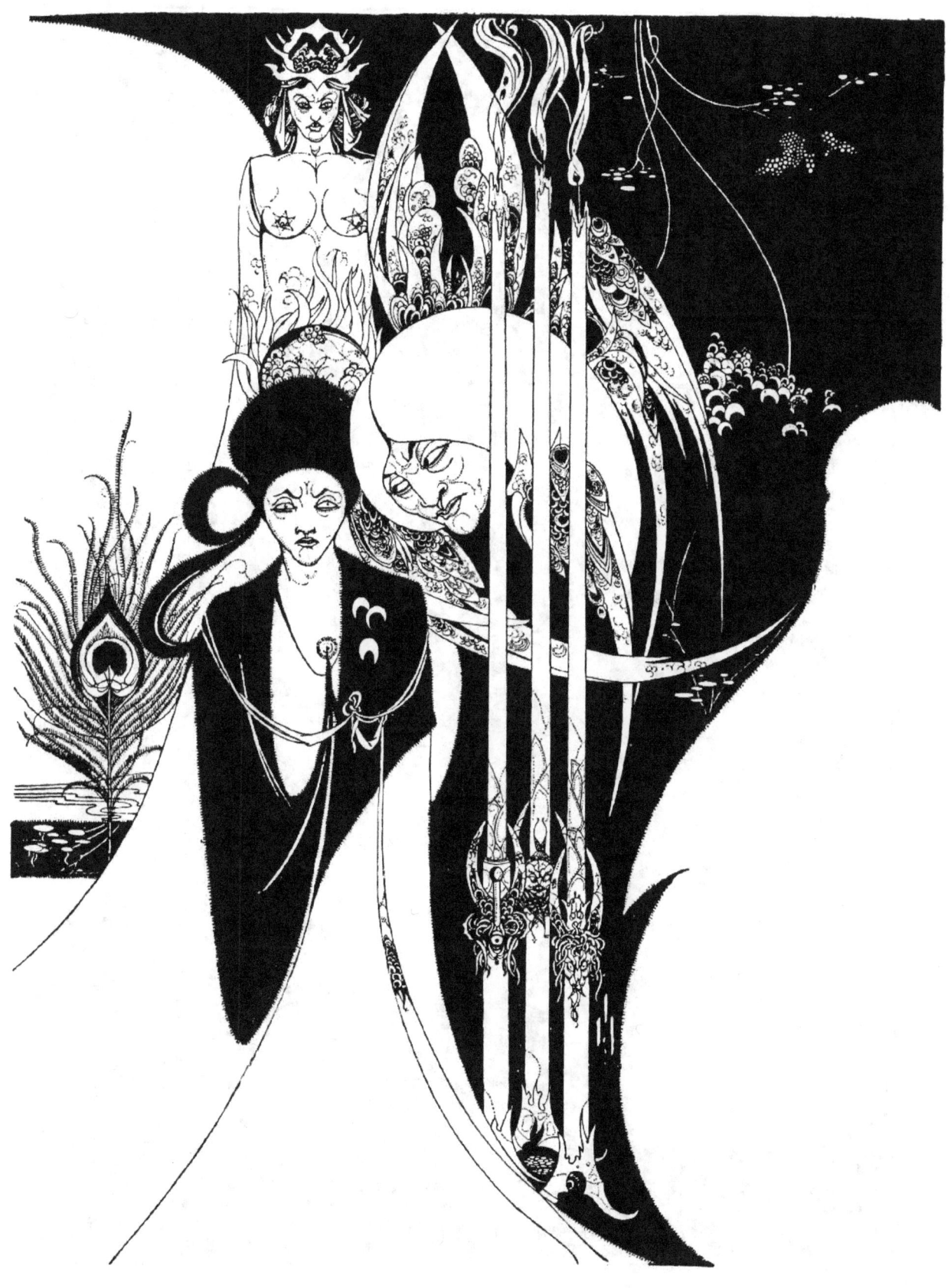

AUBREY BEARDSLEY: "Of a Neophyte, and how the black art was revealed to him."

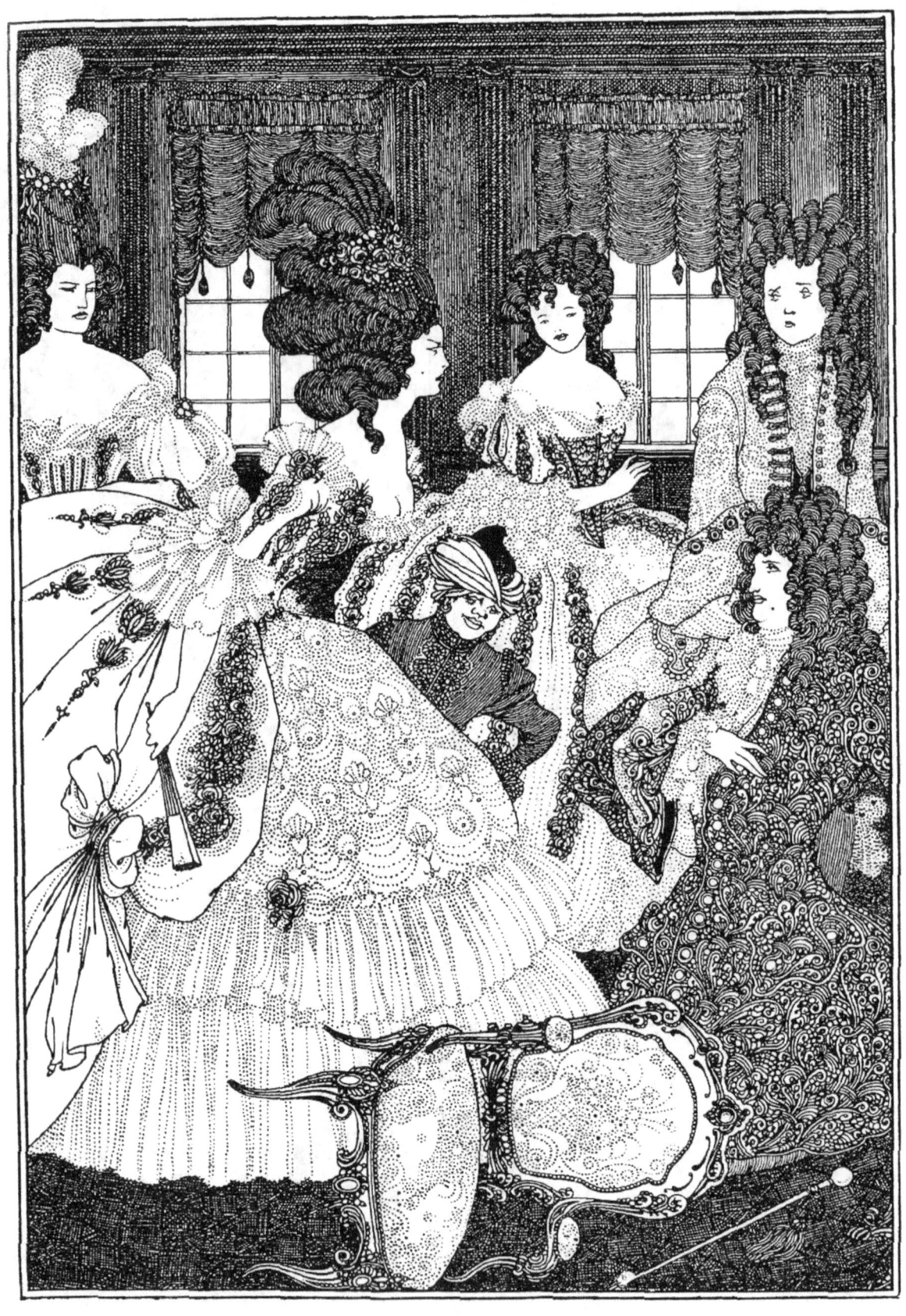

AUBREY BEARDSLEY: The Battle of the Beaux and the Belles. From 'The Rape of Lock'

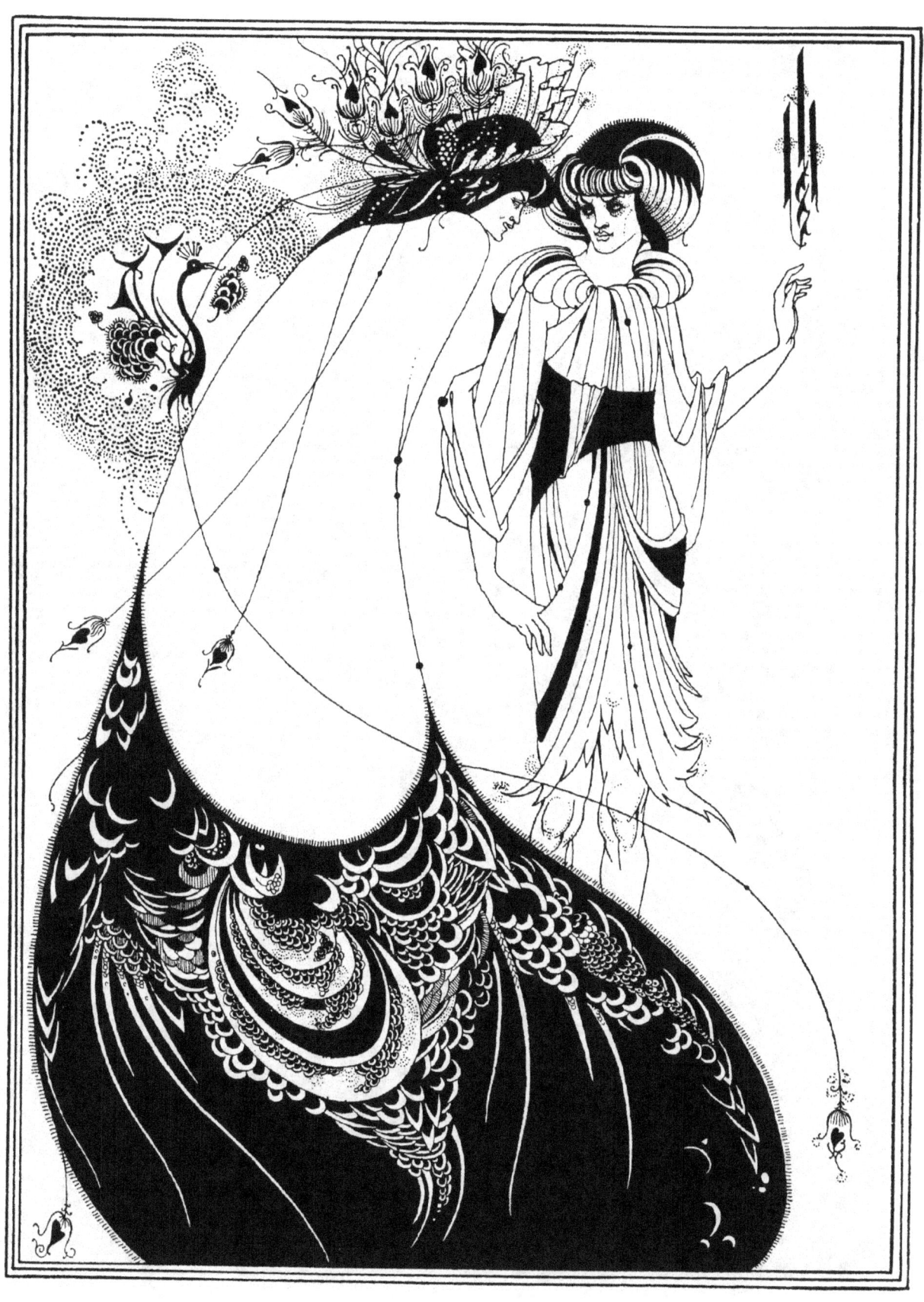

AUBREY BEARDSLEY: The Peacock Skirt. Illustration for Oscar Wilde's play 'Salomé'.

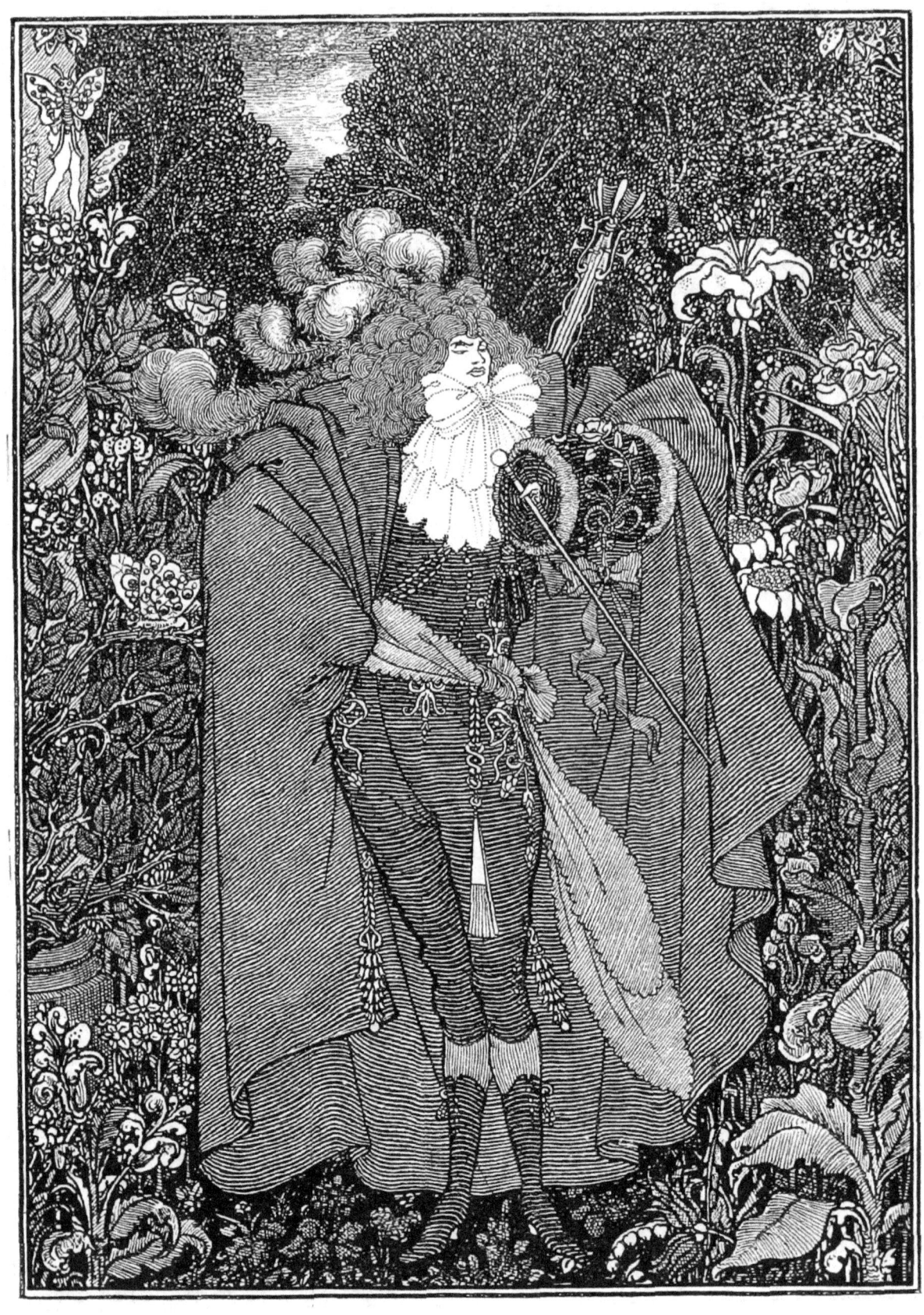

AUBREY BEARDSLEY: The Abbe. Illustration from 'Under the Hill'

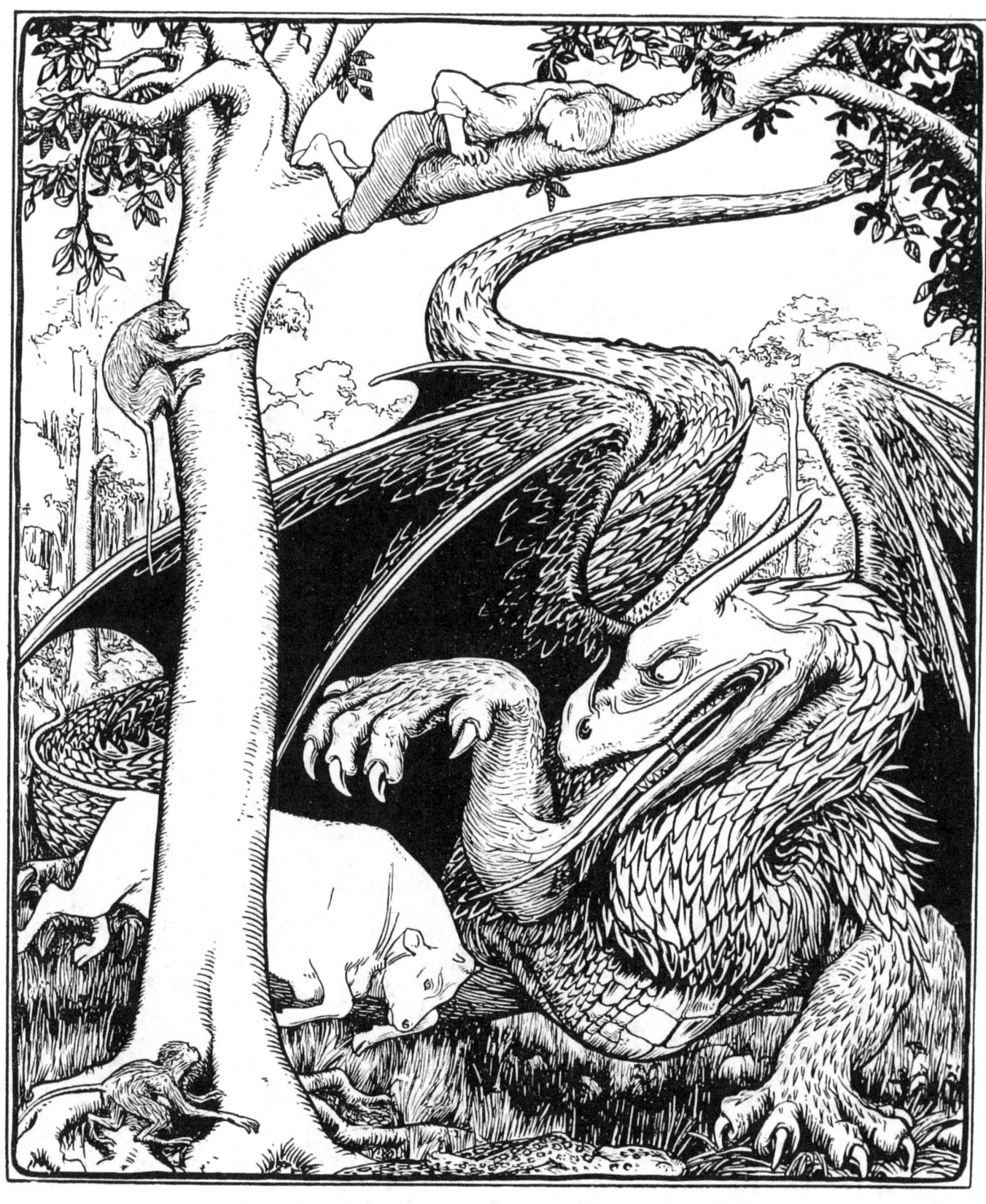

JOHN D BATTEN: The little Bull-Calf. From 'More English Fairy Tales'

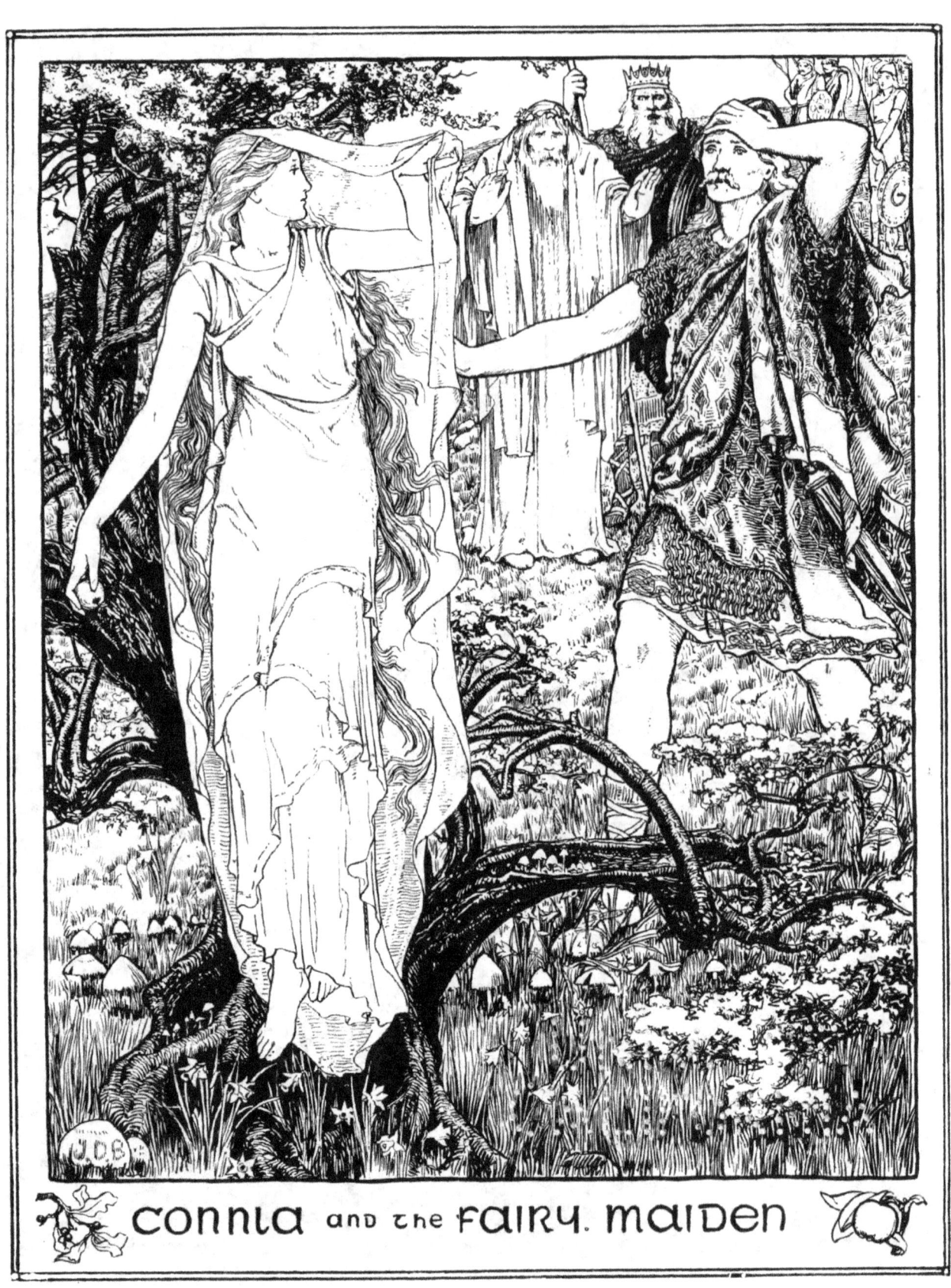

CONNLA AND THE FAIRY MAIDEN

JOHN D BATTEN: Above, From 'Celtic Folk & Fairy Tales'
Right, In-text embellishments from various books.

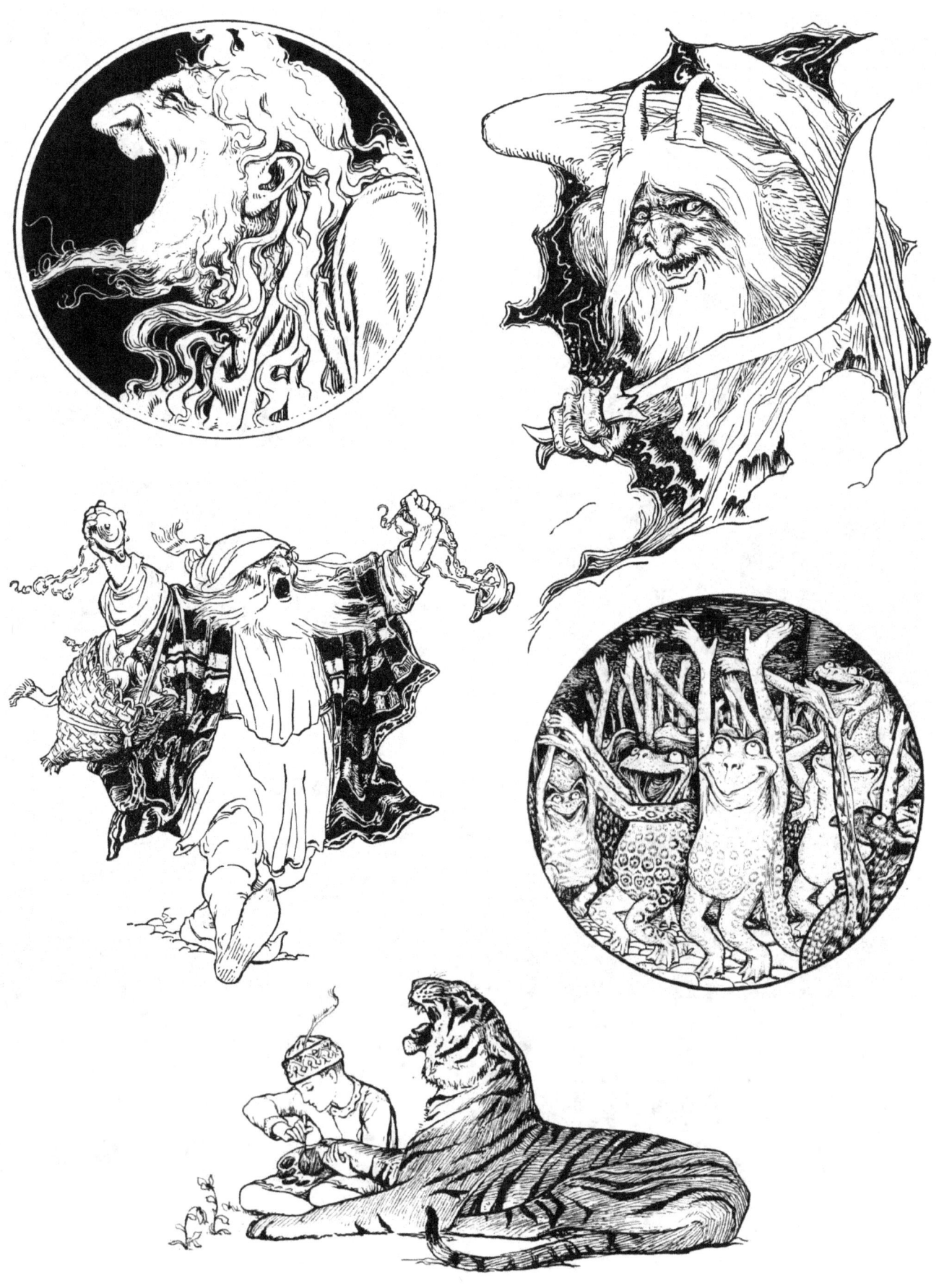

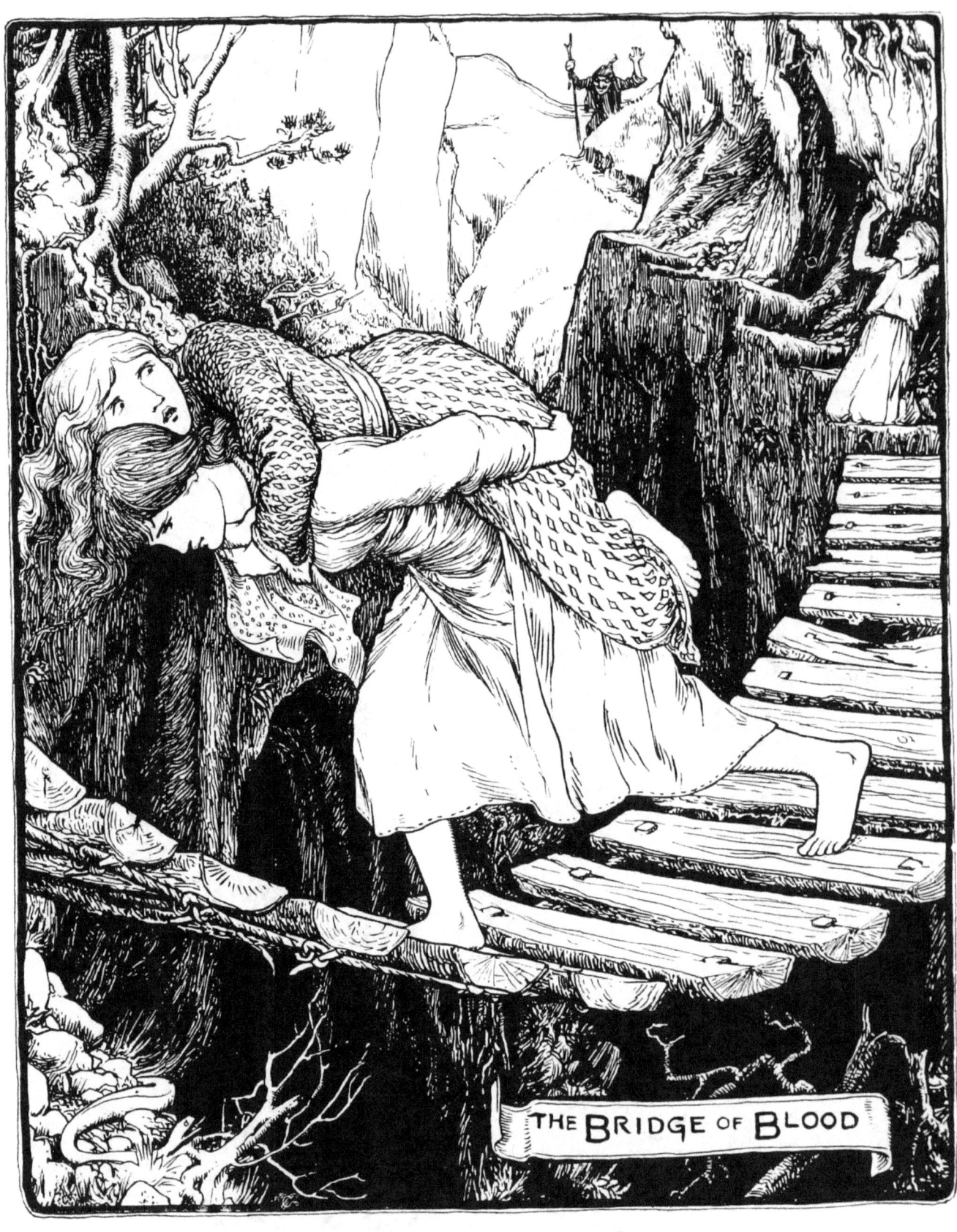

JOHN D BATTEN: Illustration from 'More Celtic Fairy Tales' (Above)
HENRY OSPOVAT: Book-plate Design. (Right)

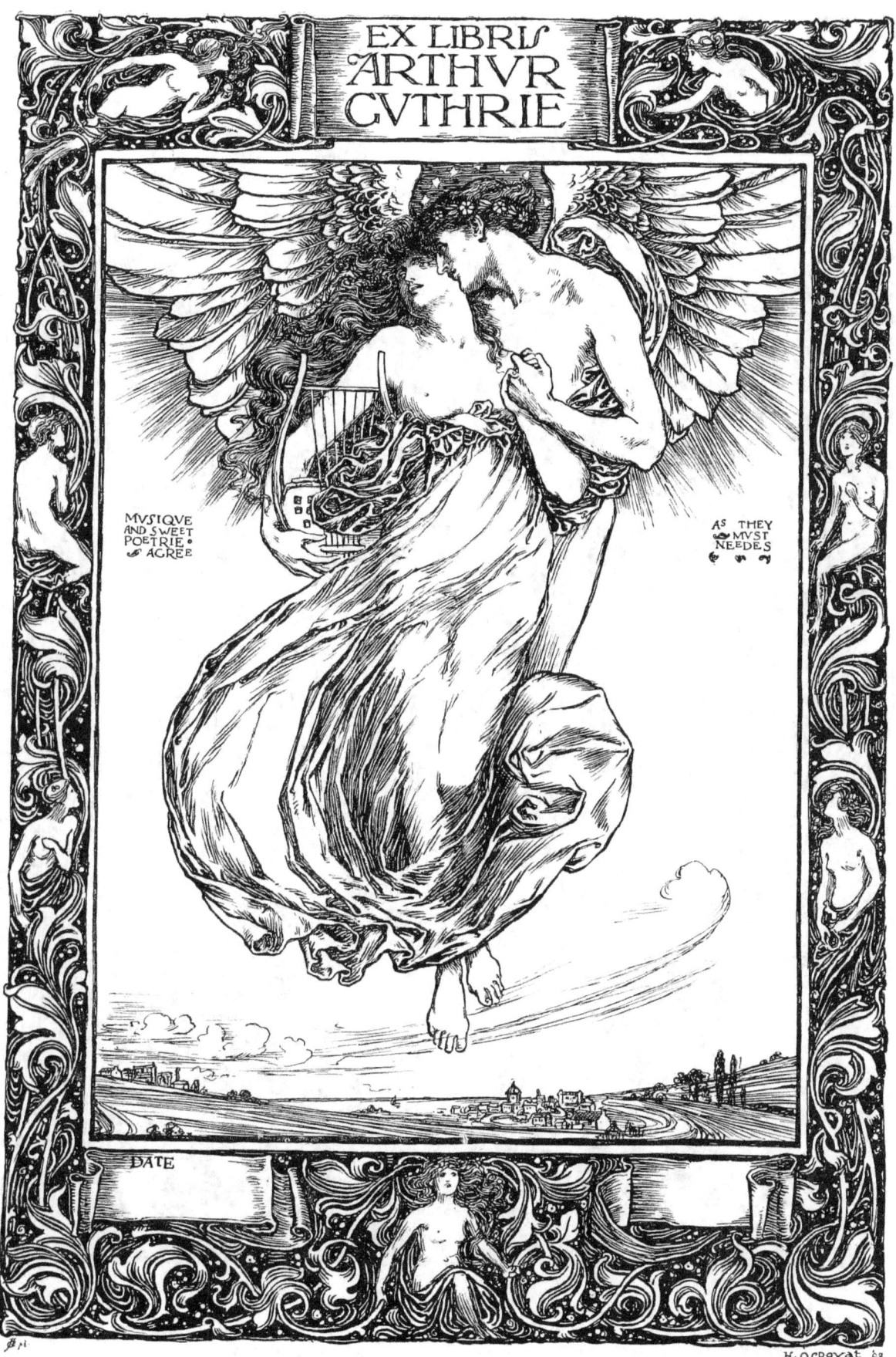

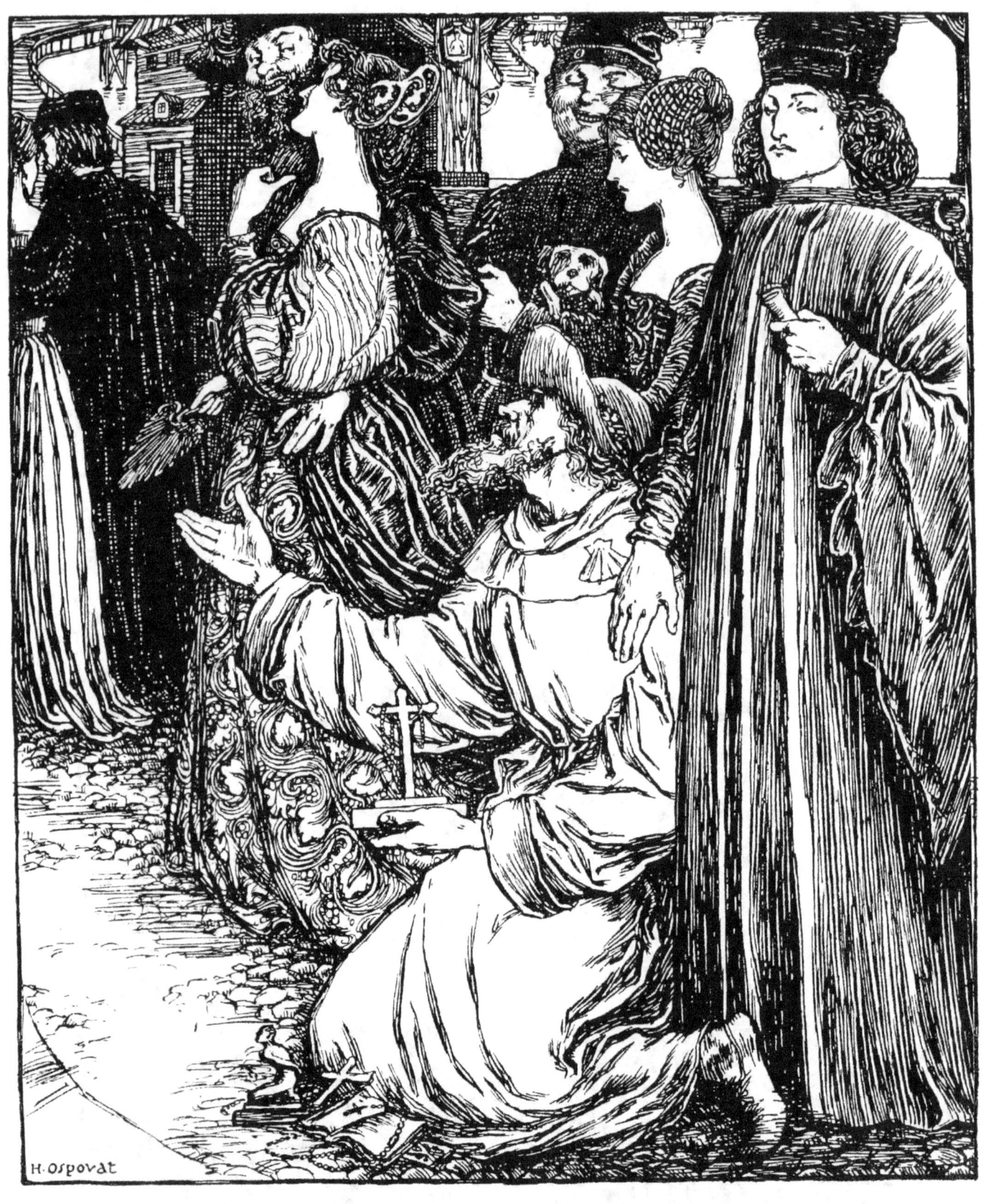

HENRY OSPOVAT: Illustration from 'Shakespeare's Sonnets' (Above)
PETER BAUER: Magazine decorations. (Right)

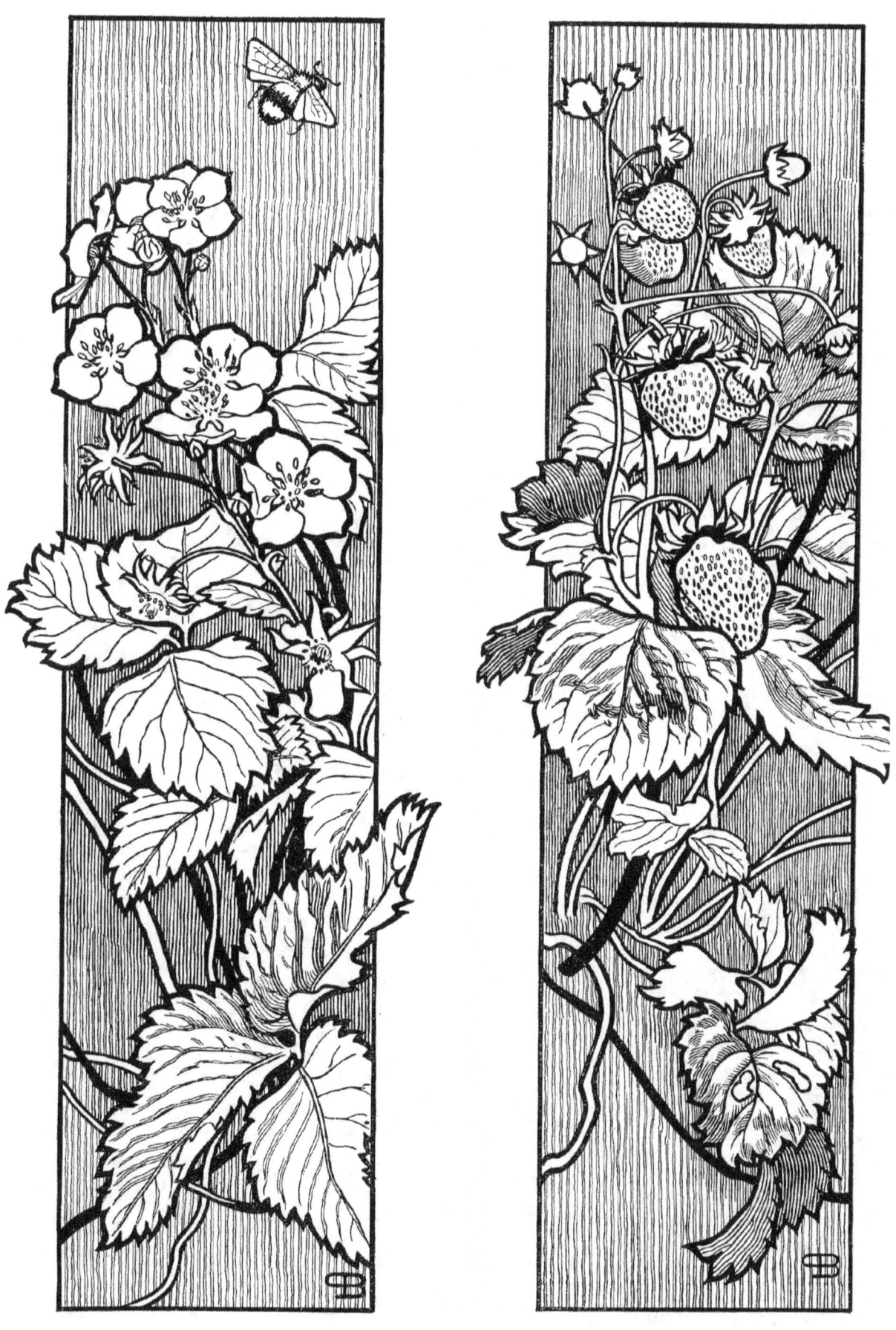

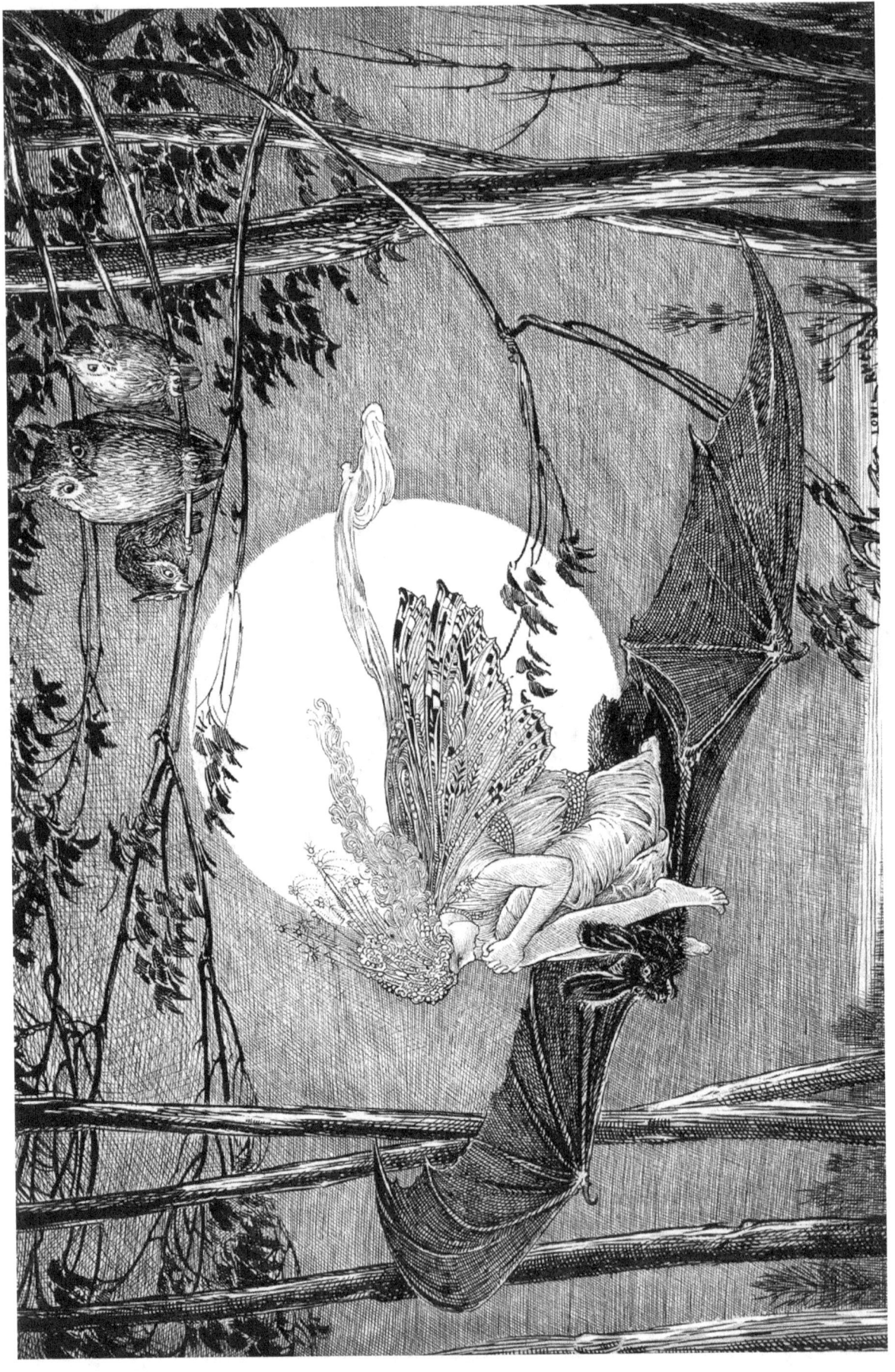

LOUIS RHEAD: 'Aerial'

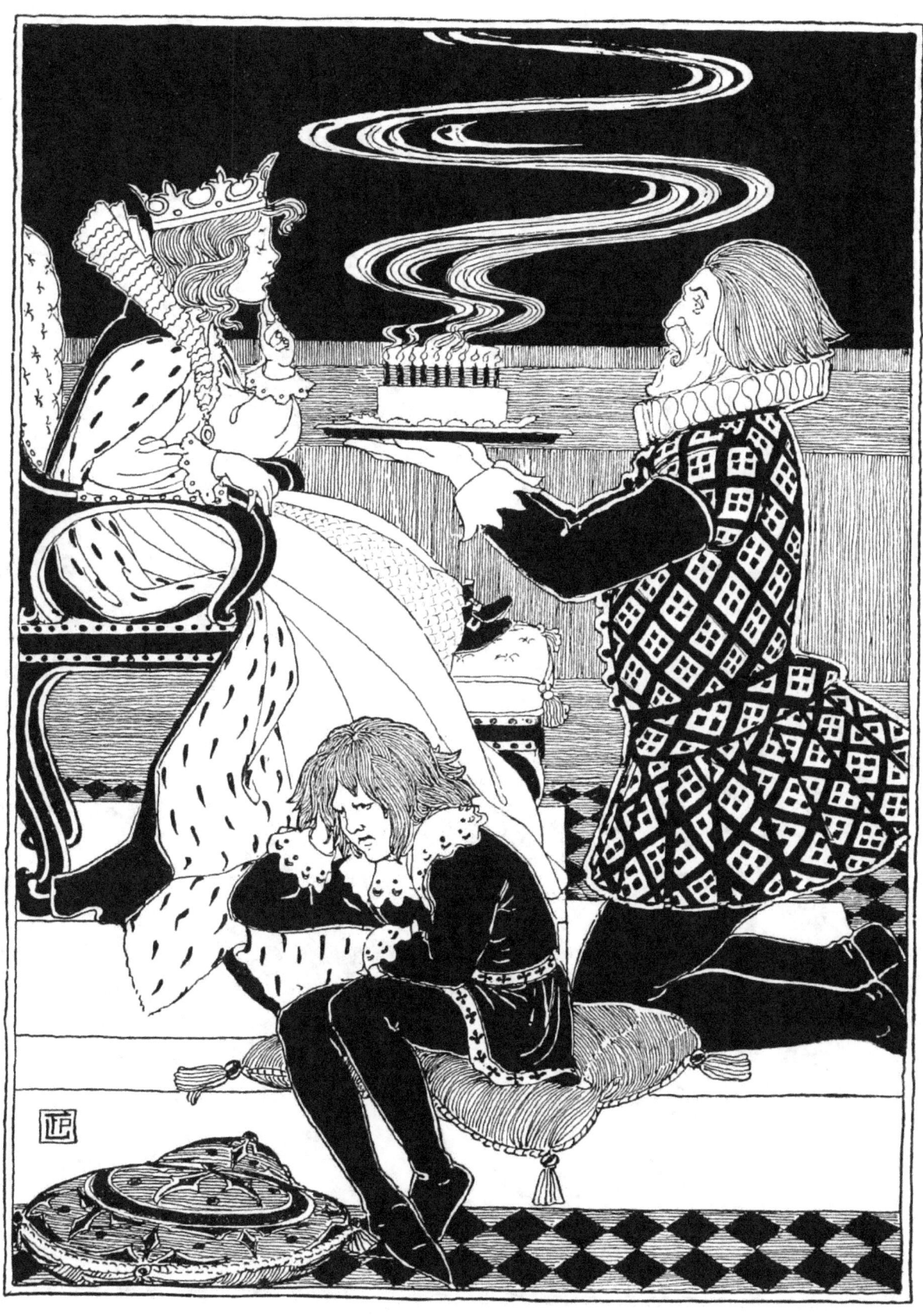

LUCY F PERKINS: If I were Queen.
From 'Boys' and Girls' Bookshelf' Vol 19.

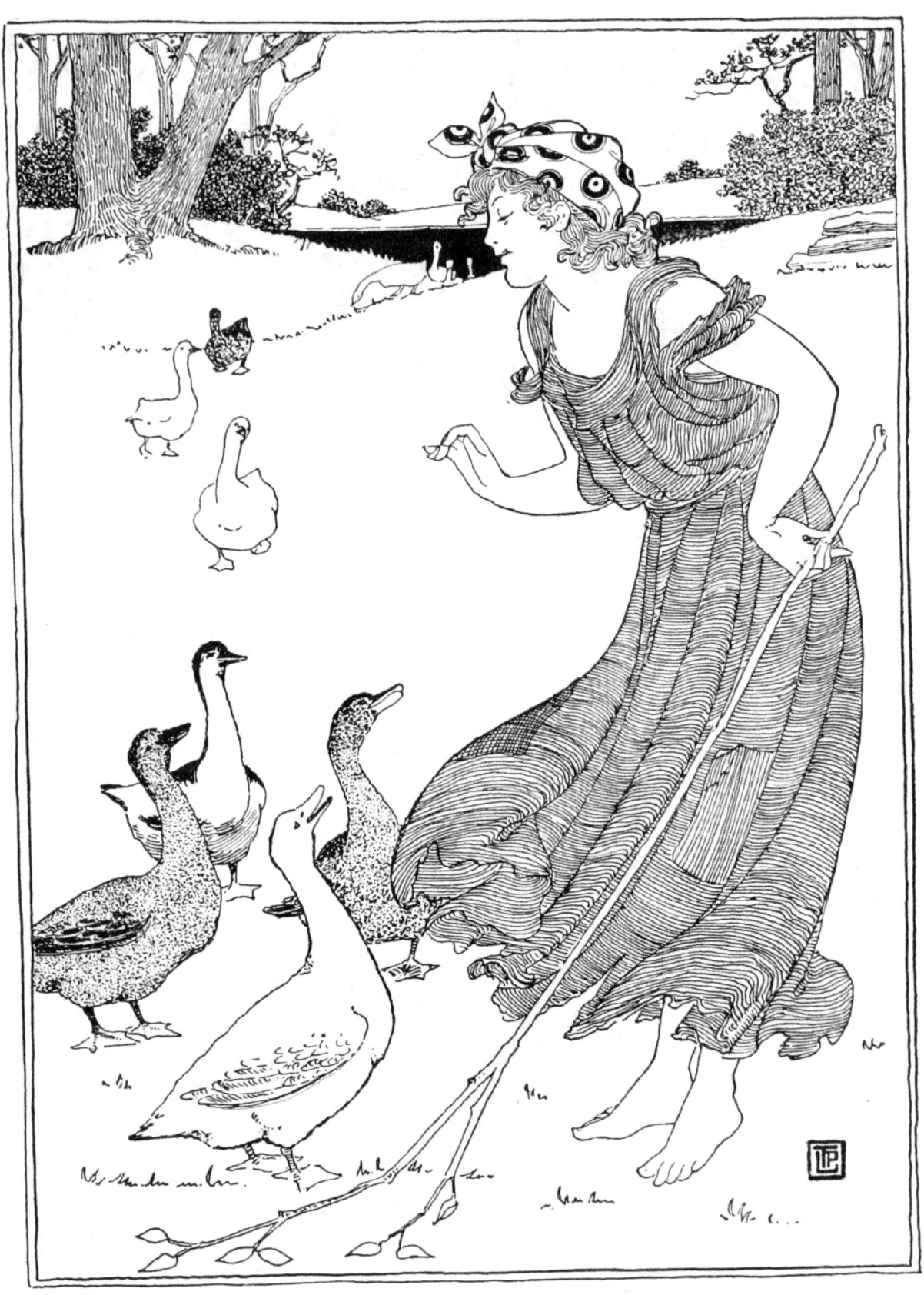

LUCY F PERKINS: The Goose Girl.
From 'Boys' and Girls' Bookshelf' Vol 4.

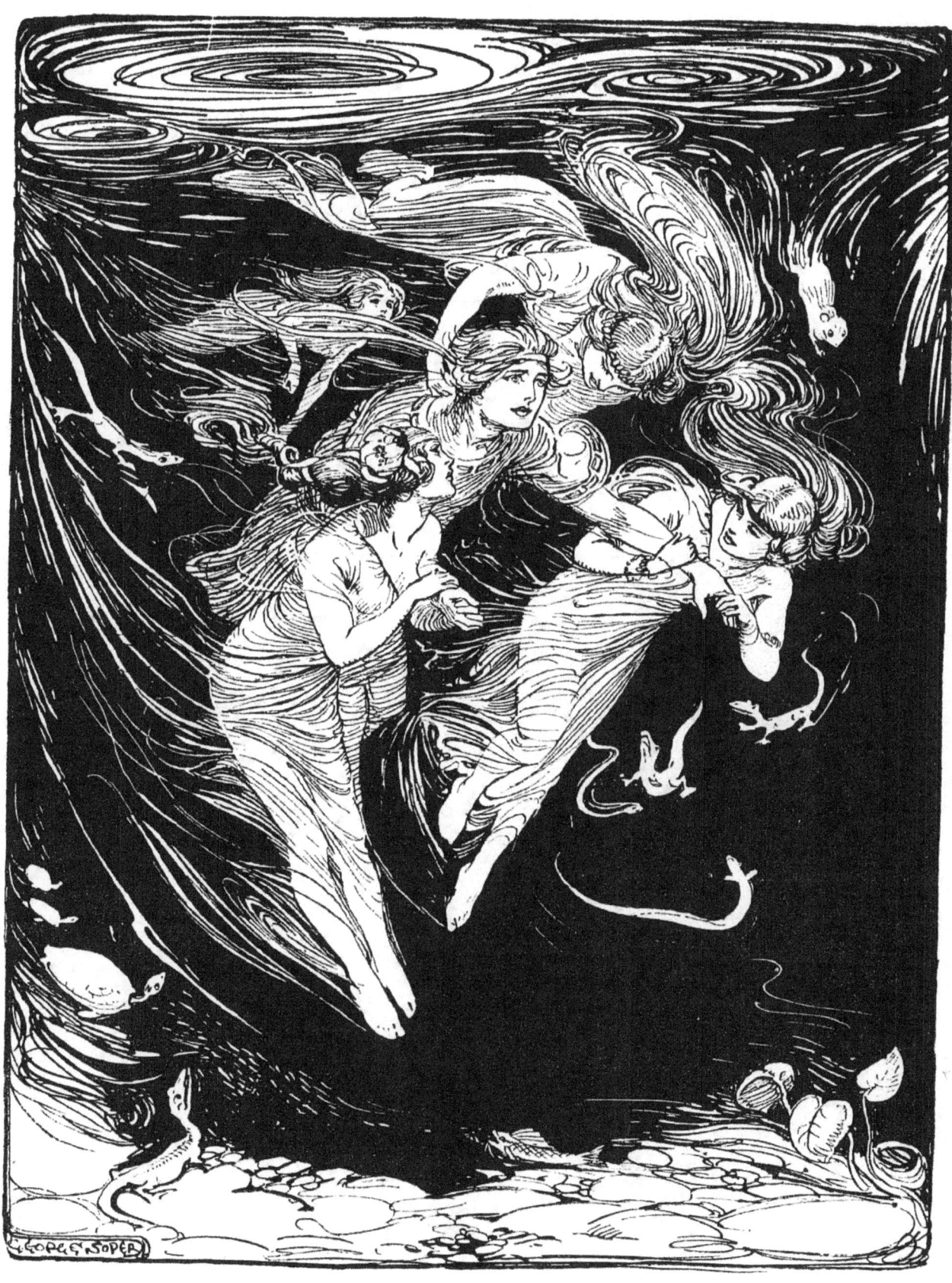

GEORGE SOPER: "The Water Nymphs carried him down under the lake to be their playfellow"
From 'Greek Fairy Tales'.

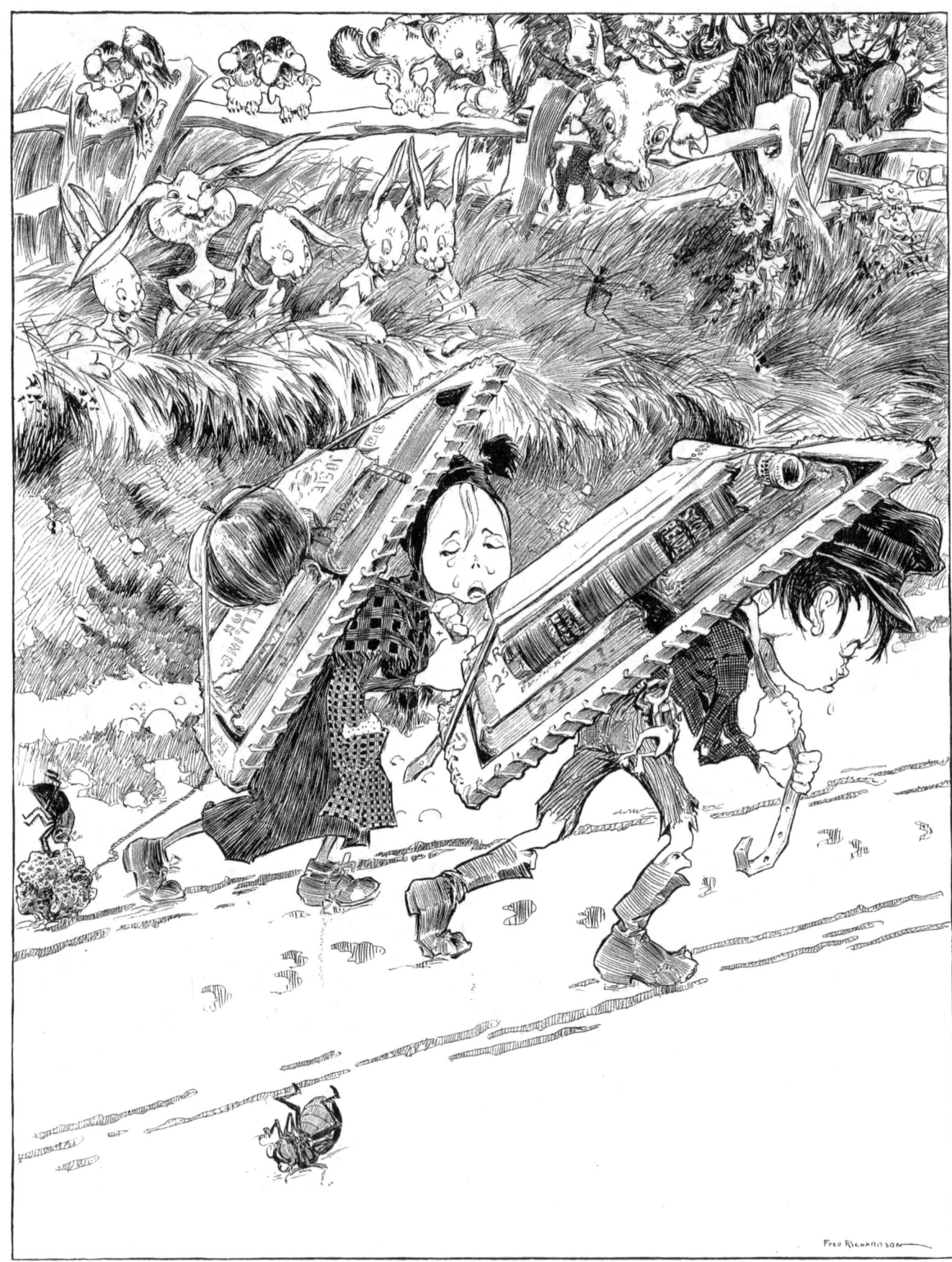

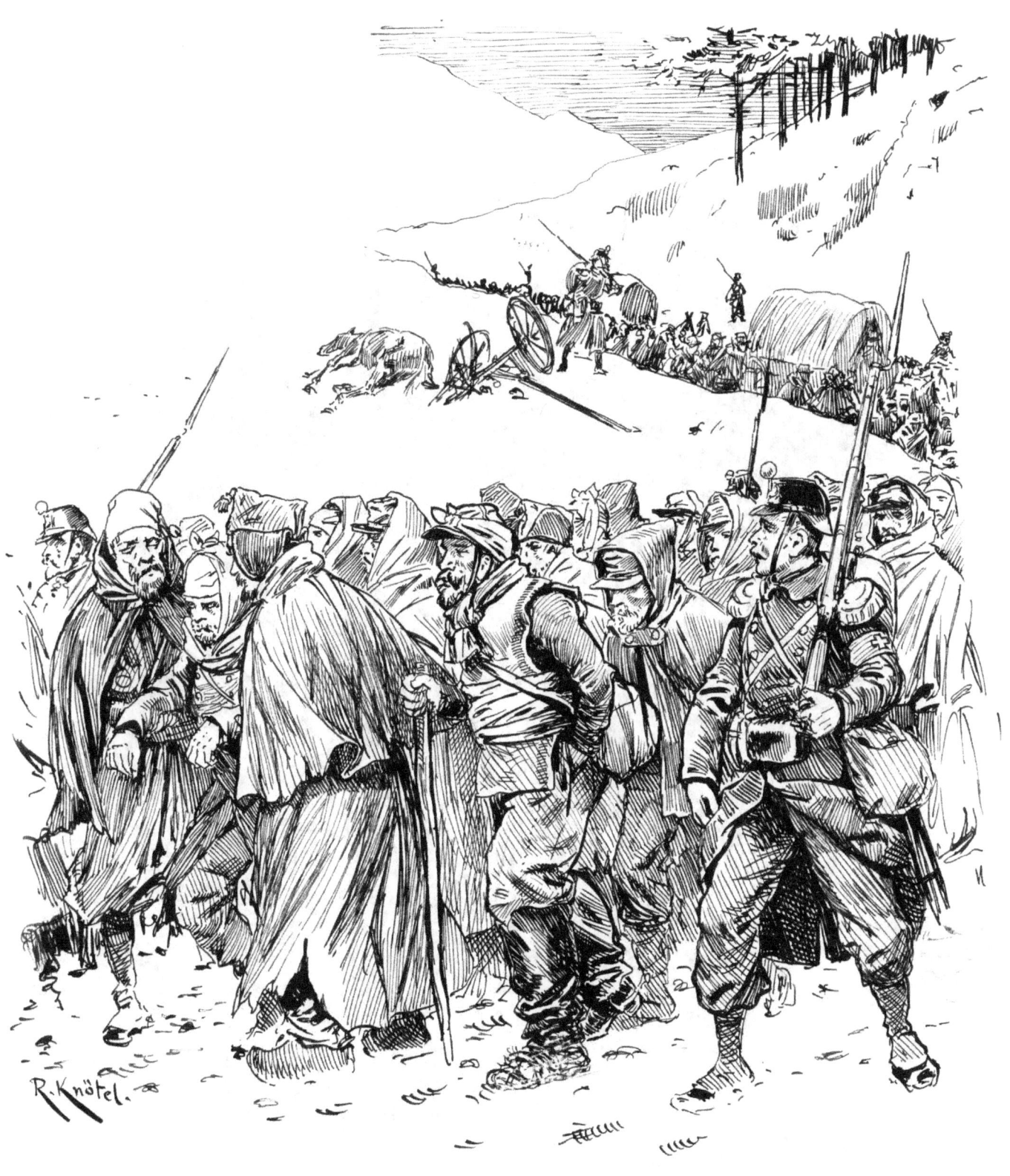

RICHARD KNÖTEL: Prisoners of War (Above).

FREDERICK RICHARDSON: When school began ... as we remember it
Illustration for the 'Chicago Daily News' (Left).

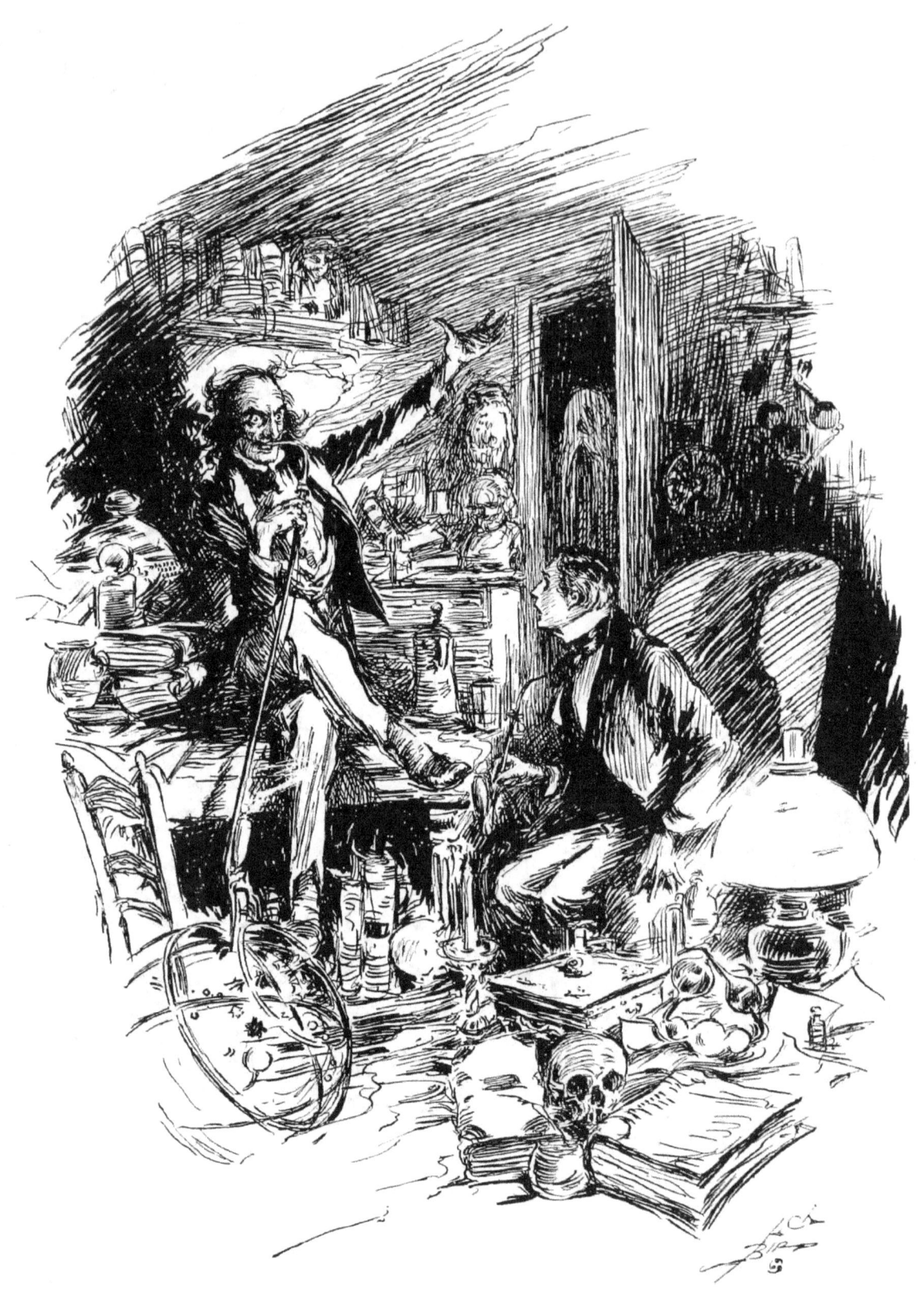

REGINALD BIRCH: Above, "This is the Tachypomp. Does it justify the name?" From 'The Tachypomp and Other Stories'.

At top right, A-Gallop, came the doctor and his nag. At lower right, A throng of frightened village folk.
Two illustrations for 'The Battle of Durley'. From 'St. Nicholas' Illustrated Magazine.

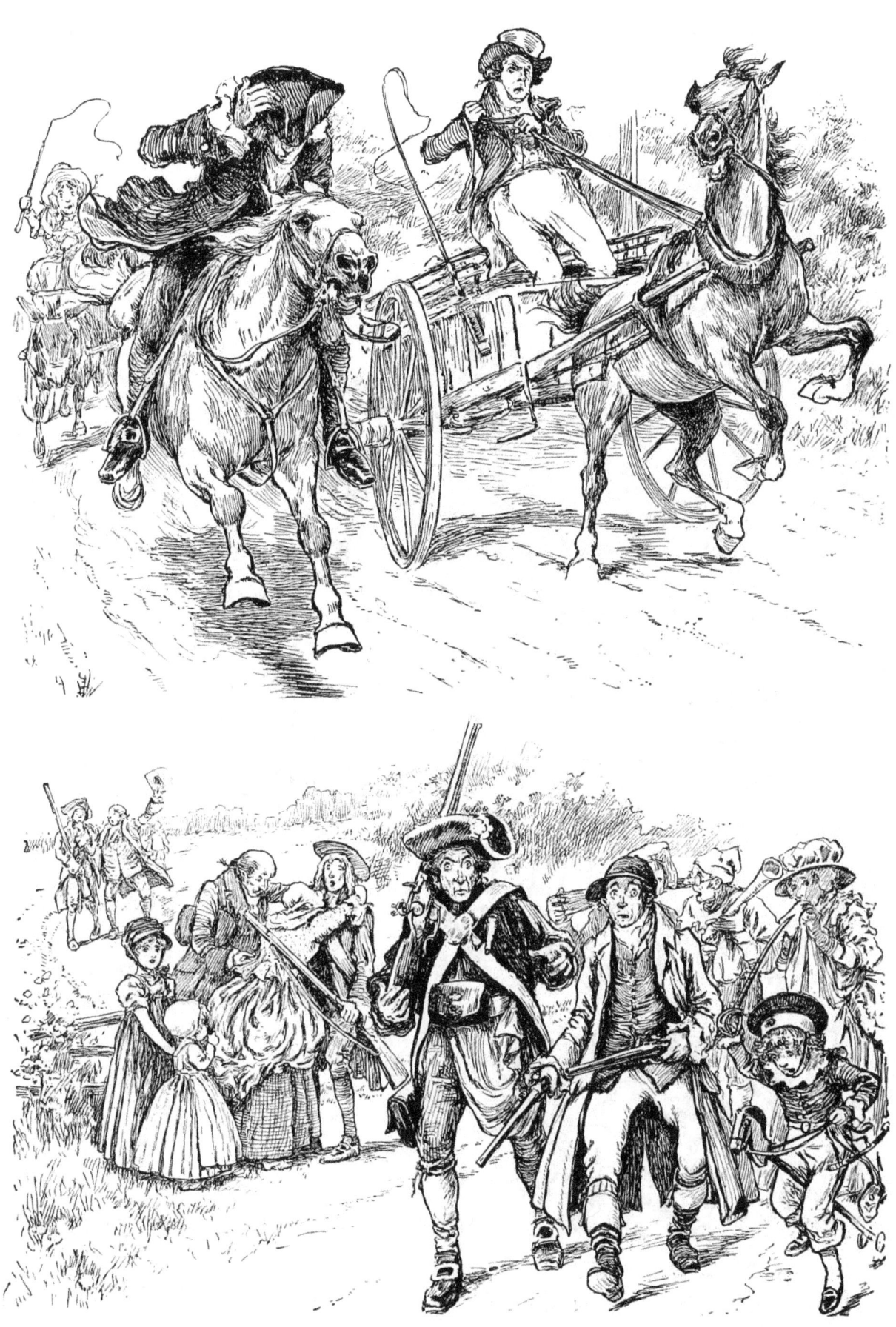

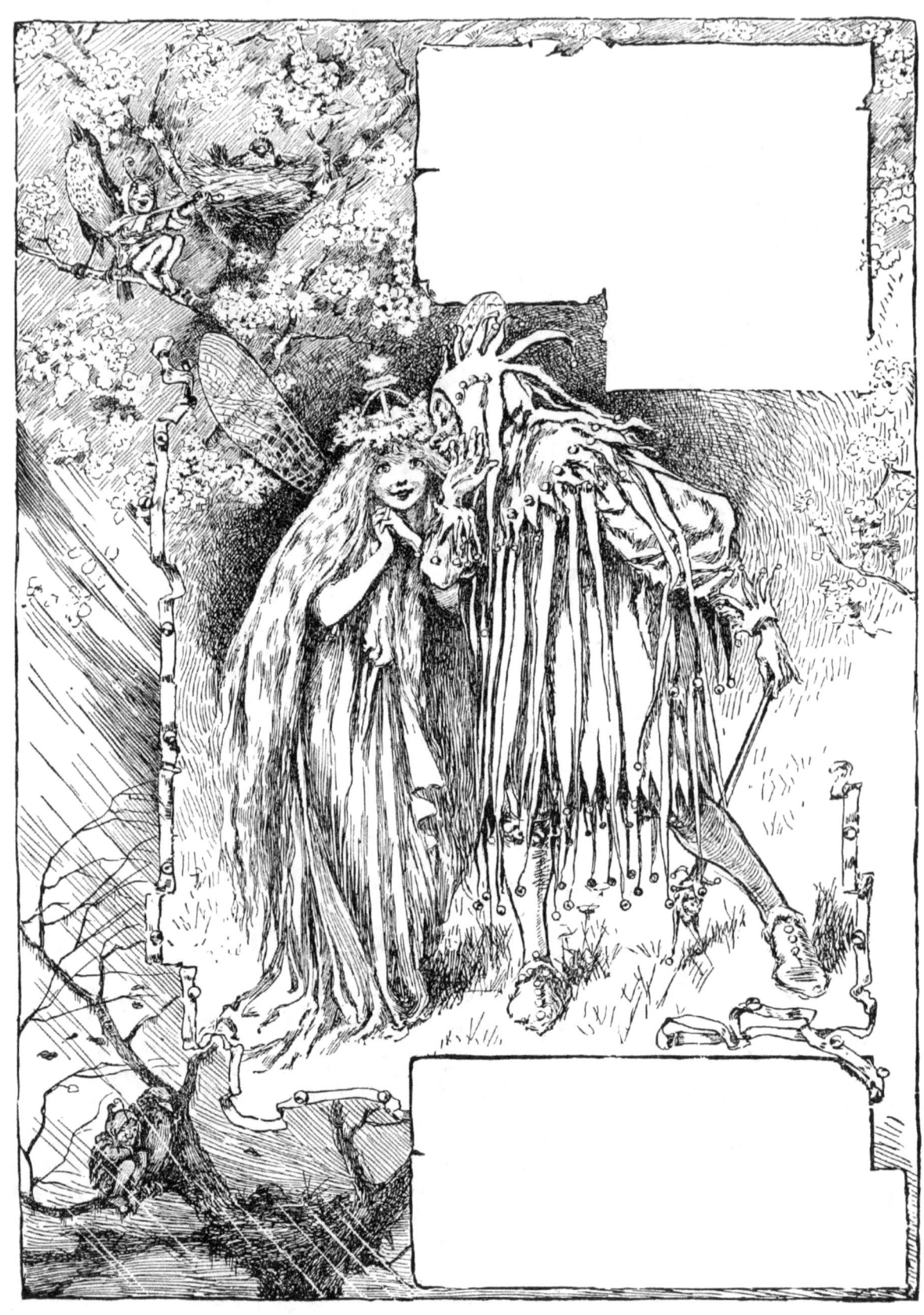

REGINALD BIRCH: Illustration for the Poem, 'An April Joke'. From 'St. Nicholas' Illustrated Magazine.

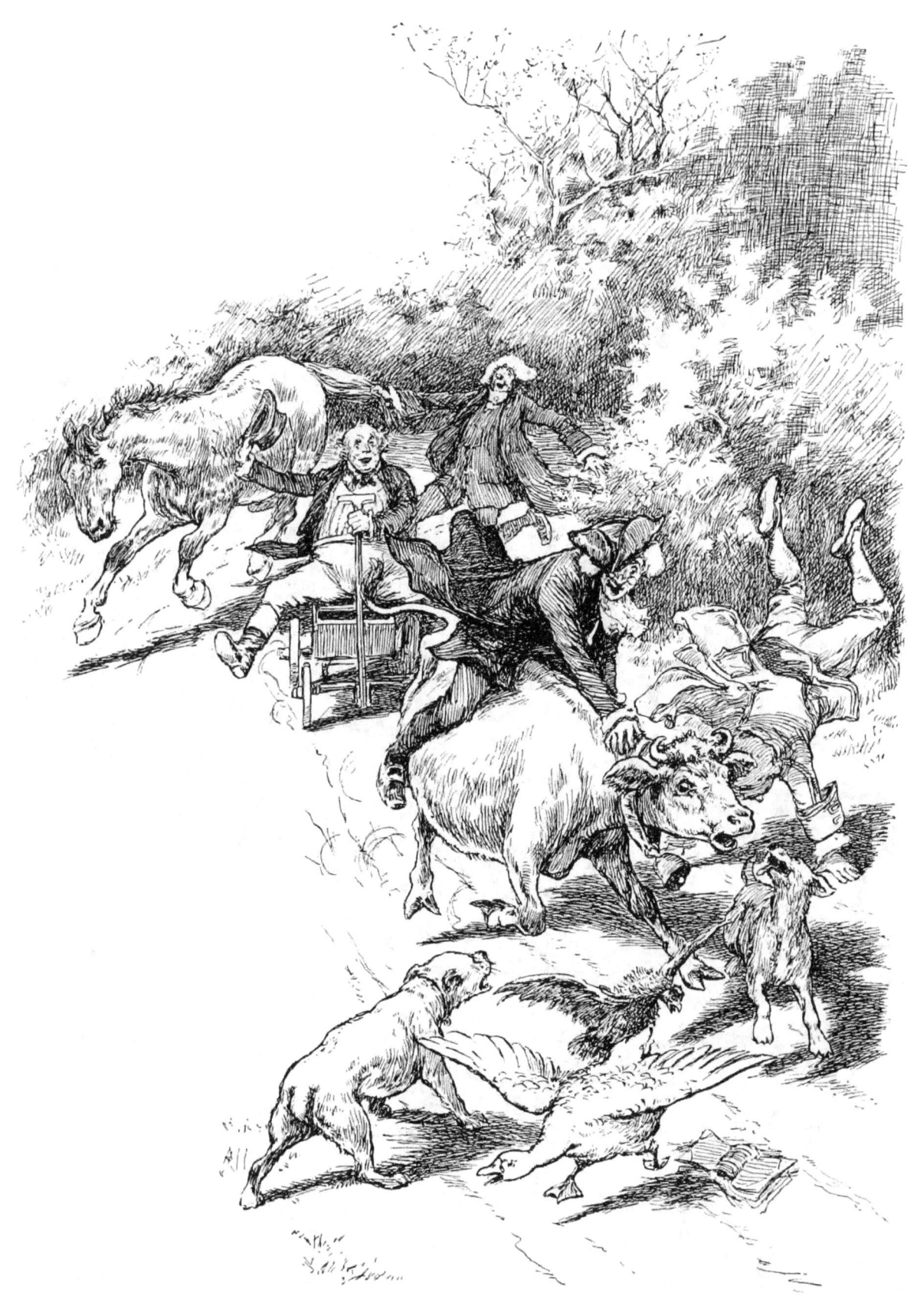

REGINALD BIRCH: Illustration for 'Mistress Pinch's Happy Thought'. From 'St. Nicholas' Illustrated Magazine.

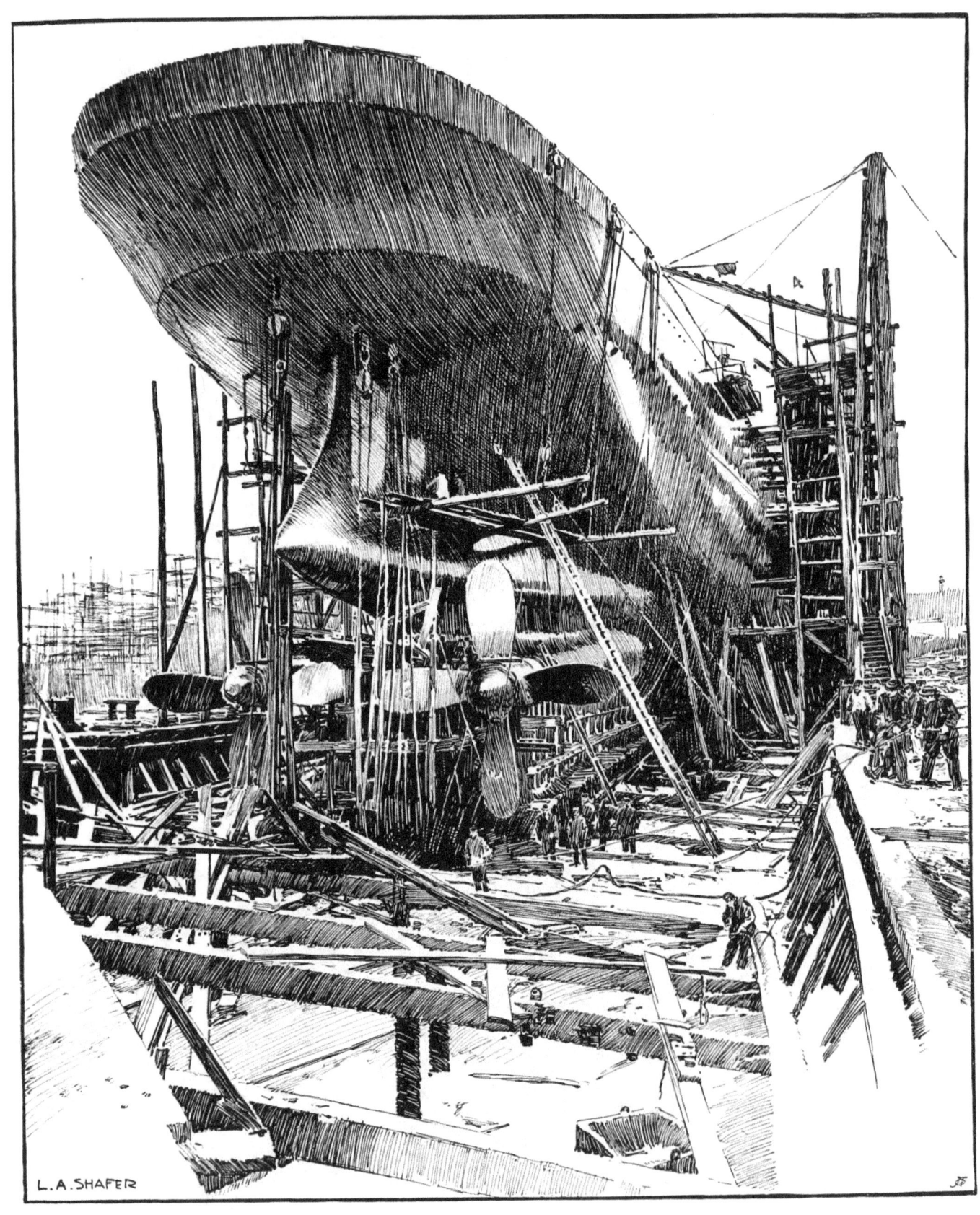

L A SHAFER: Drawing of the 'Germanic' in dry dock.

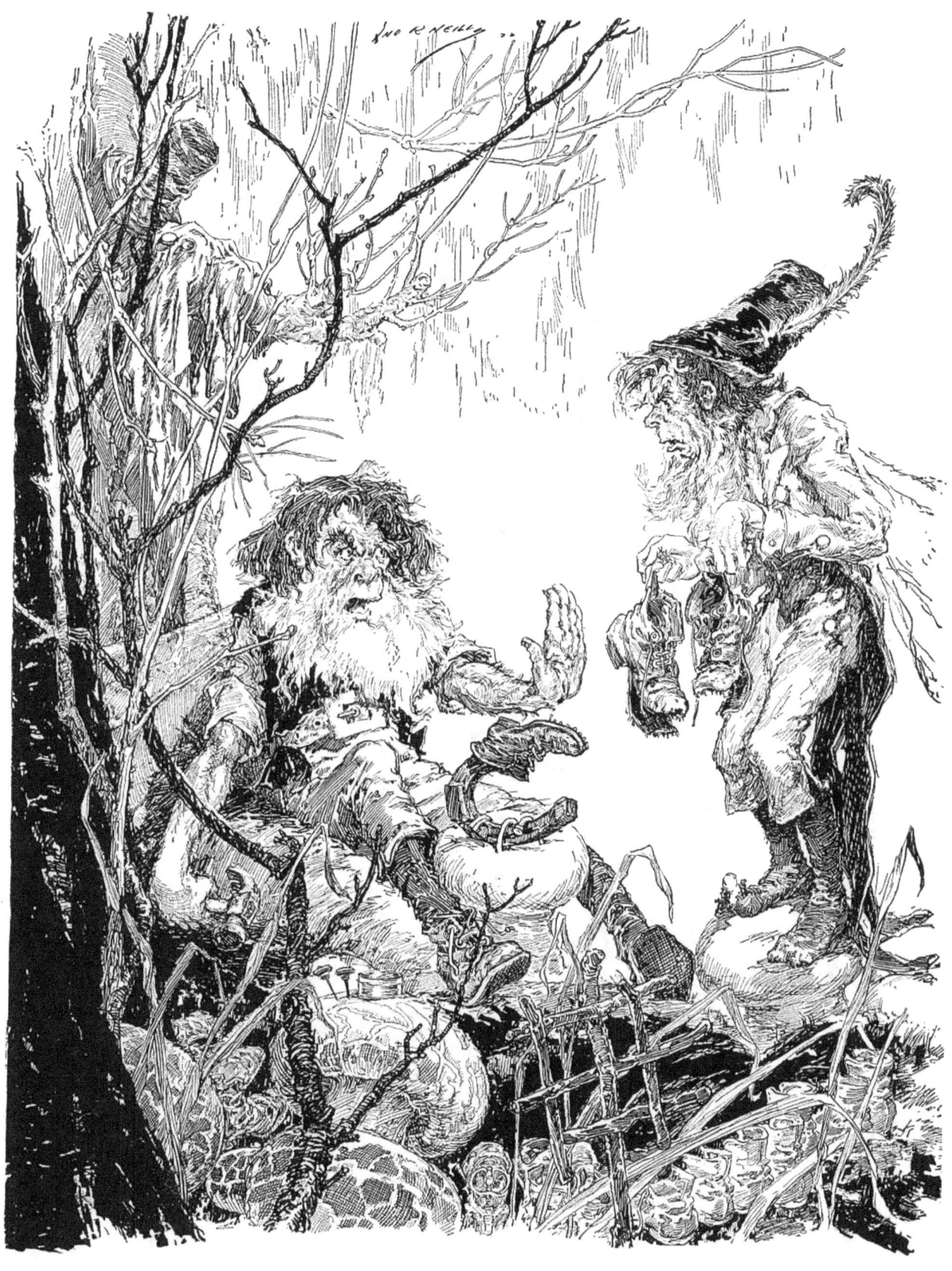

JOHN R NEILL: 'The Cobbler'.

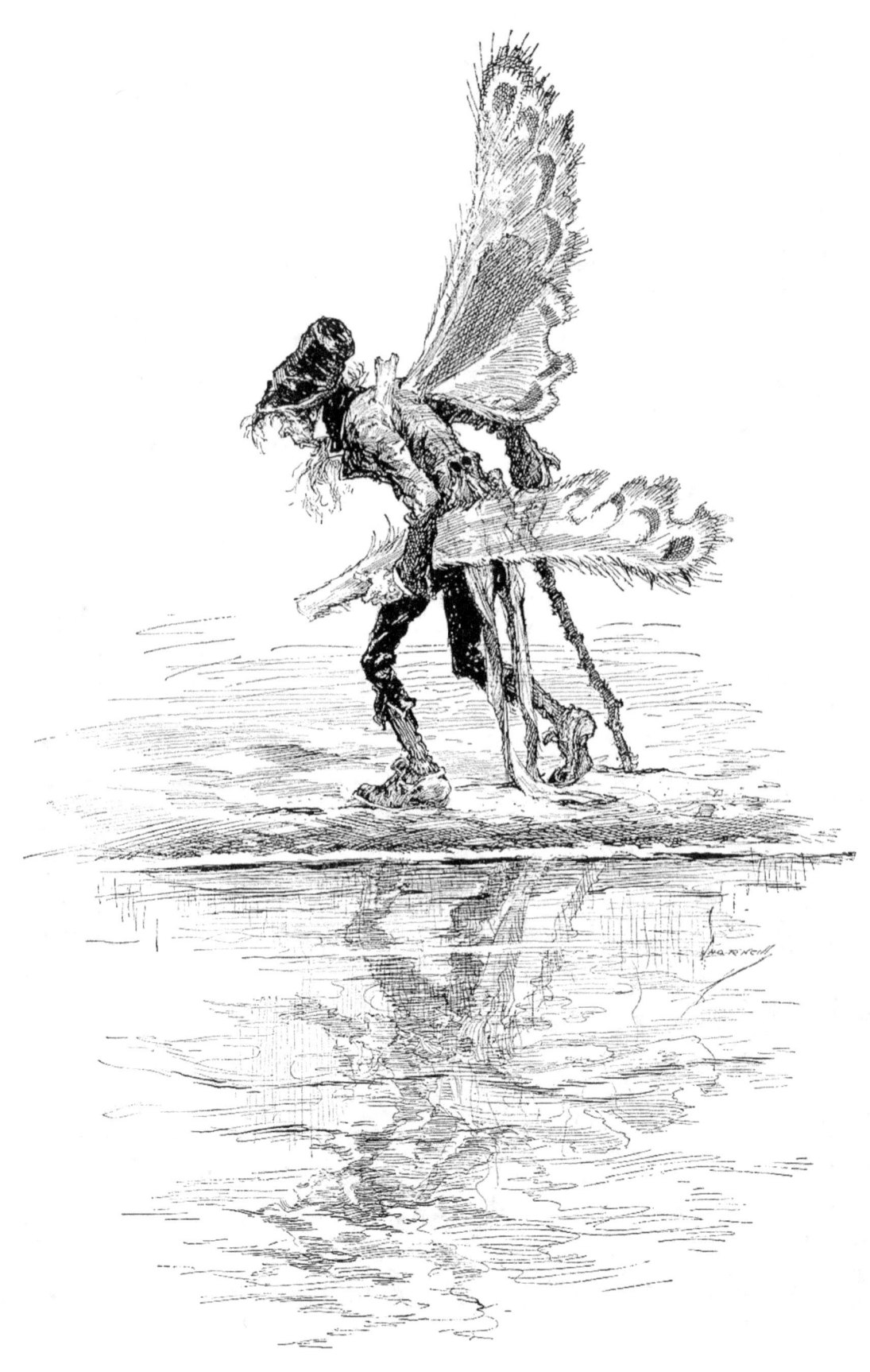

JOHN R NEILL: 'The Romancer'.

www.ingramcontent.com/pod-product-compliance
Lightning Source LLC
Chambersburg PA
CBHW081017240526
45471CB00017B/3246